Revise
AS&A2

ICT
Information & Communication Technology

Chris Jones, Mark Reader and Joan Vallely

Contents

Chapter 10: Implementing ICT systems

Chapter 11: Implementing and managing change

Chapter 12: ICT and society

Chapter 13: Working in and with ICT

Specification lists

Module (Unit)	Specification topic	Chapter reference
1 (INFO1)	Health and safety in relation to the use of ICT systems	11.2
	Analysis	3.2, 3.3, 4.1, 4.2
	Design of solutions	3.1, 3.2, 3.3, 4.1, 4.2
	Selection and use of input devices and input media	2.2, 2.3
	Selection and use of storage requirements, media and devices	2.2, 2.4
	Selection and use of output methods, media and devices	2.2
	Selection and use of appropriate software	2.5, 5.1, 5.2, 5.3, 6.1, 6.2, 6.3, 6.4, 6.5, 7.1, 7.2, 7.3, 7.4
	Implementation of ICT-related solutions	3.1, 3.2, 3.3, 4.1, 4.2
	Testing of ICT-related solutions	3.3, 4.1
	Evaluation of ICT-related solutions	3.2, 3.3, 4.1, 4.2
2 (INFO2)	An ICT system and its components	2.1, 2.5, 8.1
	Data and information	1.1, 1.2, 1.3
	People and ICT systems	2.3, 2.5, 8.1, 8.2, 8.3, 11.3, 13.2
	Transfer of data in ICT systems	9.1, 9.2, 9.3
	Safety and security of data in ICT systems	6.5, 10.1, 12.1, 13.2
	Backup and recovery	1.2
	What ICT can provide	7.2, 8.1, 8.3
	Factors affecting the use of ICT	12.1
	The consequences of the use of ICT	12.1, 12.2, 12.3, 13.2

Examination analysis

The specification comprises two unit tests at AS.

Unit 1 (INFO1) **Practical Problem Solving in the Digital World** (50% of AS, 25% of A Level)
Candidates sit a 1 hour 30 minutes examination (80 marks) and answer short answer and structured questions.

Unit 2 (INFO2) **Living in the Digital World** (50% of AS, 25% of A Level)
Candidates sit a 1 hour 30 minutes examination (80 marks) and answer short answer and structured questions.

Module (Unit)	Specification topic	Chapter reference
3 (INFO3)	Future developments	11.2, 12.1, 12.2, 12.3, 13.3
	Information and systems	3.1, 3.2, 3.3, 4.1, 4.2
	Managing ICT	11.1, 11.3
	ICT strategy	11.2
	ICT policies	10.1, 10.2, 10.3, 13.1, 13.2, 13.3
	Legislation and regulation	10.1, 13.2
	Developing ICT solutions	3.1, 3.2, 3.3, 4.1, 4.2, 5.1
	Development methods	3.1, 3.2, 3.3, 4.1, 4.2
	Techniques and tools for systems development	3.1, 3.2, 3.3, 4.1, 4.2
	Introducing large ICT systems into organisations	3.1, 3.2, 3.3, 4.1, 4.2
	Training and supporting users	10.3, 11.3
	External and internal resources	11.1
4 (INFO4)	Practical issues involved in the use of ICT in the digital world	Practical application of chapters 3–7

Examination analysis

The specification comprises one unit test and one coursework project report at A2.

Unit 3 (INFO3) **The Use of ICT in the Digital World** (30% of A Level)
Candidates sit a 2 hour examination (100 marks) and answer structured questions based on pre-release material and questions requiring extended answers.

Unit 4 (INFO4) **Practical Issues Involved in the Use of ICT in the Digital World** (20% of A Level)
Candidates complete a project (70 marks) involving the production of an ICT-related system over an extended period of time.

OCR AS

Module (Unit)	Specification topic	Chapter reference
1 **(G061)**	Data, information, knowledge and processing	1.1, 1.2, 1.3, 8.3, 9.2
	Software and hardware components of an information system	2.1, 2.2, 2.3, 2.4, 2.5, 9.2
	Characteristics of standard applications software and application areas	3.1, 3.2, 3.3, 4.2
	Spreadsheet concepts	5.1, 5.2, 5.3
	Relational database concepts	6.1, 6.2, 6.3
	Applications software used for presentation and communication of data	7.1, 7.2, 7.3, 7.4
	The role and impact of ICT – legal, moral and social issues	6.5, 8.3, 10.1, 11.2, 13.1, 13.2, 13.3
2 **(G062)**	Structured ICT tasks	Practical application of chapters 3–7

Examination analysis

The specification comprises one unit test at AS and coursework.

Unit 1 (G061) **Information, Systems and Applications** (60% of AS, 30% of A Level)
Candidates sit a 2 hour examination (120 marks) and respond to short and long answer questions.

Unit 2 (G062) **Structured ICT tasks** (40% of AS, 20% of A Level)
Candidates complete a number of structured tasks covering practical aspects of ICT (80 marks).

OCR A2

Module (Unit)	Specification topic	Chapter reference
3 **(G063)**	The systems cycle	3.2, 3.3, 4.1, 4.2
	Designing computer-based information systems	3.2, 3.3, 4.1, 4.2, 6.4, 6.5, 8.1, 8.2
	Networks and communications	9.1, 9.2, 9.3
	Applications of ICT	5.2, 5.3, 6.4, 6.5, 12.1, 12.2, 12.3
	Implementing computer-based information systems	10.2, 10.3, 11.1, 11.2, 11.3
	Implications of ICT	11.1, 11.2, 12.1, 12.2, 12.3, 13.1, 13.2, 13.3
4 **(G064)**	ICT project	Practical application of chapters 3–7

Examination analysis

The specification comprises one unit test and one coursework project report at A2.

Unit 3 (G063) **ICT Systems, Applications and Implications** (30% of A Level)
Candidates sit a 2 hour examination (120 marks) and answer short and long answer questions.

Unit 4 (G064) **ICT Project** (20% of A Level)
Candidates complete a project (80 marks) involving analysis and design over an extended period of time.

WJEC AS

Module (Unit)	Specification topic	Chapter reference
1 (IT1)	Data, information and knowledge	1.1, 1.2, 1.3
	The value and importance of information	1.1, 1.2, 1.3
	Quality of information	1.1, 1.2, 1.3
	Validation and verification	1.2, 5.2
	Capabilities and limitations of ICT	2.2, 2.4, 2.5, 3.3, 4.2
	Uses of ICT	5.1, 5.2, 5.3, 6.1, 6.2, 6.3, 6.4, 6.5, 7.1, 7.2, 7.3, 7.4, 11.2, 12.2
	Presenting information	2.1, 7.1, 7.2, 7.3, 7.4
	Networks	9.1, 9.2, 9.3
	Human Computer Interface (HCI)	2.3, 8.1, 8.2, 8.3
	Social issues	10.1, 12.1, 12.2, 12.3
	Database systems	6.1, 6.2, 6.3, 6.4, 6.5
	Modelling	5.1, 5.2, 5.3
2 (IT2)	Presenting information	Practical application of chapters 3, 4, 7

Examination analysis

The specification comprises one unit test at AS and coursework.

Unit 1 (IT1) **Information Systems** (60% of AS, 30% of A Level)
Candidates sit a 2 hour 15 minutes examination (80 marks). They are also required to prepare a spreadsheet on a specific topic, in advance of the written paper.

Unit 2 (IT2) **Presenting Information** (40% of AS, 20% of A Level)
Candidates undertake DTP and multimedia tasks (80 marks), presenting the outcome for internal assessment.

WJEC A2

Module (Unit)	Specification topic	Chapter reference
3 (IT3)	Networks	9.1
	The Internet	9.1, 9.2, 9.3, 11.3, 12.1, 12.2, 12.3
	Human Computer Interface (HCI)	8.2
	Working with ICT	13.1
	ICT security policies	10.1, 13.2
	Database systems	6.1, 6.2, 6.3, 6.4, 6.5
	Management of change	11.1
	Management Information Systems	10.2, 10.3, 11.1, 11.2
	System Development Life Cycle (SDLC)	3.1, 3.2, 3.3, 4.1, 4.2
4 (IT4)	Relational database project	Practical application of chapter 6

Examination analysis

The specification comprises one unit test and one coursework project report at A2.

Unit 3 (IT3) **Use and Impact of ICT** (30% of A Level)
Candidates sit a 2 hour 30 minutes examination (90 marks).

Unit 4 (IT4) **Relational Database Project** (20% of A Level)
Candidates complete a project (100 marks) involving analysis, design, test and evaluation of an ICT solution over an extended period of time.

CCEA AS

Module (Unit)	Specification topic	Chapter reference
AS 1	Data and information	1.1, 1.2, 1.3
	Hardware and software components	2.1, 2.2, 2.3, 2.4, 2.5
	Network communication	9.1, 9.2, 9.3
	Applications of ICT	5.1, 5.2, 5.3, 6.1, 6.2, 6.3, 6.5, 7.4, 8.3, 10.1, 11.1, 11.2, 12.1, 12.2, 12.3, 13.2
	Developing ICT applications	3.1, 4.1, 4.2, 8.3, 10.3, 11.1, 13.3
AS 2	Data processing task	Practical application of chapters 5 and 6
	Multimedia task	Practical application of chapter 7

Examination analysis

The specification comprises one unit test at AS and two compulsory tasks.

Unit AS 1 Components of Information and Communication Technology (50% of AS, 25% of A Level)
Candidates sit a 2 hour written examination (120 marks) and answer all the short answer questions presented.

Unit AS 2 Developing ICT Solutions (50% of AS, 25% of A Level)
Candidates need to produce an ICT solution to a task-related problem. The assessment is marked internally and moderated by the examination board. Assessment will be made up of a data processing task (60 marks) and a multimedia task (60 marks).

CCEA A2

Module (Unit)	Specification topic	Chapter reference
A2 1	Database systems	6.1, 6.2, 6.3, 6.4, 6.5
	Networked systems	9.1, 9.2
	Software development	3.1, 3.2, 3.3, 4.2
	The user interface	2.3, 2.5, 8.1, 8.2
	User support and training	8.1, 8.2, 11.3
	Legal and professional issues	10.1, 10.2, 11.1, 13.2
	Implications of ICT	12.1, 12.2, 12.3, 13.1, 13.2, 13.3
A2 2	Approaches to system development	Practical application of chapters 3, 4, 6, 9, 10

Examination analysis

The specification comprises one unit test and one coursework project report at A2.

Unit A2 1 Information Systems (25% of A Level)
Candidates sit a 2 hour written examination (120 marks) and answer all the short answer questions presented.

Unit A2 2 Approaches to System Development (25% of A Level)
Candidates complete an internally assessed project (80 marks) involving analysis, design, test and evaluation of an ICT solution.

AS/A2 ICT courses

AS and A2

Advanced Level ICT courses are in two sections. Students first study the AS (Advanced Subsidiary) course. Some will then go on to study the second part of the A Level course, called A2. There are two modules (units) at AS Level and two at A2 Level. The AS and A2 courses are designed so that the level of difficulty increases from AS to A2:

- AS ICT builds on GCSE ICT
- A2 ICT builds on AS ICT

How will you be tested?

Assessment units

For AS ICT, you will be tested by two assessment units. For the full A Level in ICT you will take a further two units. AS ICT forms 50% of the assessment weighting for the full A Level.

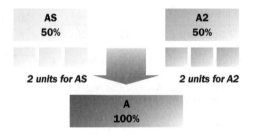

Depending on the exam board, a unit can be taken in January or June, or both. Alternatively, you may be able to study the whole course before taking any of the unit tests. There is some flexibility about when exams can be taken, and the diagram below shows just some of the ways that the assessment units may be taken for AS and A Level ICT.

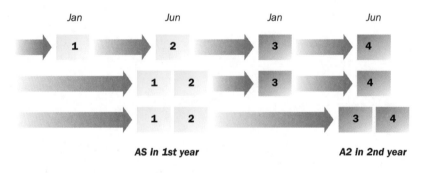

If you are disappointed with a module result, you can resit a module. The higher mark counts.

A2 and synoptic assessment

After having studied AS ICT, you may wish to continue studying ICT to A Level. For this you will need to take two further ICT units at A2. The A2 units assess the course using a 'synoptic' approach to assessment. Synoptic assessment tests your ability to apply knowledge, understanding and skills you have learnt throughout the course, and to make connections between different areas of the subject. It takes place across the two A2 units and encourages candidates to gain a holistic understanding of ICT.

What skills will I need?

The Advanced Subsidiary GCE and Advanced GCE in ICT draw on the subject criteria for ICT, which are prescribed and are compulsory. AS and A Level ICT should encourage you to:

- become effective and discerning users of ICT, with a broad range of ICT skills, and knowledge and understanding of ICT
- apply creative, innovative, analytical, logical and critical thinking skills to the solution of ICT problems across a range of contexts
- develop collaborative approaches to the solution of a range of ICT problems
- understand the consequences of using ICT for individuals, organisations and society
- understand the social, legal, ethical and other considerations about the use of ICT
- be aware of emerging technologies and have an appreciation of the potential impact these may have on individuals, organisations and society.

It is important that you develop your key skills throughout your AS and A2 courses. These are important skills that you need whatever you do beyond AS and A2 Levels. The main key skill areas relevant to ICT are:

- communication
- application of number
- information and communication technology
- working with others
- improving own learning and performance
- problem solving.

Each examination board will 'signpost' where key skill developments can best take place whilst studying A Level ICT. You will have opportunities during your study of A Level ICT to develop your key skills.

You will have to meet the following assessment objectives:

- Demonstrate knowledge and understanding of the specified content.
- Apply knowledge and understanding to problems and issues arising from both familiar and unfamiliar situations.
- Investigate and analyse problems, issues and situations to produce a specification.
- Design and evaluate the effectiveness of solutions in relation to the tested outcomes and the relevant documentation.

Types of exam questions

In ICT examinations, different types of question are used to assess your abilities and skills. Unit tests mainly use structured questions requiring both short answers and more extended answers. These questions are often linked directly to a given context, requiring you to read and study the stimulus material (a paragraph or short article about a real or imagined ICT problem).

Short-answer questions

Short-answer questions can be set at AS and A2 Level. A short-answer question may test recall or it may test understanding. Short-answer questions may have space for the answers printed on the question paper.

Here is an example (a brief answer is shown below):

Mr Smith sends a monthly email from the national organising body to members of his local classic car club. He likes to add a digital photograph of a member's classic car each month.

State three functions of email software, and explain how each one would help him to carry out the above task efficiently.   (6)

Email software allows users to forward (1) emails to other recipients without having to retype or copy it (1). The capacity to attach files (1) is a common feature in email software. This allows Mr Smith to attach his digital photograph to the email he is forwarding to members (1). By setting up a group in his address book (1) Mr Smith will be able to forward the email to all members in the local classic car club without having to email each member individually (1).

Structured questions

Structured questions are in several parts. The parts usually have a common context and they often become progressively more difficult and more demanding as you work your way through the question. A structured question may start with simple recall, and then test understanding of a familiar or an unfamiliar situation. Many of the questions in this guide are structured questions, as this is a popular type of question used in A Level ICT exams.

Here is an example of a structured question that becomes progressively more demanding.

(a) Explain the benefits and drawbacks for an organisation deciding that they need to have bespoke software to meet their business needs.   (8)

(b) 'The majority of business operations can be fulfilled using off-the-shelf software that can be tailored to meet their needs.'
Given that this might well be the case, explain why some organisations require bespoke software to fulfil their operational and strategic outcomes.

(12)

When answering structured questions, do not feel that you have to complete one question before starting the next. The further you are into a question, the more difficult the marks are to obtain. If you run out of ideas, go on to the next question.

You need to respond to as many parts to questions on an exam paper as possible. You will not score well if you spend so long trying to perfect the first questions that you do not reach later questions at all.

Extended answers

In A Level ICT, questions requiring more extended answers may form part of structured questions or they may form separate questions (e.g. linked to a case study or a structured problem that you need to resolve). These questions are often used to assess your abilities to communicate ideas, relate your knowledge to the case study or problem in the question, and put together a logical argument.

The 'correct' answers to extended questions are often less well-defined than those requiring shorter answers. Examiners may have a list of points for which credit is awarded up to the maximum for the question.

Marks for your answer may be allocated using a 'levels of response' mark scheme. Such a scheme for a 12-mark question might be written as follows:

- **10–12 marks:** You have seen all the consequences and produced an evaluative answer.
- **7–9 marks:** You see all the consequences but do not consider all issues (e.g. you ignore quality or cost issues).
- **4–6 marks:** You limit your answer to basic points (e.g. you do apply some of your knowledge, but show gaps in understanding).
- **1–3 marks:** You show only a limited knowledge (e.g. of some theory points).

AS and A Level specifications will assess your quality of written communication (QWC). Marks are likely to be allocated for legible text with accurate spelling, punctuation and grammar, and for a clear, well-organised answer in which you use specialist ICT terminology and acronyms effectively.

Exam tips

Exam technique

Examiners use instructions to help you to decide the length and depth of your answer:

State, define, list, outline: These key words require short, concise answers, and often recall of material that you have memorised.

Explain, describe, discuss: Some reasoning or some reference to theory is needed, depending on the context. Explaining and discussing require you to give a more detailed answer than when you are asked to 'describe' something.

Apply: With an 'apply' question, you must make sure that you relate your answer to the given situation (this is always good practice in ICT exams).

Evaluate: You are required to provide full and detailed arguments, often 'for' and 'against', to show your depth of understanding.

Calculate: A numerical answer is required here.

What grade do you want?

Everyone would like to improve their grades but you will only manage this with a lot of hard work and determination. Your final A Level grade depends on the extent to which you meet the assessment objectives listed earlier. The hints below offer advice on how to improve your grade.

A* or A grade

To achieve a grade A* or A you have to:
- show in-depth knowledge and critical understanding of a wide range of ICT theory and concepts
- apply your knowledge and understanding to familiar and unfamiliar situations, problems and issues, identifying the use of appropriate hardware, software and problem-solving techniques
- evaluate effectively evidence and arguments
- make reasoned judgements in presenting appropriate conclusions.

You have to be a very good all-rounder to achieve a grade A* or A. The exams test all areas of the syllabus, and any weaknesses in your understanding of ICT will be found out.

C grade

To achieve a grade C you need to have a good understanding of the aspects shown in the criteria to gain an A grade (shown above), but you will have weaknesses in some of these areas. To improve, you will need to work hard to overcome these weaknesses, and also make sure that you have an efficient and effective exam technique.

1 Processing data for information and deriving knowledge

The following topics are covered in this chapter:

- **Data types, sources and structures**
- **Handling and checking data**
- **Deriving, conveying and presenting information**

1.1 Data types, sources and structures

LEARNING SUMMARY

After studying this section you should be able to:

- understand the relationship between data and information
- identify the key features of different data types
- describe the advantages and disadvantages of using direct and indirect data sources
- explain the difference between dynamic and static data structures
- explain the purpose of encoding and encrypting data

Data and information

AQA   **INFO 2**
OCR   **G061**
WJEC   **IT1**
CCEA   **AS 1**

> **KEY POINT**
>
> **Data** is simply raw sets of facts and figures that have absolutely no meaning until they are processed and turned into something that has a useful purpose (e.g. 21111805).
>
> **Information** is data that has been made meaningful by being processed, formatted and put into context. Once a user knows what the raw data means (e.g. that 21111805 is 21st November 1805), the data has become information.

Whilst we usually think of data as taking the form of text, numbers and symbols, it can also come in the form of audio, still and moving images. The smallest piece of information that can be processed by a computer is called a **bit** and most computers store bits together in groups of eight, known as **bytes**. Each byte contains enough information to represent a number, letter, symbol or screen pixel, and provides the computer with enough information to process the data effectively. No matter what type of data is entered into a system, the computer stores it as **binary code** (a series of '1's and '0's) and processes it by creating **digital** signals that correspond to the binary digits.

In order for data to be read and processed by a computer's **Central Processing Unit** (**CPU**), the individual items need to be formatted in a way that best suits their content.

Characters are single units of information that represent letters, numerical digits, punctuation marks and symbols. In most cases, characters are grouped together into **strings**.

Integer data consists of whole numbers (i.e. those numbers that do not include decimal points or fractions). Integers can be stored with both positive and negative values (e.g. 0, 2, -78 and 18829).

Real data (also referred to as **floating-point numbers**) is numerical data (both positive and negative) that includes a decimal point so cannot be represented by integers (e.g. 35.6, 274.9385, 7.92). Real data is frequently used to represent quantities (e.g. currency and measurement), but can only store the numerical component and not the unit of measurement. This means that in order to make sense of real data it needs to be placed into context.

Alphanumeric strings (also referred to as **text** or **string**) consist of sequences of characters representing combinations of text, numbers and symbols. This includes data such as house numbers (e.g. 28 The Laurels), postcodes (e.g. M12 8BS), passwords (e.g. G29*m-9) and email addresses (e.g. info@letts.co.uk).

Boolean is the most basic data type in that it can only have one of two values, true or false (sometimes referred to as **truth values** or **logic**). Boolean data fits nicely with the binary numbering system used by the computer's CPU, where each bit has a value of either 1 or 0 and can be used to represent the two values true or false (also on/off, yes/no and other values that represent either one thing or its opposite). Examples of Boolean logic include asking a question such as 'Are you under the age of 21?' (expecting an answer of yes or no), asking if a statement is true or false, or programming an electronic timer to activate an electrical item (i.e. to turn it on or off).

Date/time data is, as the name describes, the way in which dates and times are stored (e.g. the time of a doctor's appointment or a person's date of birth). There are many variations in the way in which this data is entered and displayed. For example, in the UK the date 7th December 1964 can be displayed as either 07/12/64, 07/12/1964, 07-12-64, 07-12-1964 or 7-Dec-1964, whilst in the US the position of the month and date are reversed (i.e. 12/07/64).

Although software will allow dates to be entered in different formats, the data is stored as a single number which represents the number of days that have passed since a fixed date (in the case of Microsoft® Excel this is 1st January 1900, and for Open Office this is 31st December 1899). This means that the number stored by the software is exactly the same no matter what format it has been entered in.

Deciding how to store data so that it meets the needs of particular situations involves asking questions such as:
- Will calculations need to be carried out on the data?
  - If yes, then the data will probably need to be stored as integer or real
  - If no, then the data can probably be stored as alphanumeric

---

Currency can be stored as both integer and real data. Small figures that include pennies (e.g. £28.46) need to be stored as real data because they include a decimal point. But with large figures (e.g. car and house prices) pennies are rarely included so the data can be stored as integer.

Remember that numerical data (e.g. integers and real data) cannot be stored or displayed with a zero as the first digit (e.g. 072), therefore numbers that need to be displayed in this way such as telephone numbers (e.g. 01316631971), catalogue and membership numbers (e.g. 01078), or account numbers (e.g. 002901029385), need to be stored as an alphanumeric string.

Try checking out the date algorithm yourself. Open a spreadsheet and enter the number '1', and then format the cell as date. Excel® will display the contents of the cell as 1 January 1900. If you enter the number 32 into a formatted cell it will be displayed as 1 February 1900. In reverse, if you enter the date 30 May 2011 and change the format from date to number, it will display the figure 40693 (the number of days that have passed since 1 January 1900).

- Does the numerical data involved large or small figures?
  - If small figures (e.g. cost of a CD) the data will need to be stored as real
  - If large figures (e.g. cost of a car) the data can be stored as integer
- Does the data involve logic?
  - If yes, then it will need to be stored as Boolean

Sources of data

AQA	**INFO 2**
OCR	**G061**
WJEC	**IT1**
CCEA	**AS 1**

Data is usually categorised as either being **direct** or **indirect**.

Direct data

When data is collected for a specific purpose (e.g. hourly weather readings used to make comparisons across a region), it is referred to as direct data. Direct data can be collected either by the organisation itself, or by third-party agents acting under the instructions of the commissioning organisation.

Direct data is data that has been gathered:
- for a particular purpose
- from original sources
- using methods such as:
  - direct observation (e.g. watching and recording events, occurrences, actions and reactions)
  - indirect observation (e.g. automated logging of actions and transactions using sensors)
  - face-to-face questioning (e.g. through interviews, surveys, questionnaires, phone polls)
  - indirect questioning (e.g. through printed and online surveys, questionnaires, forms).

Advantages of direct data	Disadvantages of direct data
<ul><li>Being able to verify the source and quality of the data (e.g. its accuracy and the way in which it was collected).</li><li>Having control over the type of data that is collected.</li><li>Ensuring that no bias is introduced into the data as it is collected.</li><li>Being in control of decisions about where the data is collected from (e.g. particular socio-economic, age and/or interest groups).</li><li>Being in a position to collect additional data if the initial responses gathered indicate that changes are required.</li></ul>	<ul><li>Being constrained by the high costs involved in collecting from direct sources.</li><li>Not being able to gather data at the optimum time (e.g. research on Christmas shopping patterns carried out in August is likely to be less effective than if it was carried out during the Christmas period).</li><li>Finding that it is not possible or financially viable to directly collect the data required (e.g. to compare shopping habits of people across the globe).</li></ul>

Indirect data

When data is used for a purpose other than that for which it was collected (e.g. data that records credit card transactions being used to examine buying trends), it is referred to as indirect data.

Indirect data is data that has been:
- collected for one purpose and used for another
- borrowed or purchased from a third-party
- created as a result of the additional processing of an original set of direct data
- assembled as a sub-set of a larger data set
- created as a result of merging two or more sets of data
- stored in archives (whether previously used or not).

Advantages of indirect data	Disadvantages of indirect data
- Being able to access larger sets of data than it might be possible to gather from direct sources. - Being able to access data from geographical locations that would otherwise be inaccessible. - Having access to data that was collected at the optimum time (e.g. able to analyse data on Christmas shopping patterns any time of the year). - Being able to compare your own analysis of the data with similar results that have been previously processed from the same data.	- Having no control over the original sourcing of the data. - Not being able to confirm the impartiality of those providing the data, or of the way in which it was collected. - Not knowing if the data is the result of several other data sets that have been merged together (making it less reliable). - Being unable to fill any gaps in the data.

Confidentiality of data

Whilst it is always possible for abuses of data to occur, when it comes to the use of personal data (i.e. information about people) the **Data Protection Act** sets out clear rules that have to be followed by organisations that use data for any purpose other than that for which it was collected. Breaking these rules can result in heavy fines and, in extreme cases, imprisonment.

Dynamic and static data structures

AQA **INFO 2**
OCR **G061**
WJEC **IT1**
CCEA **AS 1**

KEY POINT

A data structure is a way of organising and storing data so that it can be used efficiently. Whilst there are many ways of doing this for specialised purposes, in general terms these structures can be classified as consisting of either **dynamic data** or **static data**.

Dynamic data structures

FaceBook, YouTube and Twitter are typical examples of websites based upon the use of dynamic data.

Dynamic data structures contain information that changes over a period of time. The data can be added to and edited as it changes or as updates become available. In some cases data may only be updated after fairly long intervals. For example, the rate at which value added tax (VAT) is paid rarely changes, but the fact that it can (and does) change from time to time means that information about VAT needs to be stored as dynamic data. In other cases data may need to be updated every few weeks (e.g. club membership lists and monthly progress reports). Data may also need to be updated on a very frequent basis (e.g. the price of stocks and shares, information on sales and warehouse stock control).

The Internet has considerably increased the number of people who access dynamic data and who actively contribute to the regular updating of data, not only in their own private domains, but also in the public domain (e.g. contributing to social blogs, uploading photographs and video recordings, creating specialist interest and club websites).

Dynamic data can easily be kept up-to-date in order to reflect ongoing changes. However, due to the rapid turnover of data, it is likely that less effort will be put into checking its quality.

Static data structures

Static data structures contain information that does not change. It is data that occurs just once in the lifespan of the data set, and cannot be edited, added to or deleted. Because of the design of static data structures adding, editing or deleting a single item of data is a time-consuming and costly business. Static data structures are usually only used where it is clear that no changes are likely to occur during the lifetime of the data set. Static data is commonly used for the purpose of creating paper-based archives, CD-ROMs (e.g. encyclopaedias, directories), e-books (e.g. electronic downloads), and some websites.

Static data can be linked with dynamic data to provide increased accessibility to data. For example, a directory of businesses might be distributed in the form of a CD-ROM containing static data, but by including hyperlinks it could provide access to additional dynamic data on each of the businesses listed.

Static data can quickly become out of date. However, due to the amount of time the data will be live, it is likely that more effort will be put into checking the quality of the data.

Quality and usefulness of information

AQA	INFO 2
OCR	G061
WJEC	IT1
CCEA	AS 1

The quality and usefulness of information generated from data is initially dependent upon the quality of the source data gathered in the first place. However, it is also dependent upon the way in which the data is processed and presented to the end-user. The age-old saying 'garbage in, garbage out' (often referred to as GIGO) is perfectly true but it is also possible to generate 'quality in, garbage out'.

Each of the factors described below affect the quality and usefulness of information:

Accuracy

There is a distinct difference between information that is wrong, and information that is inaccurate. If a user knows that information is wrong, it can be discounted. However, if a user discovers an error in a data set (e.g. an incorrect date of birth in a list of club members) it raises the question, 'Does the data contain any other errors?' As soon as questions begin to arise relating to the accuracy of the data being used, it can no longer be relied upon or trusted. Having to check the accuracy of data after its initial entry is a time-consuming and costly process, which is why it is important to invest time in checking, validating and verifying data at its point of entry. Inaccurate information is of little use to an end-user.

Age

When processing information it is important to know how long it has been since the data was collected. Whilst some data may have a reasonably long shelf life (i.e. it doesn't change very often), other data changes frequently. When considering whether or not data is up-to-date, it is important to consider the context in which it was collected. For example, because the price of groceries in shops regularly changes, last month's price list will be of little use to someone shopping this week. In contrast, a membership list (e.g. of clubs and societies) will be valid for a much longer period, because each person remains a member for the full year following payment of their membership fee.

Completeness

It is important that information meets the full requirements of the task in hand. Having only part of the information required is of little use. For example, providing a passenger with information about the time of their flight and the airport they will leave from is of no use whatsoever unless they are also told the departure date.

Incomplete data can also be extremely misleading. For example, it might sound quite reasonable to ask a courier to make a delivery to 23 Abbey Road, London, but without including the postcode the courier is likely to have problems because there are five different Abbey Roads in London. Without the postcode the package could easily end up being delivered to the wrong address.

Level of detail

Sometimes there is a fine balance between including too little and too much data. Too little information results in creating an incomplete picture, whilst too much information can easily lead to confusion and result in the end-user missing the point altogether.

For example, if a person asks what time a film starts at a cinema and is told, 'It starts between three o'clock and four o'clock', they do not have enough information to ensure that they arrive on time. In contrast, if they want to know what time their train arrives at a particular station, being given a list of the times at which the train reaches every station on its journey provides much more information than is required and could be confusing.

Presentation

It is important that information is presented in a way that can be easily understood by the target audience. There needs to be consistency in the way in which information is presented (e.g. in the use of headings and sub-headings within a written document). It is also helpful if, where possible, tables, graphs and/or images are used to illustrate or summarise complex text.

Relevance

In order for information to be useful, it needs to be relevant to the purpose for which it was requested. Information that is not relevant can easily result in confusion, with the user wasting time by having to wade through the additional data in order to find what they need.

Encoding and encryption

AQA	INFO 2
OCR	G061
WJEC	IT1
CCEA	AS 1

Many people think of **encoding** and **encryption** as being the same thing, when in fact they are quite different.

Encoding data

Although the term encoding data has other meanings, it is commonly applied to the process by which information is reduced in length in order to make it more manageable. Very often codes are based on the initials or abbreviations of the things they represent. For example, many clothes are coded as S, M, and L, which represents small, medium and large. Likewise, codes are frequently used when referring to days and dates (e.g. DEC represents December and SAT represents Saturday). Although most people can interpret this type of code very easily, we also use more complex codes that computers can recognise easily, even though people find them more difficult to interpret.

For example, standard British car registration plates use a seven figure code, each part of which has a specific meaning. The car registration plate **LA57 FGW** is made up of the following components:

Code	Purpose	Meaning
L	Area code (region) – to identify the DVLA area where the car was first registered	The car was registered in the London area
A	Area code (local office) – to identify the local DVLA office where the car was first registered	The car was registered in the Wimbledon office
57	Age identifier – to identify the six-month period in which the car was first registered	The car was first registered between September 2007 and February 2008
FGW	Random letters – to identify individual cars registered at the same DVLA office	The car's unique identifier

Using codes considerably speeds up data entry. Consider the time and effort needed just to enter the word 'Female' when recording data collected from a survey of hundreds of interviews. Using codes also simplifies the validation process as the operator is less likely to make a mistake when entering the code. In addition to saving time, coded data takes up much less space; the smaller the size of the saved data set, the quicker queries and searches will run.

In some cases it is not possible to code items/responses accurately, particularly where responses require people to make value judgments or give detailed descriptions. The problem with this type of response is that there is no single measurable value because the data collected is a result of someone's opinion. Researchers often use graduated scales to record this type of response but (given that there are hundreds of possible responses) if a researcher were to ask the question 'What is your favourite shade of green?' and use a code (where 1 = light green, 10 = dark green) they would have problems coding the responses because one person's idea of 'light green' is likely to be very different from another's. Using coding in this instance results in some of the finer details in the data being lost. This loss of detail is referred to as **coarsening** of data.

Encryption of data

Encryption is the process of disguising information so that it can only be understood by people with authorised access. It is a key component of keeping data secure. Encryption software is used to convert the original data into a format that is totally unintelligible, ready for on-site storage or electronic transmission to another user. Then, once received, the software converts the encrypted data back into its original format.

Use of encryption keys and/or passwords by the sender and receiver ensures that the data remains secure during storage and/or transit. This process is also sometimes referred to as **scrambling** data. Although originally used to protect diplomatic and military secrets, encryption is now widely used by the banking and financial sector to protect client confidentiality and the transfer of money.

PROGRESS CHECK

1. Identify the data types for the following:
   (a) 6.92   **(b)** 30289   **(c)** M52 6GN
2. List three disadvantages of using indirect data sources.
3. List four factors that affect the quality and usefulness of information.
4. Describe the difference between dynamic and static data structures.

4 Dynamic data structures contain information that changes over a period of time, and static data structures contain information that does not change.
3 Any four from: Accuracy, age, completeness, level of detail, presentation and relevance
2 Any three suitable answers, e.g. No control over the original source; being unable to confirm the impartiality of data; not knowing if the data is a combination of several data sets; inability to fill any gaps in the data.
1 **(a)** real or floating-point **(b)** integer **(c)** alphanumeric string

---

1.2 Handling and checking data

LEARNING SUMMARY

After studying this section you should be able to:

- understand the different types of errors and how they occur
- describe the difference between validation and verification
- produce a graphical representation of the processing cycle
- explain the purpose of backing up and archiving data

Reducing the occurrence of errors

AQA	INFO 2
OCR	G061
WJEC	IT1
CCEA	AS 1

In order for the information derived from the processing of data to be of any value to the user it is essential that the data that has been entered into the system is both accurate in its content and has been entered in the correct format.

KEY POINT

It is important to build in a range of checks that can be used to minimise the possibility of entering incorrect or invalid data.

Transcription errors occur when the data entered is different from that shown in the source. When paper-based data collection methods are used (e.g. printed forms that have been filled out by researchers or by clients), the operator is required to read the form and to key the information it contains into the system (i.e. to turn the data into an electronic format). This process of copying something from one medium to another is called transcription, and errors made during this process are called transcription errors.

There are many reasons why transcription errors occur. These include:
- Unclear source information – the writing on the form might be poor or faint, which makes it difficult for the operator to read.
- Inaccurate source information – the person who completed the form may have misinterpreted the question being asked, or simply have made a mistake when writing their response to the question.
- Poor quality source documents – folds, creases, splashes and stains can make parts of a paper-based source document more difficult to read.
- Miss-keying data – one of the most common causes of transcription errors arises as a result of the operator hitting the wrong keys as they enter data.
- Tiredness – in all walks of life as people become tired they are liable to make mistakes that they would normally not expect to make. In the case of entering data, operators tend to make more errors towards the end of a work session than they do at the start.

Transposition errors occur as a result of the operator entering two numbers or letters in reverse order (e.g. the number '12' being entered instead of '21', or the word 'trail' being entered instead of 'trial'). This type of error is most common among operators/users that touch type, possibly as a result of the operator's brain getting a step ahead of their fingers. Transposition errors are commonly made by human operators, but can also occur when **Optical Character Recognition software (OCR)** is used (see page 42).

Electronic errors commonly occur when using forms and other documents that are designed for automatic reading by scanners and Optical Character Recognition software. These can occur when:
- the paper gets crumpled before being scanned
- the ink or pencil marks on the form become smudged
- unusual fonts have been used
- the document slips as it passes through the scanner resulting in an uneven scan.

Validation

AQA **INFO 2**
OCR **G061**
WJEC **IT1**
CCEA **AS 1**

Validation is the process by which data is checked, as it enters the system, to make sure that it meets a set of pre-prescribed rules and falls within pre-defined boundaries (i.e. that it is valid). Any data falling outside of these boundaries is rejected. For example, if collecting data on the year in which clients were born, the software would check that only numbers had been entered (and not letters), that each entry consisted of four numbers and that, given that no clients are likely to be more than 110 years old, all entries would start with the numbers 19 or 20 (e.g. 1974, 2003).

Validation procedures are usually written as part of the original program code and are consequently invisible to the user, who might be asked to check and re-enter specific items of data. However, whilst validation can check that data meets the requirements of the system, it cannot check its accuracy (e.g. although a year of birth entered as 1963 meets the requirements of the system and passes all validation checks there is no guarantee that this entry is accurate because the operator may have entered 1963 instead of 1983. Therefore, further checks are required to minimise the possibility of inaccuracies occurring. Some of the most commonly used validation rules are explained below.

Allowed character checks ensure that only the type of characters that are expected are accepted. For example, an email address field can be set to require a '@' sign and reject the data if it contains less than or more than a single '@'. Similarly, a text field into which a person's name is to be entered can be set to disallow characters such as '+' and '/'.

Check digit checks (which is a **checksum** function) are used for numerical data. The check digit is an extra digit added to the end of a number which is the result of a calculation performed on the other digits in the number. This process is commonly used as part of the International Article Number system (EAN-13) that is used to generate 13 digit bar codes, and was also part of the original 12 digit Universal Product Code (UPC) coding system. Whilst the first 12 digits represent the maker's identification number and the unique item number for the product, the final digit in the code (the check digit) is used by a scanner (e.g. at a supermarket checkout) to check that the number has been correctly recognised by the system. Given that a scan can register incorrect data (due to things such as inconsistent scanning speeds, poor quality barcode printouts, folded/crumpled labels, and marks and stains on the barcode), it is important to verify that the data contained within the barcode has been interpreted correctly.

> Even though hundreds of thousands of items are scanned every day, the use of check digits on barcodes is the main reason why so few errors are made at supermarket checkouts.

The following example uses the EAN-13 barcode for the Letts ICT GCSE Success Revision Guide (9781843156505) to demonstrate that the check digit (the final digit '5') is correct.

ISBN 978-1-84315-650-5

1. Remove the check digit from the number (i.e. the '5'), to leave 978184315650.
2. Starting on the right (and not the left as you would normally expect) label the first digit as odd and then work towards the left labelling all other digits as being in odd or even positions. In this case, the pattern of numbers would look like this:

9	7	8	1	8	4	3	1	5	6	5	0	Start from this end
even	odd	even	odd	even	odd	even	odd	even	odd	even	odd	

3. Add up all the digits in 'odd' positions (except the 13th digit – the check digit) and then multiply the result by three (e.g. 7 + 1 + 4 + 1 + 6 + 0 = 19 x 3 = 57).
4. Add up all the digits in 'even' positions (e.g. 9 + 8 + 8 + 3 + 5 + 5 = 38).
5. Add the totals for the odd and even positions together (e.g. 57 + 38 = 95).
6. The check digit is the number which, when added to the total (in this case 95) can be divided by 10. So in this case, for the total to be divisible by 10, the number 5 needs to be added to the total of 95. Therefore, the check digit is 5

(as shown in the original barcode). Note that if the total is already divisible by 10, the check digit would be '0'.

Check digits are also used in international bank account numbers, vehicle identification numbers (VINs), EU cattle passport numbers and ISBN and ISSN book/publication numbers.

Consistency checks ensure that data in two or more fields correspond with each other. For example, if 'Mrs' is entered into the 'Title' field on a client database, the consistency check makes sure that the 'Gender' field equals 'F' (female).

Format checks (also referred to as picture checks) ensure that data has been entered in the correct format (e.g. Boolean, integer, real, text/string, date/time) and, where appropriate, uses a predetermined pattern of letters and numbers. For example:

- A UK postcode would take the format (pattern) of two letters, a single number, an optional single number, a space, a single number, and two letters (e.g. CV3 1AF or CV35 2LZ).
- A date of birth could take on the format of DD/MM/YY or DD/MM/YYYY where D = day, M = month and Y = year (e.g. 15/04/79 or 15/04/1979).

Length checks ensure the data has the correct number of characters. For example, that a year includes four characters or that a bank account number includes eight characters.

Look-up checks compare the entered data with existing stored data to ensure that the entry is correct. Look-up checks are also used to trigger searches for other relevant data. For example, when working with online shopping accounts, following the entry of one or two key items of information (e.g. logon, password and account number) a look-up check is used to find and display all of the client's account details.

Presence checks are used to ensure that required data is entered into specific fields (i.e. that the required data is present and has not been missed out). For example, an email cannot be sent unless an address has been entered into the 'To' box. Every time a user clicks the 'Send' button, the software carries out a presence check to see if a valid email address has been entered. Presence checks are often used with online electronic forms (particularly with e-commerce). Without certain key items of information the order would not be able to be processed and delivered, so instructions are usually included along the lines of 'Fields marked * must be completed'.

> Often, several different kinds of checks are applied to the same data. For example, when completing an online form the name field might include a presence check, a type check and an allowed character check.

Range checks determine whether or not a set of data falls within a specific range (i.e. within two pre-defined values), and reject any entries that fall outside of the range. For example, the 'month' part of a date must be within the range 1–12.

Spell checks look-up words in a dictionary in order to ensure that they have been correctly entered into text fields and text documents. Spell checks are most commonly used in word processing applications but they can also be applied to data entry.

Type checks (also referred to as 'data type' checks) determine whether or not the data is of the right type. For example, dates of birth should be entered using whole numbers (integers), and family names should be entered using text (letters). Likewise, if the number zero is entered into a field that only accepts text (instead of the letter 'O'), the check would generate an error message.

Verification

AQA **INFO 2**
OCR **G061**
WJEC **IT1**
CCEA **AS 1**

KEY POINT

Whilst validation can check that data meets the requirements of the system, it cannot check its accuracy. **Verification** is the process of checking data that has been entered into the system to make sure that it is accurate.

Manual verification

Manual verification is usually referred to as **proofreading**. This initially occurs when the operator carries out a visual check by comparing what they have entered on-screen (or by looking at a printout of what has been entered) with the document from which they are transcribing (copying) the data. Whilst this may pick up some errors, it is a relatively slow process and there is no guarantee that an operator will spot their own errors. Many computer users refer to the problem of 'being too close to their own work', meaning that no matter how many times the user reads a passage of information, they may never spot some errors.

This is usually addressed by ensuring that a second or third person looks at the entered data to proofread and to check it against the source document. However, this is a time-consuming and expensive process with no guarantees of 100% success.

Automated verification

Double entry verification (sometimes referred to as **double keying**) is the process by which each item of data is entered twice and the computer then checks that both versions are identical before accepting them. A common example of double entry verification occurs when users create an online account. In order for an organisation to make sure that they have at least one valid way of communicating with the person who has set up the account, double entry verification is carried out on the client's email address by asking the customer to enter it twice. By doing this, the system checks that the email address has been entered as the user intended (e.g. with no transposition errors or miss-keying of data), and will not allow the set up procedure to continue until the two entries are identical.

For the purpose of commercial data entry, requiring operators to enter every item of data twice is time-consuming and can still result in potential errors.

In order to overcome 'single operator' transcription and transposition errors, the same set of data can be entered by two different operators. Then, when both sets have been entered the computer compares them and generates a report which highlights any errors. Whilst this effectively doubles the amount of work that needs to be done by operators (making it more costly), the result is that only verified data is added to the system.

Transfer and migration of data occurs when data is moved from one storage or processing environment to another. Although transfer and migration are both done automatically, it is still possible that errors may occur (i.e. some items of data in the new location differ from those in the original source location). In order to reduce transfer errors, automatic comparison of the two sets of data can be carried out using **parity checks**. This is where an extra **bit** is added to each binary character before it is transferred and then, once in its new location, the **parity bit** is used to check that the data has arrived correctly.

The processing cycle

AQA **INFO 2**
OCR **G061**
WJEC **IT1**
CCEA **AS 1**

In the vast majority of cases, raw data does not provide enough information upon which action can be taken or decisions can be made. The data needs to be processed so that it can be interrogated and used to produce meaningful results.

The **processing cycle** involves data being entered into the system (input) and programs being used to retain (store) and manipulate (process) the data, after which it can be displayed (output) in a meaningful way. In many cases output information (feedback) is also used to help inform input.

The processing cycle

Term	Meaning
Input	The term given to the process of feeding data into a computer. This can be done using a range of input devices such as keyboards, mice, scanners, cameras and sensors.
Processing	The term given to the computerised manipulation of data carried out by software applications and utilities. The type of software used to carry out the processing will depend upon the nature of the data involved and the type of output that is required (e.g. manipulation of financial data would be best carried out by a spreadsheet application, and data that is predominantly in a text format would require the use of word processing software).
Output	The term given to anything that comes out of a computer (output can be both meaningful and meaningless). In most cases the output of processed data is presented in a way that can be easily accessed by a user (e.g. on-screen images, printed documents, sound) or in a format that can be passed on to another source (e.g. data transfer, CD, DVD).
Storage	Where data is held after it has been input, while it is waiting to be processed and once it has been processed. In order to ensure that it is always available, data needs to be stored on non-volatile media (see page 50).
Feedback	The process by which output from the system informs additional input. This is often referred to as a **feedback loop** and is used as an integral part of many control systems. For example, when entering data on a form (input) the computer verifies that it has been entered (processing) and, if a problem is identified, displays an error message (output), after which the data is re-entered (input).

Backing up and archiving data

AQA	**INFO 2**
OCR	**G061**
WJEC	**IT1**
CCEA	**AS 1**

Backing up

The primary purpose of **backing up** data is to ensure that you have a spare copy that can be accessed in the event of the original data being compromised. During backing up, copies of files are saved to an external medium (e.g. an external hard drive, USB flash drive, CD or DVD), but the original versions of the files remain on the computer system.

There are many ways in which data can be compromised, including:

- **Corruption** – errors that occur accidentally within the computer as the data is opened, saved, processed or transmitted.
- **System crash** – even the most reliable computers can break down, and when they do it invariably results in a loss of some data.
- **Disk crash** – errors that occur as a result of damage caused if the read/write head touches the rotating disks in a hard disk drive. This is sometimes caused by incorrect start-up or shutdown procedures (e.g. turning off the power without shutting down the system).
- **Power failure** – no matter how many times users are reminded to save files at frequent intervals, large quantities of data are frequently lost as a result of power cuts/failure.
- **Sabotage** – data that has been deliberately infected, changed, or deleted by another person.
- **Viruses** – data that is infected by a computer virus (in most cases the virus can be removed using antivirus software but there are occasions when it is not possible to clean up the data file).
- **Theft** – whilst most thieves target hardware, once the computer or laptop has gone, so has the data.
- **Loss** – it is surprising how many laptops get left in cafes, in public places, and on trains and buses. Unfortunately, as with theft, when the laptop gets lost so does the data.
- **Deletion** – files are frequently lost when users tidy up the contents of their directories/folders and accidently delete the files they wanted to keep.
- **Overwriting** – perhaps one of the most common causes of lost/compromised data arises from using an existing document as a template, making changes to it and then saving it without giving it a new name. Consequently, most of the content of the original document is lost.

Most modern software offers users the opportunity to activate **auto-save** and **auto-recovery** modes, which saves any open documents at regular intervals and re-opens them when the computer is started up after a crash or power failure. However, no matter how frequently files are saved, they are still vulnerable and can easily become compromised.

Types of backup

Type	Purpose
Full backup (also referred to as a full system backup)	This not only creates a backup copy of data files, it also makes a copy of the Operating System (see page 52), all system settings and all installed software. However, this is generally a time-consuming process because every time a full backup is run all files are backed up whether they have been changed since the last backup or not.
Incremental backup	This only makes copies of the files that have been changed since the last incremental backup was run. However, if a file has been changed for a second or third time since the last full backup, rather than replace the backup file, it creates additional copies.
Differential backup	This makes copies of all files that have been changed since the last backup, and overwrites the previous versions. This type of backup is only suitable if only the latest version of the data is required.

Archiving

The primary purpose of **archiving** is to store data that is no longer in current use but that may be required at some point in the future. During archiving, copies of files are saved to an external medium, and the original versions are removed from the computer system in order to free up space.

It is always difficult to know if redundant data will ever be needed again. For example, it might seem quite reasonable to delete records of employees who no longer work for a company. However, these records might be required for legal and/or tax purposes at some point in the future, so will need to be kept. Archive data can easily be stored on an external medium (e.g. an external hard drive, CD or DVD), or can be sent to a networked or online backup/archiving service. Some key benefits of archiving data include:

- Data storage space is relatively expensive, so archiving old data frees up space for new data.
- By removing old data from the system, the performance of the computer system can be improved considerably (the system has less data to work through during virus checking, backing up and searching procedures, so these processes will take less time).
- Because it will only be accessed on rare occasions, archive data can be compressed in order to minimise the space required for its storage.
- Even though it may not be needed for regular use, being able to refer to archive data allows individuals and organisations the opportunity to refer back if required.

PROGRESS CHECK

1. Describe the purpose of a presence check.
2. Explain how double entry verification works.
3. List three ways in which data files can be compromised.

1. A presence check is used to ensure that required data is entered into a specific field.
2. Each item of data is entered twice and the computer checks that both versions are identical before accepting them.
3. Any three from: Corruption, system crash, disk crash, power failure, sabotage, viruses/malware, theft, loss, deletion, overwriting.

1.3 Deriving, conveying and presenting information

LEARNING SUMMARY

After studying this section you should be able to:

- describe the relationship between information and knowledge
- describe the process by which information is derived
- explain the advantages and disadvantages of using different formats for conveying information
- identify key factors involved in the cost of producing information

Information and knowledge

AQA **INFO 2**
OCR **G061**
WJEC **IT1**
CCEA **AS 1**

Note that inference is the logical process by which new facts are derived from known facts, thus resulting in knowledge.

Many people think of **information** and **knowledge** as being the same thing, whilst others think of knowledge as being the possession of information. However, in terms of ICT, information only becomes knowledge when it is placed into a context that aids decision-making or permits **inference** by the user. For example, 'Tomorrow will be a good day to go sailing', might be the knowledge gained by interpreting weather forecasts.

In order to use information to derive knowledge the user needs to apply a set of rules. In some cases the rules are based on known certainties (e.g. a car engine will not start if there is no fuel in the tank). In other cases the rules are based on probabilities (e.g. I can drive from my home to Oxford in less than one hour *if* the weather is fine *and if* there are no hold-ups on the road). Similarly, if we know two pieces of information (e.g. that Kelly is Susan's daughter and that Brian is Susan's brother), we can use the rules that apply to family relationships to infer that Brian is Kelly's uncle.

However, we can also use existing knowledge to help us to develop sets of rules that will help us interpret new information. For example, inexperienced dinghy sailors tend to require lots of help because they capsize frequently so, using this knowledge, we could develop a rule that during sailing lessons there should be at least one powered safety boat for every six sailing boats.

> **KEY POINT**
>
> It is important to remember that information is based on facts and that knowledge is based on rules of certainties and probabilities.

When a body of information, knowledge, concepts and rules that apply to a particular topic or area of interest are gathered together in a subject–problem–solution format (e.g. the online support services provided by Adobe® , Apple® , Corel® and Microsoft®) it is known as a **knowledge base**. Programs that are designed for extending and/or querying knowledge bases are known as **knowledge-based systems**.

Deriving information

AQA **INFO 2**
OCR **G061**
WJEC **IT1**
CCEA **AS 1**

As we already know, on its own raw data has no meaning. However, once the data has been processed in order to give it meaning it becomes information.

A simple formula for creating information would be:

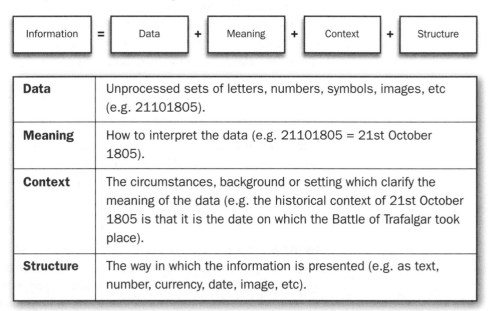

| Information | = | Data | + | Meaning | + | Context | + | Structure |

Data	Unprocessed sets of letters, numbers, symbols, images, etc (e.g. 21101805).
Meaning	How to interpret the data (e.g. 21101805 = 21st October 1805).
Context	The circumstances, background or setting which clarify the meaning of the data (e.g. the historical context of 21st October 1805 is that it is the date on which the Battle of Trafalgar took place).
Structure	The way in which the information is presented (e.g. as text, number, currency, date, image, etc).

Presenting information

AQA **INFO 2**
OCR **G061**
WJEC **IT1**
CCEA **AS 1**

Information can be presented in a wide range of formats and through the use of different media (see Chapter 7). For any system to present information effectively it is important that it uses the most appropriate form and that it meets the needs and requirements of the people who will use it. The method of presentation selected for any particular purpose will need to take into account a range of factors. For example:

- What is the nature of the information that needs to be communicated? (Is it complicated information? Is it technical information? How important is the information?)
- Who is the target audience and do they have any particular requirements? (Will the audience be able to read text easily or can the information be presented in an alternative format?)
- Does the target audience need to understand the information in detail or will they only need an overview? (Do they need to see detailed figures or will a bar chart give sufficient information?)
- How quickly does the information need to be assimilated? (Use of lights to aid instant recognition of motorway lane closures, use of icons to speed up the use of software, use of graphs to illustrate complex numerical data, use of text to report on the outcome of a project).
- What sort of lifespan will the information have? (Will it need to be looked at a second time? Will it need to be updated regularly?)

Text is one of the most common ways that we communicate information, either in hard copy (i.e. printed material) or in soft copy (i.e. on-screen). Textual information forms an integral part of our lives – not only do we read text but we also generate text in order to communicate with others (e.g. emails, text messages, reports, etc). The advantage of text is that it can include lots of detail and has the ability to make things very clear and easy to understand. The use of titles and layout can also help make information much clearer. However, it can take a long time to read and is less accessible for people who find reading difficult, who have impaired eyesight and for speakers of other languages (unless they are bilingual).

Images are visual representations of objects that are displayed on a surface. We use images to communicate information in many different ways. The names we use for these images are often interchangeable (e.g. the word 'graphics' can be used to mean graphs, pictures, symbols and moving images such as animation and video). Images can be used to overcome the problem of language barriers and the recognition of images is generally much quicker than reading text. However, images can be confusing if you do not know how to interpret them, and some images have different meanings in different countries.

Digital images are made up from large numbers of pixels, each of which can consist of one or more bits of information, which represent colour and brightness. In photography, the advantage of working with digital images is that the stored image can be edited using specialist software, and then saved in a range of different formats (e.g. TIFF, JPEG, GIFF).

Symbols are signs that have been given a specific meaning. The Internet and the increased globalisation of communications media have resulted in an ever-increasing commonality of the use of symbols. Some of this arises from the use of symbols and icons that commonly appear on the toolbars used in a wide range of programs; others because of the need to standardise images in commonly used environments (e.g. airports and transport hubs). Although some symbols vary slightly from country to country, there is enough similarity for a user to easily interpret their meaning (e.g. in a public place a sign showing any of the symbols (☎ ① could easily be interpreted as identifying the location of a telephone). However, the meaning of some symbols changes depending upon the context in which they are used. For example, the symbol 'x' is often used to indicate that something is wrong but it is also used to indicate kisses at the end of personal letters or to show that two items should be multiplied.

Pictures are most often thought of as photographs, though in terms of ICT cartoons and drawings are also frequently referred to as pictures. In fact, the terms 'picture' and 'image' can often be interchanged.

Graphics is another overarching term that can be applied to pictures, symbols and graphs. When talking about graphics we are referring to any kind of visible output, which can include individual or combined items of pictures, symbols, graphs, video, animation, photographs and artwork.

Vector graphics are images that are stored as a collection of geometric shapes, the position of which is identified as a set of coordinates and mathematical equations rather than appearing as a bitmap (i.e. a group of pixels). Both the image as a whole, and individual elements within the image, can be edited, resized and rendered independently (see page 169).

Videos are primarily recordings of moving images, most of which are recorded in a format that also includes a synchronised soundtrack. The moving images are stored as a sequence of still images (frames) that are, in effect, photographs taken at regular intervals. The more frequent the frame interval, the smoother the moving image will appear when played back (30 frames per second is the equivalent to film projected in a cinema). Videos can be digitally compressed to allow them to be transmitted across different media (e.g. broadband, wireless laptops and 3G mobile phones), and 'streaming' allows users to start watching videos before the whole thing has finished downloading. Videos can include multiple types of information and if used effectively, can transcend language barriers. They can be used to illustrate concepts more effectively than most other methods of communication. However, their use can be time-consuming (e.g. users may have to watch a long video clip in order to extract a single item of information), and the soundtrack is likely to be difficult to understand by speakers of other languages.

Animation is a **simulation** of movement achieved by displaying a series of frames of man-made images (e.g. drawings, cartoons) or edited photographs (e.g. stop frame animation). Completed animations can be recorded as videos or presented in alternative formats for use in multimedia and web-based applications. Whereas video records **continuous motion** and breaks it into a series of discrete frames, animation does exactly the reverse by starting with individual frames and putting them together in order to create the illusion of continuous motion.

Sound is a key component of video and multimedia products. In the case of computers, all sound is recorded, processed and played in a digital format. Not only can it be used to provide live soundtracks to video clips, it can add considerably to multimedia presentations and also be used to create voice-over commentaries. The advantage of sound is that it can be can be replayed if not easily understood and can be accessed without seeing the source. Sound can easily be accessed by people with visual impairments and can be used in conjunction with speech synthesisers where it is inappropriate or not possible to use text. However, it may be difficult to understand when working in noisy environments and is less accessible for people with hearing difficulties.

Light is a frequently overlooked means of communicating information and something that is used much more often than realised. LEDs (light emitting diodes) emit light when an electrical current is passed through them. Standard LEDs are frequently used within equipment that is controlled either by computer or by a microchip both as indicator lights and in order to create moving message panels. Infrared LEDs form an integral part of remote-controlled devices. Light outputs can be seen from some distance (e.g. overhead warning messages on roads can be seen from several hundred yards), and can be seen in daylight, darkness and adverse weather conditions (e.g. fog warnings on motorways). Lights can be activated very quickly and are ideal for conveying simple information. LEDs are very small so can be grouped together to create screens that display changeable images. However, they can generally only display a limited amount of information and are of no use where there is no direct line of sight. They can also be difficult to understand unless the user is familiar with the context in which they are displayed.

The cost of producing information

AQA **INFO 2**
OCR **G061**
WJEC **IT1**
CCEA **AS 1**

It is important to remember that information does not come free; even if you collect, process or generate information yourself there are key costs that need to be considered.

Personnel

Even though it could be argued that the computer does the hard work of processing the data, people are involved in collecting and/or collating data, deciding how to process the data, deciding how the resulting information will be presented, and distributing the results. These processes all take time, and in a commercial environment the time of personnel is paid for in the form of wages. In addition to the time spent working with the data, personnel need to be trained in order to carry out their work effectively. Training also incurs costs in the form of paying for the trainer, the cost of any materials used, the wages of people attending the training, and the cost of lost productivity (i.e. the work trainees would be doing if they were not at a training session).

Hardware

When considering the cost of hardware, a number of factors need to be taken into account. There is the initial cost of purchasing the hardware and setting up the system, the cost of upgrading and replacing hardware (e.g. as it wears out, breaks down or becomes obsolete), the ongoing costs involved in maintaining the hardware (e.g. IT support, technicians, network managers), and the cost of storage for information as it is gathered, processed and presented (e.g. the cost of initial storage; the cost of backing up and backup storage media, the cost of online backup and archiving services).

Software

The cost of the software will depend upon the type of information being produced. In many cases the use of a generic office suite will be suitable for most purposes. However, for some purposes more specialised software (which is much more expensive than generic software) will be required. In both cases, the way in which the software is used is likely to incur differing costs. For example, most off-the-shelf packages allow the software to be loaded on a single machine, which means that only one person can use it at a time. Rather than buy multiple copies of the same software, it is more cost-effective to buy a **multi-user licence** (the cost of which is based upon how many users need to access the software at the same time). The advantage of licensing is that, as an organisation grows bigger, additional licences can be purchased without requiring additional software to be loaded.

In many cases organisations need to customise the way in which the software they have purchased can best meet their needs (e.g. the way in which their operators will interface with the company database). Therefore, the cost of setting up the customisation of the software (whether done in-house or by consultants) will need to be accounted for. In addition, as with hardware, the cost involved in maintaining and upgrading the software also needs to be taken into account.

Consumables

Despite claims made many years ago that the use of computers would result in a **paperless office**, that day has still not arrived. In fact, it could be argued that organisations now generate much more paper-based information than they did before the introduction of computers. Consequently, the cost of generating paper-based documents needs to be taken into account when considering the overall cost of producing information. Whilst these costs can be cut (e.g. by using recycled items such as recycled paper, ink and toner cartridges), there needs to be a balance between reducing costs and maintaining the quality of the products produced. It should also be remembered that computer hardware runs on electricity, which needs to be paid for.

PROGRESS CHECK

1. Describe what is meant by the term 'knowledge'.
2. Draw a simple diagram to illustrate how information is created.
3. Describe one advantage and one disadvantage of using images to convey information.
4. List the four key factors that need to be taken into account when considering the cost of producing information.

1. Knowledge is the human capacity to understand the relationship between different pieces of information and know what to do with it.

2. | Information | = | Data | + | Meaning | + | Context | + | Structure |

3. Any suitable answers, e.g. An advantage is that the recognition of images is generally much quicker than reading text. A disadvantage is that images can be confusing if you do not know how to interpret them.

4. Personnel, hardware, software and consumables.

Sample questions and model answers

1. Describe two advantages of collecting direct data. **(4)**

Collecting direct data allows you to verify the source and quality of the data, such as its accuracy and the way in which it was collected. Collecting direct data also allows you to make decisions about where the data is collected from, such as particular socio-economic, age and/or interest groups.

2. An airline database needs to store numerical information as either integers or real data. Describe what is meant by the terms 'integer' and 'real data', and in each case give an example of a suitable piece of information that the airline could store in this way. **(4)**

An integer is a whole number that does not include decimal points or fractions. The number of people on an aircraft would be recorded as whole numbers, so could be stored as integers. Real data (also known as real numbers and floating-point numbers) are numbers that include a decimal point. The weight of passengers' luggage is usually recorded in kilograms (e.g. 28.45 Kg), so could be stored as real data.

3. Explain the purpose of using check digits. **(6)**

A check digit (which is a checksum function) is an extra digit added to the end of a number, and is used to check that the main part of the number has been entered into the system correctly. Check digits are commonly used on barcode labels, and are often entered into a computer system via a scanner. Unfortunately the scanning process can result in inaccurate data entry because it is fairly easy for the scanner to misread the barcode (e.g. because there are marks on it, because the paper is torn, because the label is creased). To overcome this, the computer carries out a calculation on the scanned number and compares the answer with the check digit (i.e. the last number on the barcode). If the calculation and check digit match, the data will be accepted. If the calculation and check digit do not match, the system will reject the data and the barcode will need to be rescanned or entered manually.

4. Operators often make transposition errors when entering data. Explain what a transposition error is. **(3)**

Sometimes an operator's mind gets out of step with their fingers, and they enter digits in the wrong order. For example, even though the operator clearly sees the figure 38, they enter the two keys in the wrong order, which means that the figure 83 gets entered instead. This type of error is called a transposition error.

Practice examination questions

1 Describe two factors that could have an effect on the quality of information produced from a data source. **(4)**

    (i) _____

         _____

         _____

         _____

    (ii) _____

         _____

         _____

         _____

2 Explain the relationship between information and knowledge. Give an example to illustrate your answer. **(3)**

_____

_____

_____

_____

_____

_____

3 Explain why data is encoded before being entered into a computer system. Give an example to illustrate your answer. **(3)**

_____

_____

_____

_____

_____

_____

2 Hardware and software components of a system

The following topics are covered in this chapter:

- Computer systems
- Input and output devices
- Accommodating the needs of users
- Data storage
- Software

2.1 Computer systems

LEARNING SUMMARY

After studying this section you should be able to:

- identify the key components of a computer system
- describe the difference between hardware and software
- explain how standardisation affects the choices made by organisations and individuals when selecting hardware and software

Components of a computer system

AQA **INFO 2**
OCR **G061**
WJEC **IT1**
CCEA **AS 1**

When referring to computers the word '**system**' can be used in a number of ways. These include:

- the entire computer system (including the input and output devices, the Operating System and other software)
- the Operating System which provides the user with an interface when no other software applications are running
- a programmed sequence (e.g. system) designed to accomplish a planned task.

ICT systems range in physical size from large **main-frame** computers down to small **microprocessors** that are used to control mobile phones and household equipment such as washing machines and DVD recorders.

In the case of an entire computer system, the system is made up of **hardware** and **software** which, together, enable **data** to be processed electronically and be presented as information.

- Hardware is the parts of the computer that can be physically touched (e.g. the case and its contents). A typical computer system is made up of hardware that includes electronic components (e.g. the motherboard, CPU, solid state memory, display screen) and mechanical components (e.g. the hard drive,

CD/DVD drives, speakers, keyboard, printer), all of which work together to facilitate the input, processing, output and storage of data.

- Software is programs (utilities and applications) that are stored in the computer's memory and that control what it can do (e.g. word processing applications, browser applications, spreadsheet applications).
- Data is basic information which, on its own, has no particular meaning (e.g. 1405, 0511 or 1127), but that can be put into context and given meaning when processed by software.
- Information is data that is presented in context (e.g. that Sunita's PIN code is 1405, that John's birthday is on the 5th November, or that a servo switch should be turned on or off).

A typical computer system (e.g. the type used at home, school or in the workplace) is made up of a number of separate components, including the computer itself, plus any other hardware devices and **peripherals** that are connected to it (e.g. a keyboard, mouse, printer/scanner, speakers, etc). The number and type of peripherals varies considerably depending upon the needs of the people using the system.

Standardisation

AQA **INFO 2**
OCR **G061**
WJEC **IT1**
CCEA **AS 1**

KEY POINT

A **standard** is something against which items, products, processes and services can be measured or judged. In terms of ICT, standards are generally specifications that set out the requirements for a particular item or process.

You can read more about standardisation on pages 62–66.

In the early days of ICT development different organisations competed with each other to create products for an ever expanding market. Whilst this encouraged creativity and innovation from manufacturers, it soon led to confusion and dissatisfaction amongst consumers. When upgrading from one manufacturer's computer to another, consumers discovered that they often needed to purchase a whole new range of peripherals rather than simply plugging in the ones they already owned (e.g. their old Acorn printer would not work with their new Sinclair computer). Manufacturers quickly became aware that some form of standardisation would be of benefit both to them and to their customers, so they began to develop standards that could be applied across the whole industry rather than just within their own organisations.

Types of standards

In some cases standards are incorporated within legislation (i.e. they become law). These standards are often referred to as **de jure** standards. However, within the ICT industry the majority of standards are voluntary and have come about through custom and practice arising from agreement amongst organisations working within the sector. These standards are often referred to as **de facto** standards.

De jure is a term which means 'concerning law'. De jure ICT standards are those that have been agreed by a regulatory body, and to which products/services have to conform. Some standards are set by national organisations such as BSI (the British Standards Institution) and ANSI (the American National Standards

Institute), whilst others are set by international organisations such as ISO (the International Organisation for Standardisation). Because manufacturers make products that are used across the globe, it is important that they conform to the de jure standards of all the countries to which they sell products.

De facto is a term which means 'by fact' or 'in practice'. De facto ICT standards are those that have developed as a result of custom and practice (i.e. because they have been widely used/applied across the ICT sector). For example, there are no laws that insist that a standard keyboard needs to be of a QWERTY format, but because most users have become accustomed to using QWERTY keyboards manufacturers might well find it difficult to sell large quantities of keyboards in an alternative format (see page 40). Likewise, because the Operating Systems used by Microsoft® and Apple® are so dominant within the market, manufacturers need to ensure that their software works effectively on these platforms in order to make their products available to the widest possible audience.

> Note that although most English speaking nations have become accustomed to using QWERTY keyboards, other layouts are used for other languages such as German, Greek and Japanese, etc.

Protocols

> **KEY POINT**
>
> **Protocols** are agreed formats (standards) used by developers to ensure that data can be transmitted between different devices.

Protocols set out rules that developers must use to manage how:
- the receiving device knows when the sending device has started to send data
- the receiving device knows when the sending device has finished sending its data
- the receiving device tells the sending device that it has received the data
- both devices check for errors
- data compression (if any) is used by both the sending and receiving devices.

There are lots of standard protocols that programmers can call upon and they can be an integral part of the hardware or incorporated into the software (or both). Examples of protocols include:
- **Bluetooth®** – a standard for the short-range radio link which allows computers, mobile phones and other portable devices to communicate with each other.
- **FTP** (file transfer protocol) – this sets out the way in which files can be downloaded from, and uploaded to, another computer over the Internet.
- **POP3** (post-office protocol) – computers without a permanent network connection need to use a 'post office' to look after their email until they go online to download it.
- **PPP** (point-to-point protocol) – this is the standard way of connecting a computer to the Internet and checking that the connection is working correctly.
- **TCP/IP** (transmission control protocol/Internet protocol) – this is a combined protocol. Whilst the TCP component enables computers to establish a connection with each other ready to transfer **packets** of data, the IP component allows those packets of data to be labelled and dropped into the system ready for transfer by the TCP. Together, they create a connection that facilitates the effective transmission of data between computers (i.e. sending messages backwards and forwards).

As indicated above, in the early days of ICT development, organisations competed with each other to create innovative new products, resulting in a total lack of standardisation. In an ideal world all ICT products would be totally compatible and totally interchangeable. However, even now, when there is a much greater degree of consultation/collaboration and when organisations use common protocols in the designs, many products are still incompatible.

As quickly as the processing power of CPUs is increased, organisations create new software designed to make use of the expanded processing capacity. As a result of this, if a user tries to load new software more than three or four years after buying their computer, they might well find that the computer's CPU struggles to cope and performs some actions even slower than their original software would have done. Consequently, in order to make best use of the latest software many users update or replace their computer every two or three years.

The format of Operating Systems varies considerably, and software purchased for use with one particular Operating System is unlikely to work with others.

> Note here how the software demands may have a negative impact on processing speeds. You could give examples of how this can impact on personal use of computers – especially in relation to gaming.

Advantages and disadvantages of standardisation

Advantages of standardisation	Disadvantages of standardisation
<ul><li>Minimises compatibility problems (i.e. it ensures that the various components of the system can communicate effectively with each other).</li><li>Facilitates effective transfer of data (i.e. a common data management system is used, which ensures that errors aren't introduced when transferring data from one part of the system to another).</li><li>Reduces training costs (i.e. staff and network managers need to be trained to use/maintain a single system rather than trying to use multiple systems).</li><li>Reduces the cost of technical support (i.e. it is much less expensive to support a single system than multiple systems).</li><li>Helps to maintain corporate identity (i.e. it facilitates the use of common presentation and reporting formats which, in turn, promotes familiarity with content and helps users to identify key items within documents much quicker).</li></ul>	<ul><li>Reduces the opportunity for individual departments within organisations to select software and hardware that best suit their needs (e.g. the sales team in a small organisation have to rely on a standard database rather than being able to select a specialised stock control package).</li><li>Organisations have to make a major investment in new hardware in order to upgrade a relatively inexpensive software application (e.g. if a new Operating System was required by the Finance Department, old PCs may need to be replaced across a whole organisation, even though the PCs would still be fit for purpose within other departments).</li><li>Having to compromise by purchasing an item simply because it's a 'best fit' solution that works for the rest of the organisation's systems (e.g. selecting a Windows-based design package when the design team would prefer to use a Mac-based design package).</li></ul>

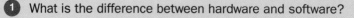

PROGRESS CHECK

PROGRESS CHECK

1. What is the difference between hardware and software?
2. Why is standardisation important?
3. What are de facto standards?

1. Hardware is the parts of the computer system you can touch, and software is the parts that you cannot touch (e.g. the Operating System and application programs).
2. Standardisation helps to minimise compatibility problems and facilitates the effective transfer of data. It also helps reduce training costs and the cost of technical support.
3. De facto standards are those standards that have been developed as a result of custom and practice rather than arising through legislation.

2.2 Input and output devices

LEARNING SUMMARY

After studying this section you should be able to:

- describe the relationship between input and output devices
- explain the advantages and disadvantages of different types of input and output devices
- justify the selection of input and output devices for a specific purpose

Manual and automated input devices

AQA **INFO 1**
OCR **G061**
WJEC **IT1**
CCEA **AS 1**

KEY POINT

Peripherals that are used to feed information into a computer are known as **input devices**. Input devices are used to enter, collect or capture data, convert it into electrical signals and send it to the computer system for further processing.

Data can be input using a manual device (e.g. keyboard or mouse) or it can be input using an automated device (e.g. scanner or barcode reader).

Keyboards

Keyboards are probably the most common form of data input device, and come in a variety of formats including standard, ergonomic, specialist and concept designs. Most English keyboards use a standard **QWERTY** layout, with the main set of keys arranged in exactly the same way as they were on traditional typewriters. The 'QWERTY' name comes from the first five letters as they appear on the top line of the keyboard. In addition to letters, numbers and symbols, most keyboards also include cursor controls to help the user navigate around a page, a separate numerical keypad (similar to those on a calculator), and a series of function keys that can be used as shortcuts for commonly used actions. Each time the user presses a key on the keyboard, an electronic signal is sent to the computer for further processing.

The main problem with using keyboards is that until the user becomes familiar with the layout of the keys, entering information can be quite slow. However, even though most users tend to 'type' with only a few of their fingers, it is surprising how quick this method of data entry can be.

Ergonomic keyboards are similar to standard keyboards, but instead of the keys being laid out in straight rows, they are positioned in a way that is much more comfortable to use when touch typing using all ten fingers and thumbs.

Specialist keyboards are designed for use where a traditional or whole keyboard is not required, such as with Braille keys for use by a blind operator, for use on a bank cash dispenser, or for controlling specialist equipment.

Concept keyboards usually take the form of a flexible plastic membrane covering a set of contact switches. Instead of letters, the membrane is printed with images, symbols or words, each of which represents a particular item of data (e.g. the price of an object). Because they can easily be wiped clean, concept keyboards are very useful in situations where people may have wet or sticky fingers, such as for teaching young children. This type of keyboard is also particularly popular in shops and restaurants, as they are easy to use and require very little training for employees.

Detachable keyboards can be used with most hand-held computers (PDAs). These are usually small QWERTY keyboards that fold up to a size not much larger than the PDA itself. They are particularly popular with people who need to work 'on the move' but who do not want to carry a much larger laptop.

Point and touch input devices

Mice are probably the most useful (and most commonly used) point and touch input devices for use in home, office and school situations. A wide range of mouse types are now available, including traditional 'ball' designs (connected directly to the computer by a cable), wireless ball designs (which 'talk' to the computer via radio signals rather than via wire), and digital tracker designs (which use sensors to identify movement, rather than a ball). Mice can be used to position the cursor when editing text, select images or areas of text, select icons and items from menus, control tools in design software and draw simple objects. However, they are less useful when using portable systems (e.g. laptops and palmtops).

Tracker balls work a bit like an upside down mouse, but instead of moving the mouse to control the cursor, the device remains still while the operator rolls the ball to move (or track) the cursor. Some users find these difficult to use.

Touch sensitive pads (also called track pads) are fitted to most laptops. These allow the user to move their finger across a pad in order to control the position of the cursor on the screen. Although they do not take up much space, many users find them difficult to use.

Touch sensitive buttons (sometimes referred to as pimples or mini joysticks) are fitted to many types of laptop. These react to pressure from the user's finger to move the cursor around the screen. Again, although they take up hardly any space, many users find them difficult to use.

Game pads and **joysticks** are the most popular devices for entering data when playing computer games. They only require cursor movement and the use of a few buttons to control functions and actions. The buttons on these devices can often be programmed to carry out the specific tasks required for each game, which allows users to react more quickly to what they see on screen.

Touch screens are not always the best solution because fingertips are extremely big in comparison with a mouse pointer, which makes it difficult to 'tap' the screen at a precise place or to control fine movements.

Touch sensitive screens are fitted to most hand-held computers and an increasing number of mobile phones. These allow the user to tap and/or drag items shown on the screen by using their finger or other pointing device (e.g. a stylus). Whilst this is a convenient way of operating a hand-held computer, it is a fairly slow process, so is not a good way of inputting large amounts of data. Larger computers can also be fitted with touch sensitive screens for use in specialised environments. On a much larger scale, the interactive whiteboards used in classrooms and training facilities also work by using touch sensitive technology.

Light pens can be used as an input device, but are only usually available for use with specialist design software.

Graphics tablets are two-part devices that include a tablet (or pad) and a stylus (pen). As the user moves the stylus over the tablet, its position is registered and the results appear on the screen. This means that a tablet can be used in a similar way to using traditional pen and paper. Most modern graphics tablets are also pressure sensitive and can be modified to suit the user's needs (e.g. the harder you press, the thicker the line produced).

Graphics digitisers are used to transfer data from an image or drawing into the computer. They work in a similar way to a graphics tablet, but use a puck instead of a stylus. The puck looks a little like a mouse with a small window containing crossed lines that allow the operator to position it accurately. The drawing is laid on the digitiser pad, the puck is positioned over the line to be traced and each time the user clicks the puck a signal is sent to the computer for processing.

Hand-held scanners are, as the name suggests, held in the hand and pulled slowly over the item to be scanned. Although these are small and extremely useful, they tend to be less accurate than flat-bed scanners.

Automated input devices

Scanners can be used to turn images (e.g. text, photos and drawings) into digital data, which can then be processed using appropriate software. The scanner 'maps' the image by turning the colour, shade and tone of each part of the image into different digital codes. The resulting set of data is usually referred to as a bitmap. Unfortunately bitmap files are usually very large and take up a lot of memory, so most graphics packages also include file compression techniques to help make the management of large bitmap files easier.

Flat-bed scanners work by placing the source document face down on a static glass plate (the flat-bed), while the scanner head (which is under the glass) moves mechanically from one end of the document to the other. Some flat-bed scanners also offer document feeder facilities.

Document feeder scanners take a document and (using rollers) pass it steadily across a static scanner head in order for the digital image to be created.

Optical Character Recognition software (OCR) allows scanners to turn the bitmap of a text document (e.g. a report or news cutting) into a digital document that can be edited using word processing software. Whilst it is an extremely useful tool, OCR is completely reliant upon the quality of the scanner, which means that if the scanned image is not particularly clear the OCR software might misinterpret the data (e.g. recognise the shape of the letter 'm' as 'rn' or 'nn').

Therefore the results of an OCR scan always need careful proofreading and editing before further development takes place.

Optical Mark Reader equipment (**OMR**) can be used to recognise marks that have been made on a pre-printed form. OMR equipment works in a similar way to traditional scanners, but because it needs to pick up less detail, the scanner head is able to move much faster. This means that automated OMR scanners can process pre-printed forms very quickly indeed. OMR forms are printed with very light ink (often a pale red), which the computer is programmed to ignore, leaving the computer to recognise only the additional marks that have been made on the form and turn them into electronic data. OMR forms are often used when answering multiple-choice tests.

Barcode equipment is used to identify items (e.g. in libraries, shops and warehouses), by scanning labels on which a unique combination of thick and thin lines and spaces (i.e. 'bars') are printed. This system allows the computer to identify an item very quickly and process the data appropriately (e.g. automatically add the price of an item to a shopping bill). The advantage to retail outlets is that the system is very fast and allows for automatic re-ordering as stock levels fall low.

Magnetic strip and **Personal Identification Number** (PIN) equipment is usually used to identify individual people. This allows a range of actions to take place, such as gaining access to a secure area, making a purchase using a credit card, getting money from a cash point machine, etc.

Other types of input devices

Microphones can be used to capture sound and turn it into a digital format. Amongst other things, this digital signal can be used for audio or video recordings, for VOIP (Voice Over Internet Protocol) telephone calls or for natural dialogue interfacing (e.g. speech recognition activities).

Web cams are mainly used to capture still and moving images ready for either internal processing, importing into multimedia applications or for transmission across the Internet (e.g. for web video-conferencing).

Midi keyboards send musical signals to a computer in a digital format (usually from electronic piano keyboards). The digital signal can then be electronically edited using specialist software.

Output devices

AQA **INFO 1**
OCR **G061**
WJEC **IT1**
CCEA **AS 1**

Screens

A **screen** allows an operator to monitor what the computer is doing (i.e. its output), which is why most screens are referred to as monitors. Clearly, the larger the screen the more expensive they become, and with many people using their computer for multiple purposes (including watching TV and films) wider and larger screens are becoming less expensive and more readily available. The resolution of a screen is a measure of the number of pixels it can display (e.g. 800 x 600 = low resolution and 2048 x 1536 = high resolution). A single pixel is the smallest amount of a screen that can be controlled by a computer.

The first computer screens used Cathode Ray Tube technology (CRT) consisting of a pressurised glass 'tube' in a case (similar to an old television set). However, as the technology evolved, the 'flat' screens that had initially been developed for use on laptops quickly became the preferred solution for desktop display. These used Liquid Crystal Display technology (LCD), and whilst they allowed for high resolution and good quality colour, they had a fairly narrow viewing angle (i.e. the image was only visible if the operator sat directly in front of the screen). Modern flat screens use Thin Film Transistor technology (TFT), which produces an excellent display and can be viewed from much wider angles than the early LCD screens. TFT screens use a much 'softer' light and do not create 'flicker', so are much friendlier to the user's eyes.

Printers

Dot matrix printers work by pressing a series of pins against an ink ribbon that creates an image (made up of a pattern of dots) on the surface of the paper. Although this method of printing is still in use it has largely been replaced by the use of inkjet and laser printers. The dot matrix method of printing cannot produce good quality graphics; it is slow, noisy and produces low quality printouts.

Inkjet printers (also referred to as bubble jet printers) are quiet to run and produce good quality images by spraying tiny drops of ink onto the paper, creating many hundreds of dots per inch. Even fairly basic inkjet printers can produce high quality text and images in full colour, and the market is now full of 'photo quality' inkjets that can be used to produce very high definition photographic prints. However, most inkjet printers are designed for low volume work (i.e. for personal use) so they are not economic to use for large print runs or where they will be in use constantly (e.g. in a busy office). It is also important to remember that the price of consumables is increased considerably when printing full colour graphics and photographs, as each print uses large quantities of ink.

Laser printers are the most expensive type of printers to purchase, but are the most economical to run. Originally only used for black and white printouts, colour lasers are now much more affordable (some models are available for under £300) and produce excellent quality output. Laser printers work by using laser beams to form an electrostatic image on a rotating drum. Toner powder is attracted to the electrostatic image on the drum and is then rolled onto the paper before being fused to the paper by being heated. Although this is a more complex method of printing, it can produce very high quality images and operate at high speeds. Colour laser printing is much slower than black and white, as it uses four toner cartridges to transfer the different coloured inks (Cyan, Magenta, Yellow and Black) onto the drum before printing each copy. Laser printers have many more moving parts than inkjet printers, so in addition to the toner refills, other parts (e.g. the transfer drum and fuser unit) need replacing at regular intervals. Nevertheless, laser printers provide a quiet, fast and efficient method of printing small and large quantities in both black and white and colour.

Thermal printers are commonly used to create receipts in cash registers and hand-held credit card machines. They work with a special type of paper that is coated with a surface that changes colour (usually black) when exposed to heat. The paper, which is usually in rolls, is passed over a line of pins (heating elements) which burn the dots onto the paper. This type of printer rarely suffers from paper jams because there are no paper feed mechanisms (they generally use rolls rather than sheets of paper), and they are very cost effective because they do not require toner or ink cartridges.

Plotters are used to produce precision graphics (e.g. architectural drawings and building plans) on large sheets of paper. Although they are fairly slow, they can draw accurate and continuous lines and curves by moving coloured pens across the paper on a mechanical arm. Plotters are available in both flat-bed and drum formats.

Other types of output devices

Speakers (loudspeakers) convert electrical signals into sound. In addition to providing audible warning and alert sounds (e.g. that an error has occurred or that a new email has arrived), speakers can be used to output digital music from an audio soundtrack, synthesized speech from text-to-speech software and audio from a VOIP telephone call. Although some speakers can be incorporated into the hardware (e.g. in a laptop or in a TFT screen), for high-quality sound additional external speakers are required. The main drawback of using speakers is that they can generally be heard by other people who are close by, which means that it is difficult to maintain privacy. However, in contrast, speakers can be used in a way that deliberately allows multiple users to listen (e.g. surround-sound home cinema systems).

Headphones and **earphones** are, in effect, miniature speakers that can be worn on the head. The advantage of using headphones is that the user can listen to the audio output without interfering or distracting other people, which allows the user to maintain a high degree of privacy.

Digital projectors can be used to display digital images onto large surfaces. They are particularly useful for giving presentations. Digital projectors have also been developed to work directly with DVD and Blu-ray players to create home cinema environments.

Smart boards are like interactive digital projectors, in that they not only display digital images but also have the advantage of including a touch-screen interface.

Control devices such as **motors** and **actuators** (both hydraulic and pneumatic actuators), can be used to turn digital signals into physical motion (e.g. to raise an automatic garage door, open a window in a greenhouse when it gets too hot, focus the lens on a security camera, or to control a robotic arm).

PROGRESS CHECK

1. What are point and touch devices?
2. Give one advantage and one disadvantage of using Optical Mark Reader (OMR) equipment.
3. What type of output device is best suited to creating hard copies of colour photographs?

1. Point and touch devices are input devices that move a symbol (cursor) around the screen. When placed over an icon or menu item, the item can be selected/opened with a single or double click.
2. OMR equipment can be used to input data by scanning documents much quicker than manual data entry. However, smudged pencil and ink marks, and creases in the paper can result in errors in the data that is collected.
3. Whilst laser printers can print colour photographs, they often struggle with specialist photographic papers and the quality of image is relatively poor. In contrast, inkjet printers can accommodate photographic quality paper and produce high-quality photographs. However, the need for specialist paper and use of large quantities of ink makes printing colour photographs much more expensive on inkjet printers than on laser printers.

2.3 Accommodating the needs of users

LEARNING SUMMARY

After studying this section you should be able to:

- describe how adaptive hardware can assist users with physical disabilities to input and output data
- describe how adaptive software can support the needs of users with physical disabilities
- justify the selection of adaptive items for users with specific disabilities

Adaptive hardware and peripherals

AQA   **INFO 1, INFO 2**
OCR   **G061**
WJEC   **IT1**
CCEA   **AS 1, A2 1**

> Try to give some practical examples of how these devices might be used – you may find examples in your school or college.

Through our own ongoing use of ICT equipment, most of us are familiar with the more common components of computer systems. However, the use of ICT is not limited to the domain of the able-bodied. For users across the whole ability spectrum (e.g. from those with limited vision to those with almost no bodily movement), the significant technological developments that have occurred in recent years have provided increased opportunities to work alongside other users on an equal basis. To accommodate individual user needs a wide range of hardware, software and peripherals has been developed. Examples of these are described below.

Braille keyboards

Two types of **Braille keyboard** are commonly available:
- The CHORD keyboard (named because it is used in a similar way to playing chords on the piano) has far fewer keys than a standard keyboard. Instead of having a separate key for each letter, the CHORD keyboard has one key for each dot used in a Braille 'cell'. In order to type a single letter, all of the keys that make up the dots in that letter are pressed at the same time.
- Braille QWERTY keyboards are also available. These usually have standard printed letters on the keys with the addition of raised Braille lettering. The advantage of this type of keyboard is that it can be used by both blind and sighted users.

Standard keyboards can be adapted using transparent Braille adhesive stickers.

Braille printers

A **Braille printer** (also referred to as a **Braille embosser**) is an impact printer that presses raised Braille letters into a surface. These printers need to use special paper, which is much thicker than normal paper in order to withstand the embosser process without tearing. Some Braille printers provide the facility to print ink and Braille characters onto the same surface.

Eye typers

In cases where severely disabled people are only capable of moving their eyes, **eye typing** provides an effective means of communication. Eye typing requires the user to select keys from an on-screen virtual keyboard by looking at a particular character for a short period of time. A video camera is used to detect eye movement, and specialist software is used to detect the period of time the user fixes their gaze upon a particular character.

Foot mice

There are many different kinds of **foot mice**, which are designed for users who are unable to use a traditional mouse or touch pad. Some take the form of a shoe with a mouse connected to it; some use a pedal which moves around within a frame; some use a tilting pedal (or pedals) that can be turned and tilted in a number of directions.

Use of a foot mouse is generally slower than that of a traditional mouse because most people have less accurate control of the movement within their legs and feet than they do with their arms and hands.

Head pointers

Some **head pointers** involve the use of a metal stick that is strapped to the user's head so that they can make physical contact with a keyboard through use of head movement alone. Other head pointers use video technology to track a defined point (e.g. a reflective spot on a headband or pair of glasses) and use this to control an on-screen cursor (similar to the movement cursor described on page 48).

Large print keyboards

Large print keyboards are designed for users with poor vision and those who work in conditions where the level of light is low. Whilst the characters that appear on standard keyboards are usually quite small in relation to the size of each key, the characters on large print keyboards are much bigger and cover most of the surface of each key.

Standard keyboards can be adapted using large print adhesive stickers on the keys.

Loudspeakers

Loudspeakers (speakers) convert electrical signals into sound, and are available in a wide range of formats ranging from tiny earphones through to the huge public address systems (PAs) used in concert halls. They can be used in conjunction with microphones to enable users to communicate audibly with other users. They can also be used in conjunction with specialist software, so users can select passages of printed text and then listen to them in audio format. Speakers provide users with the opportunity to listen to soundtracks and commentaries whilst looking at visual representations (a common format for many web pages).

Microphones

Microphones convert sound into an electrical signal. They can be used with ICT equipment to record sound in a digital format, to provide an input for speech recognition software, and as a means of direct communication via web conferencing and web telephone services (e.g. VOIP services such as Skype). Microphones can also be used in **knock sensors** to detect mechanical vibration. When used with specialist speech recognition software, microphones provide users with the opportunity to create text by speaking, and to control systems by using verbal commands.

Movement cursors

Movement cursors are motion detection systems designed to convert head or hand movements into on-screen cursor movements by processing images from a video camera.

Oversized keyboards

Oversized keyboards are designed for users who have problems with hand and finger movement (e.g. arthritis). They have larger than normal keys that provide the user with better finger contact and keyboard control, and large letters to aid readability.

Suck and puff switches

Suck and puff switches are designed to allow users with severely limited movement to independently operate electronic equipment (e.g. powered wheelchairs and communication software/hardware). The user operates equipment by either sucking and/or blowing on a mouthpiece or by squeezing a ball on the end of a tube in order to activate a switch, which in turn is connected to a microprocessor or computer.

Touch screens

Whilst the use of touch screen technology has become commonplace in recent years (e.g. on mobile phones and satellite navigation systems), it should not be forgotten that touch screens also provide an effective interface for users with limited mobility. If required, they can be used in conjunction with a head pointer.

Adaptive software

AQA	**INFO 1, INFO 2**
OCR	**G061**
WJEC	**IT1**
CCEA	**AS 1**

A wide range of software has also been developed to support the needs of users with physical disabilities. Examples of these are described below.

Predictive text

Predictive text is designed to make the entry of data much quicker than normal. As soon as a user types the first letter of a word, an on-screen prediction window shows the most commonly used words that start with the entered letters. As the user continues to enter additional letters, the selection of words is narrowed down until one can be selected.

Although available for use with QWERTY keyboards, the most common use of predictive text is with mobile telephones. Systems such as T9 and iTap make specific use of the nine letter keys on a mobile keypad to speed up the creation of messages by effective use of predictive text.

Speech recognition and speech synthesisers

Speech recognition uses specialist software to convert words spoken into a microphone into text (e.g. for word processing) and/or to control systems using spoken commands. The term 'speech recognition' generally applies when the software is able to recognise speech from a range of different users, whilst the term 'voice recognition' generally applies when the software requires training in order to recognise a particular user's voice. Speech/voice recognition software can greatly increase the input speed of users who are slow at inputting data via a keyboard. Speech recognition is also widely used for voice interfaces such as automated telephone responses (e.g. 'If you are a new customer, please say Yes'), entering basic data over the telephone (e.g. a credit card number), and voice dialling systems (e.g. 'Call John').

Speech synthesisers can turn data and text into human speech. Used in conjunction with headphones or speakers, this can provide partially sighted and blind users with an extremely effective way of interacting with output.

Sticky keys

The sticky keys feature allows users to use key combinations (e.g. those involving the Ctrl, Alt, or Shift key) by pressing only one key at a time rather than both/all at the same time. With this feature activated, a user can press and release the Shift key and then press a character key to create an uppercase character, rather than press the Shift and character keys at the same time. The sticky keys feature causes the Shift key to remain active until another key has been pressed, after which the keyboard returns to its normal state.

Zoom

Most software applications include inbuilt zoom facilities, which allow users to increase or decrease the size/scale of the on-screen image in order to make it easier to view. Many Operating Systems also include features that allow users to magnify specific parts of the screen to make them more accessible. In some cases these take the form of a magnifying glass that can be moved around the screen to enlarge the image/text below.

PROGRESS CHECK

1. What is the purpose of adaptive hardware and software?
2. Give an example of one input and one output device that could be used by a blind user.
3. What is the purpose of large print keyboards?

3 A large print keyboard makes it easier for users with limited eyesight to use a QWERTY keyboard.
2 Any suitable answer, e.g. A Braille keyboard could be used to input data and a speech synthesiser with speakers could provide an audio output.
1 Adaptive hardware and software provides people with physical disabilities suitable ways in which to access ICT.

2.4 Data storage

LEARNING SUMMARY

After studying this section you should be able to:

- explain the difference between read-only and random-access memory
- describe the difference between volatile and non-volatile storage
- justify the selection of specific types of storage for a particular purpose

Data storage is the process by which data is held in a digital format that can be read by a computer's internal (primary) and external (secondary) memory.

Internal (primary) memory

AQA **INFO 1**
OCR **G061**
WJEC **IT1**
CCEA **AS 1**

KEY POINT

The computer's internal memory consists of **read-only memory** (**ROM**) and **random-access memory** (**RAM**).

ROM

Read-only memory (ROM) contains data that the computer's manufacturers do not want to be changed (i.e. the ROM can be read from but cannot be changed or added to). The computer's ROM is '**non-volatile**' which means that it does not disappear when the computer is shut down. It is used to store the instructions that are used to boot up the computer and make sure that the Operating System is loaded correctly every time the computer is turned on.

RAM

Random-access memory (RAM) is located on the computer's motherboard alongside the processor. The RAM is the computer's **primary storage** and is used to temporarily store program code and data while the processor carries out its tasks. By adding more RAM to a computer system its performance can be increased considerably and its capacity to run multiple programs at the same time is vastly improved. The computer's RAM is '**volatile**', which means that it is wiped every time the computer is turned off.

External (secondary) memory

AQA **INFO 1**
OCR **G061**
WJEC **IT1**
CCEA **AS 1**

Only a small amount of data can be stored in the internal memory, so it is essential to have enough external memory (also referred to as **secondary memory**) to store the Operating System, the software applications and data required.

Magnetic media

In the case of ICT, magnetic media refers to the storage of data on magnetised surfaces that is accessed through use of magnetic read/write heads.

Hard drives (also referred to as **hard disks**) are sets of rigid magnetic disks that rotate between a series of read/write heads. Most computer systems include at least one hard drive that is permanently connected to the motherboard. Hard drives are capable of storing large quantities of data, and the use of 1 TB (one

A terabyte is 1024 gigabytes.

terabyte) drives is now commonplace. Additional external hard drives are frequently added to systems for the purpose of backing up and archiving data.

Floppy disks are now a thing of the past because, by current comparisons, they were capable of holding so little data (only 1.44 MB). However, many computer systems remain capable of accepting floppy disks even though they are now of limited use. They consisted of a thin, flexible magnetic disk housed in a plastic sleeve.

Magnetic tape is another medium that is rarely used nowadays. Consisting of a thin magnetic strip, housed on a reel or in a cassette/cartridge, it was commonly used for backing up and archiving data. Whilst magnetic tape is still used with some systems, the falling cost of hard drive technology has resulted in most backing up and archiving systems being switched to high-capacity hard drives.

Optical media

In the case of ICT, optical media consists of circular plastic disks which carry encoded data on their surface and which are read by reflecting a low-powered laser beam off their surface. The data is stored in binary form. Small areas that reflect light (land) represent the binary value of 1, and other areas that do not reflect light (pits) reflect the binary value of 0.

CDs (compact disks) are the most common form of optical media. They are available in a number of formats. CD-ROMs (compact disk read-only memory) contain non-volatile data that can be read from but cannot be changed; they are commonly used for audio disks and distribution of software. CD-Rs (compact disk recordable) are commonly used for storage and archiving relatively small quantities of data, and whilst they are inexpensive they can only be written to (e.g. recorded on) once, after which they cannot be erased or re-recorded on. CD-R disks can be played on audio CD players, CD-ROM drives and also on most DVD players. CD-RWs (compact disk rewritable) are similar to CD-Rs but can be written to (recorded on) on more than one occasion. CD-RWs can also be erased and re-recorded on as often as required. Whilst significantly more versatile than CD-Rs, they can only be played on CD players, CD-ROM drives and DVD drives that are specifically listed as CD-RW compatible.

DVDs (digital versatile disk or digital video disk) are high density optical disks, and although they are exactly the same size as CDs they are capable of storing up to seven times more data. DVDs were developed primarily for video and data storage, and are widely used within the entertainments industry to distribute movies. DVDs can store up to 17 GB of data. As with CDs, they are available in a number of formats, including DVD-ROM (read-only), DVD-R (recordable) DVD-RW (re-writable).

Blu-ray is a format of optical disk that has been developed to improve upon the standard DVD format by being able to store high-definition video and computer games. The name of the disk comes from the blue laser light that is used to read the data (unlike CDs and DVDs which use a red laser light). Blu-ray disks can store up to 50 GB of data.

Solid-state storage

In the case of ICT, **solid-state drives** (SSD) are devices that use solid-state memory (e.g. microchips) to store data. Because they have no moving parts, solid-state drives are silent, and are quicker and less vulnerable than electronic and optical disks. Another key advantage of solid-state drives is that most of them use **non-volatile flash memory**, which continues storing the data even when the power is turned off. Solid-state storage is available in a number of formats, including:

- CompactFlash cards (frequently found in digital cameras)
- USB flash drives (also called data sticks, jump drives, etc)
- Memory cards (commonly used in digital cameras, mobile phones, games consoles, MP3 players, etc)
- Memory sticks (found in some brands of digital cameras).

The fact that most forms of solid-state storage are small and lightweight makes them very portable and ideal for users to transfer small quantities of data from machine to machine, site to site and work to home.

PROGRESS CHECK

1. What is primary memory?
2. Why is secondary memory required?
3. What is the difference between magnetic media and solid-state storage?

1. Primary memory is the computer's internal memory. It is the CPU's ROM plus the RAM that is permanently attached to the motherboard.
2. Only a small amount of data can be stored in the internal memory, so it is essential to have enough secondary memory (such as hard drives) to store the Operating System, the software applications and data required.
3. Magnetic media refers to the storage of data on magnetised surfaces and requires the use of moving parts (e.g. disks and read/write heads) while solid-state storage stores data directly onto microchips and requires no moving parts.

2.5 Software

LEARNING SUMMARY	**After studying this section you should be able to:** - explain the differing roles of Operating Systems, utilities and applications software - describe the characteristics of different types of user interface - justify the selection of specific software applications for a particular purpose

Operating Systems

AQA **INFO 2**
OCR **G061**
WJEC **IT1**
CCEA **AS 1**

Before applications such as word processing and spreadsheet software can be loaded and run, a computer needs to know how to accept software as it is loaded, and what to do in order to make it function effectively. Therefore the starting point for any computer system is the system software which controls the way in which the computer functions. It is this system software that provides an interface between the user and the computer hardware and peripherals. At the heart of the system software is an **Operating System** (OS) which controls the way in which the computer works. The Operating System provides a software platform that enables application programs to run.

Operating Systems are generally classified in the following way:

- **Multi-user** – allowing two or more users to run software concurrently (at the same time). With some Operating Systems it is possible for thousands of users to access the system at the same time.
- **Multi-processing** – allowing a computer to use two or more CPUs in a single system (e.g. multi-core processors). This can also be referred to as **parallel processing**. OS/2 and UNIX are examples of multi-processing Operating Systems.
- **Multi-tasking** – allowing several programs to be run concurrently. Many people also refer to this as multi-processing although, technically, multi-processing involves more than one CPU (as described above) whilst multi-tasking is carried out by a single CPU which switches between the multiple programs so quickly that it seems to be running them concurrently.
- **Multi-threading** – allowing different parts of the same program (called threads) to run at the same time without interfering with each other.
- **Real-time** – providing instant response to a user's input. Most general-purpose Operating Systems (e.g. DOS and UNIX) are not real-time because they take a few seconds before they react.

The Operating System manages the use of RAM, ensuring that there is enough memory available for all open applications to run effectively. As the power and capacity of computers have significantly increased year-on-year, the ability to carry out a number of tasks simultaneously has become common practice (e.g. allowing the user to work on a PowerPoint presentation whilst simultaneously communicating with a colleague via a web conference). Consequently, the ability of Operating Systems to manage and prioritise the use of memory has become increasingly important. In cases where the system fails to carry out a command or becomes overstretched by the number of tasks being carried out, the Operating System creates a log of the errors and sends error messages to the user.

> Remember that there are times that the Operating System may fail to run things as quickly, or as efficiently, as we would like. This could cause programs to run slowly or stop responding.

The Operating System controls the transfer of data from the secondary memory (e.g. the hard drive) to the primary memory (RAM), and also controls the management of **virtual memory** (data stored on a hard drive that, when required, is transferred to the RAM in order to allow the program to work as if the RAM is larger than it actually is).

The Operating System also manages all peripherals that are linked to the computer (keyboard, mouse, printer, web cam, etc) by using **drivers** to receive instructions from them and, where appropriate, to send commands and data to them.

Operating Systems also provide the first line of defence in terms of security by managing **privileges** and regulating use according to instructions it has been given. Consequently, the Operating System will ensure that only users who use recognisable passwords are permitted to log on to the system, and that each user is only given access to the software and data defined by the computer's administrator.

Operating Systems such as Microsoft's **Windows®** and Apple's **Mac OS** are proprietary products and the **source code** used to create these Operating Systems is not in the public domain. This means that people can use these Operating Systems but cannot adapt them beyond the levels built into their design. In contrast, Operating Systems such as **Linux** are referred to as **open source** because the source code has been placed into the public domain and made available for people to use and (if they wish) modify free of charge.

User interfaces

AQA **INFO 1, INFO 2**
OCR **G061**
WJEC **IT1**
CCEA **AS 1, A2 1**

> **KEY POINT**
>
> A user interface is the part of a system that allows the computer and a human operator to communicate with each other.

Graphical user interface

You can read more about user interfaces on pages 182–185.

The **graphical user interface** (GUI) uses images (e.g. icons, buttons and dialogue boxes), rather than text, to allow the user to access control tools, applications and software, via use of a pointing device (e.g. a mouse).

Most GUI software also provides the user with the opportunity to customise the images used, and to replace them with icons and buttons of their own choosing.

WIMP interface

A **WIMP interface** is a style of graphical user interface that is now used within most Operating Systems. WIMP can either stand for: Windows, Icons, Menus, Pointers or Windows, Icons, Mouse, Pull-down Menus. Both refer to the same thing.

Windows	Rectangular areas of the screen (windows) each of which can run a different program or display different data (see also Windows system below).
Icons	Small images or pictures that represent objects, controls and programs.
Menus	A list of commands or options (in text format), that can be selected by use of a mouse or keyboard.
Pointer	An arrow or a symbol that appears on the screen, and which can be moved by a mouse, trackball, touchpad or direction keys. Pointers can be used to select menu options and icons using either single or multiple clicks. When used within word processing applications the pointer is usually referred to as a cursor.

Command line interface

Unlike a graphical user interface, which uses images rather than words to interface with software, a **command line interface** (CLI) carries out instructions that it receives as text (either directly from the user or from a pre-prepared file). With CLI the command line appears in a small window on screen and a prompt (after or below the line) indicates that the computer is waiting to receive an instruction (command) from the user. Once the user types in the instruction, the computer carries out the instruction and then issues a new prompt indicating that it is ready to receive the next instruction. In some cases the CLI carries out the instructions itself, and in other cases it uses the instructions to load and run other files.

Whilst less commonly used in modern Windows® operating environments, CLI can still prove a useful means of interfacing with computer systems.

Windows systems

Windows systems enable rectangular areas of the screen (windows) to act as interfaces with different applications/programs. When open, each window provides the user with direct access to a particular process, application, document or file.

Most windows can be:
- minimised – reduced to a tab
- maximised – enlarged to fill the screen
- resized – adjusted to meet the needs of the user
- moved – dragged around the screen by the user
- restored down – reduced from full-screen to its most recent resized size/position.

By opening/selecting different windows, the user can see the status of a number of different processes at the same time and can easily switch between different applications at will, which facilitates effective multi-tasking.

Natural language interface

Natural language interfaces enable users to interact with a computer system by using spoken language. This type of interface is becoming increasingly common in high spec models of cars, where it can be used to interact with satellite navigation systems, control radio commands, make telephone calls or adjust temperature settings. Natural language interfaces are now also common on mobile phones, where it is generally referred to as voice dialling. On small systems such as cars and mobile phones, the dialogue interfaces can generally only cope with a limited range of words, so the interaction is usually in the form of short phrases. However, many commercial speech recognition software packages (which are predominantly used with word processing applications to generate text from spoken words) contain much broader vocabularies that provide users with a wider range of commands. This allows a greater degree of control. Whilst this type of interface provides the opportunity for hands-free control (particularly useful as a safety feature in cars), many systems require time-consuming training before they will recognise the user's voice.

Forms

Forms can provide an effective interface in both paper-based and electronic formats.

Pre-printed paper forms can be completed and scanned into a system where Optical Character Recognition software translates the marks on the paper into electronic data.

Electronic forms are displayed on screen allowing the user to enter data via their keyboard and mouse. Electronic forms are often presented as interactive dialogue boxes, which support faster (and more accurate) data entry by requiring the user to enter information using methods such as check boxes, drop-down selections and free text boxes.

Desktop

The **desktop** provides the key visual interface for the user. In a similar way to which someone can look at their desk and visually see the different equipment and documents laid out before them, the computer screen (monitor, TFT, LCD etc.) provides the user with a visual representation of the tools and documents available (and in use) on their computer. Consequently, this visual representation is commonly referred to as the desktop. The user works on the desktop by using a mouse or other pointing device to open applications and documents via use of the WIMP and graphical user interface.

Utilities

AQA	**INFO 1**
OCR	**G061**
WJEC	**IT1**
CCEA	**AS 1**

Utilities are programs that perform specific tasks that are additional to the application software being run. For example:

- archiving – organising and keeping track of files
- backing up data – copying (and in some cases, compressing) files to a secure secondary medium
- file compression – storing data in a format that requires less memory space than normal
- file synchronisation – making sure the same data appears on two or more devices
- virus protection – checking incoming files for malicious attachments (malware) and alerting the user if any viral infections are detected.

Many utilities are included as part of the Operating System software. However, users can easily purchase proprietary utilities that provide additional features and that, once loaded, interact smoothly with the original Operating System.

Applications software

AQA	**INFO 1**
OCR	**G061**
WJEC	**IT1**
CCEA	**AS 1**

KEY POINT

Applications are the programs that enable users to carry out specific tasks and achieve desired outcomes.

When purchasing a new computer the Operating System is generally pre-loaded and comes as part of the overall package. Whilst some application software might be included with the package, it usually has only limited functionality meaning that the user will need to **upgrade** to the full commercial package in order to access the full functionality of the software.

Generic software is a term that refers to applications that are commonly used by large numbers of people and that are readily available for purchase by the general public. This includes word processors, spreadsheets, databases, desktop publishing and presentation software; these applications are frequently grouped together and referred to as **office software** (even though they are also commonly purchased for personal use within the home). The disadvantage of purchasing generic software is that it may not always fit the whole range of the user's needs. The advantages of purchasing generic software are that it is relatively inexpensive, it generally receives very good levels of support from the manufacturer, and as users send feedback to the manufacturers on any problems that they have encountered, regular updates and **patches** can be issued to overcome those problems.

For information on customising generic software see pages 61–66.

Task specific software is a term that refers to applications that are designed for a single or specialist purpose. This includes payroll applications (designed to process wages and keep a track on employee tax and insurance), project management applications (designed to enable managers to plan and track the various stages of a project), and mind mapping applications (designed to create diagrams using words and images to help generate ideas and visualise outcomes). Although most task specific software is readily available for purchase by the general public, because it is less commonly used, the cost of purchase tends to be higher than that of the more commonly used generic software.

See page 67 for more information on task specific and bespoke software.

Bespoke software is a term that refers to software that has been designed for a specific client or group of clients, for example, the software used by National Air Traffic Services to control UK airspace. This type of software is not available for purchase by the general public. In some cases bespoke software is built upon an existing generic platform (e.g. a stock management system that uses bespoke add-ons with a proprietary database), whilst in other cases the software is developed from scratch (e.g. missile guidance systems). The advantage of commissioning bespoke software is that it has been designed specifically for the individual client so is likely to produce as near as possible a perfect solution to the client's needs. However, because there is a significant investment in the time and resources required to develop bespoke software, it tends to be much more expensive than other software and may need considerable additional investment if changes are required at a later date.

Purchasing the most appropriate software

For many users (e.g. employees), the choice of which software they can use is limited to the applications that appear on their desktop when they log on. These applications have been chosen by managers as being the most suitable for the organisation's needs.

However, it is not as straightforward as asking, 'Do we need a spreadsheet package?' because there are many different spreadsheet applications available. Purchasers need to ask themselves a number of questions, including:
- Can the existing hardware cope with the new software?
- Is the software going to be used as a stand-alone application or does it need to integrate with other applications (e.g. as part of an office suite)?
- Does the software provide the full range of options that our organisation requires?
- Is the software expandable and can we purchase/add additional functions if we discover that we need them?
- Is the high cost of some of the additional functions worth it, or can we do without them and purchase a cheaper product instead?
- Can the software be loaded onto a network so that several employees can use it at the same time?
- Is the software available with a multi-user licence, or will we need to purchase lots of copies?

Selecting software for use

There are four main groups of generic application software, though there is considerable crossover between some of these:
- **Text software**, such as word processors and text editors, primarily provide users with the facility to manipulate and present text. However, modern word

processing software is becoming increasingly sophisticated in the way it handles images and tables, which means that it is increasingly being used as an alternative to specialist presentation and desktop publishing software.

- **Numerical software** is frequently referred to as spreadsheets, and provides users with the facility to enter, process, analyse and present numerical data in a wide range of formats. However, modern spreadsheet software is becoming increasingly sophisticated in the way it manages the interrogation of data, which means that it is increasingly being used as an alternative to simple database software.

- **Data-handling software** is frequently referred to as databases, and provides users with the facility to enter, manage, process, analyse and present different forms of data (e.g. text, numeric, alphanumeric). Most users find database software to be more complicated to use than other generic software.

- **Graphics software** primarily provides users with the facility to create, edit, and manage two-dimensional (2D) graphics. This can include digital photographs, scanned images, clip art, logos, headings, web graphics and other forms of digital images.

There are also several common groups of task specific software:

- **3D graphics software** primarily provides users with the facility to create, edit, and manage three-dimensional (3D) graphics for use in animation and modelling.

- **Multimedia software** provides users with the facility to bring text, still images, audio, animation and video together in a range of combinations for use in presentations, games and simulations.

- **Presentation software** provides users with the facility to display information, normally taking the form of slides, which they have created using a combination of text, still images, audio, animation and video. Most modern presentation software packages provide a wide range of multimedia capabilities.

- **Desktop publishing software** provides tools for both professional and amateur designers to create documents and publications that can be viewed on-screen, printed in-house or sent electronically to a commercial printer.

- **Web authoring software** allows users to develop and upload web pages without the need to understand HyperText Markup Language (HTML).

PROGRESS CHECK

1. Describe the purpose of a user interface.
2. Explain what utilities are and give examples.
3. What is the difference between Operating Systems and application software?

1. A user interface allows the user to input data in a way that the computer will understand, and allows the computer to output data in a way that the user will understand.
2. Utilities are programs that perform specific tasks that are additional to the application software being run. For example, archiving, backing up data, file compression, file synchronisation and file protection.
3. Operating Systems are software packages that control the way in which the computer functions and permit applications to be run. Applications are programs that enable users to carry out specific tasks and achieve desired outcomes (e.g. create a spreadsheet).

Sample questions and model answers

1. An independent travel agency is opening a new office. Identify three different output devices they will need to install and give an example of how each of these could be used. **(3)**

TFT screens would be used to display the data stored in the computer system. A laser printer would be used to print booking forms and to generate hard copies of information for clients. Speakers would be used to generate sounds from error messages, and could also be used (with the screen) to show video clips of holiday destinations as advertisements for holidays in its shops.

2. The computers at an airline's check-in desks are all fitted with keyboards and mice. Identify three other input devices that would be appropriate for the airline, and give an example of how each could be used. **(6)**

A scanner could be used to scan details from printed 'e-tickets' and to make copies of documents required for security purposes (e.g. passports), and a touch-screen monitor could be used by the operator to interact with the computer system (e.g. to select and allocate seats). Sensors could be used under the conveyor belt to detect the weight of the luggage, and a point-of-sale credit card reader could be used to make any additional payments required (e.g. excess luggage).

3. Utility software and Operating System software are installed on a computer. Describe the role of each of these types of software. **(6)**

Utility software is designed to help the user carry out basic tasks (e.g. format a CD). It carries out additional tasks that are not included in either the Operating System or applications (e.g. defragmentation of hard drives). Operating System software allows the computer to communicate with the hardware and peripherals. It manages the computer's resources (e.g. use of memory) and prioritise its tasks, providing a platform on which the applications software can run. The Operating System provides the interface which allows the user to communicate with the computer.

4. Explain why somebody would choose to use a USB memory stick. **(3)**

Most computers have a USB port that will accept this type of device and because they are inexpensive, light-weight and robust they are easy to carry around, which allows for easy transfer of data. These qualities make USB memory sticks an ideal choice for the storage and transfer of data.

Practice examination questions

1 Touch sensitive screens are becoming an increasingly common component of mobile phones. Describe two advantages and one disadvantage of using a touch sensitive screen. **(3)**

_____

_____

_____

_____

2 Describe three possible uses for USB memory sticks. **(3)**

(i) _____

_____

(ii) _____

_____

(iii) _____

_____

3 Describe the main features of a WIMP interface. **(6)**

_____

_____

_____

_____

_____

_____

_____

_____

_____

_____

3 Standardising and developing software applications

The following topics are covered in this chapter:

- Customising generic software to meet the needs of organisations
- Developing software
- Ensuring that software applications are fit for purpose

3.1 Customising generic software to meet the needs of organisations

LEARNING SUMMARY

After studying this section you should be able to:

- identify the basic tasks required of generic software applications
- describe key requirements of automated and customisable features
- explain why tailored and customised features are important for organisations and end-users

Identifying basic tasks of generic software applications

AQA **INFO 1, INFO 3**
OCR **G061**
WJEC **IT1, IT3**
CCEA **AS 1, A2 1**

Business use of ICT includes the use of **generic software** and **industry/task specific software** (see also pages 56–57). For example, schools and colleges make use of generic word processing, spreadsheet, data handling, presentation, publishing and web authoring software. They are also likely to use specialist registration, forecasting, registration and analytical software, which are designed specifically for the education market.

Software application	Uses
Word processing	Letter writing Memos Reports
Publishing	Flyers Brochures Posters Business cards

Have some examples in your mind if you're asked about how generic software can be applied. Use examples of documents and files from your project work to add to your descriptions.

Software application	Uses
Spreadsheets	Data handling Modelling Graphs Forecasting Financial analysis
Database	Data storage Data handling Sorting Searching Mail-merging
Web page authoring	Web pages Video presentations Sound files
Presentation software	Presentations

Using software tools to customise applications

AQA **INFO 1, INFO 3**
OCR **G061**
WJEC **IT1, IT3**
CCEA **AS 1, A2 1**

There are many software tools that can be used to customise applications to meet the needs of an organisation. The most common tools are:

- **wizards**
- **templates**
- **style sheets**
- **macros**

Tool	Definition	Advantages of use	Disadvantages of use
Wizards	Wizards are automated tools within software applications that make common and/or complex procedures more accessible.	• Wizards can make the design and layout of complex documents, graphs, and presentations much more straightforward. • They can be time-saving and increase efficiency.	• They often have their own pre-set styles and formats that may not comply with the **house style**.
Templates	Templates are ready-made outlines of pages. They will include text that organisations want to see on every page (like address and contact details on a letter). They will also set preferred fonts and layouts for everyone to use. They may also include company logos and other images to reflect the organisation's house style.	• Templates are already set up so that users don't have to worry about formatting documents each time they create a new one. • Templates ensure that all documents are standardised and consistent. This is especially useful when organisations want everything to have a house style.	• If the generic templates that are provided within the software aren't appropriate then users have to spend time making their own – this of course is important if the company wants its own house style. • Designs are often restrictive and users may have to make changes manually. • New users will need specific training in how to use them – it's not as straightforward as simply creating a document.

Tool	Definition	Advantages of use	Disadvantages of use
Style sheets	Style sheets are templates for desktop publishing. They enable documents like brochures and flyers to have a consistent style by establishing the layout and format of the pages. They may also be referred to as **master sheets** (or **master slides** in presentation software).	• Style sheets save time when designing new pages for a publication. • Like templates they make sure that publications are consistent even if they are being produced by lots of different people (a house style).	• Style sheets can lead to documents being rather too similar in style – this may mean that the impact is lost. • It can be difficult to adapt publications to meet the needs of a particular audience. For example, a style sheet may impose a particular font that users with a visual impairment may find difficult to read.
Macros	Macros automate regular tasks. They are created by recording the steps taken to complete a task in a scripting language, or by a wizard within the software application.	• Macros make the completion of repetitive tasks much more efficient: less time, fewer errors. • They can be attached to buttons to give the user control over certain actions. • Macros can run automatically as soon as a program is run. A macro could, for example, automatically insert the current date into a document without interaction from the user.	• The recording of macros can take some time to master – it may require a specialist within the organisation. • Macros are used by hackers to create viruses: this means that some organisations and users will not allow the use of files that contain macros.

KEY POINT

More than likely you will have used templates, wizards, style sheets and macros in your project work. When describing the advantages and disadvantages of automated tools in generic software refer to real examples. Examiners like that sort of thing.

Customising generic software for users

AQA **INFO 1, INFO 3**
OCR **G061**
WJEC **IT1, IT3**
CCEA **AS 1, A2 1**

You will know from your own experiences of using generic software packages that **menus** guide you through the use of the program. If software packages are bundled together in a suite then these menus will have a consistent structure that help you move quickly and easily from one program to another.

Organisations that have decided upon a **house style** will have determined that users, wherever they are in the organisation, will work with documents that follow a pre-determined layout and format. Most often this is done through the use of templates, **style sheets** and **master slides**. This tailored or customised approach can be extended further by customising the way users interact with the software by using:

- user-defined menus
- buttons
- forms
- form controls

These features can make generic applications faster and easier to use.

> Customised interfaces make it easier and quicker to enter data. This increases efficiency as users are less likely to make mistakes.

> Systems can appear to be more user friendly. This makes it easier for less experienced users – and can reduce the amount of time spent on training.

> Where text or numbers are validated on entry this reduces errors and again increases efficiency.

Feature	How the customisation works
User-defined menus	Menus can be used to make the software appear to be more user-friendly: a user working with a relational database (see page 127) might find the process of selecting the right table to search data a little daunting. A menu-driven system can make that selection much more straightforward. Menus also provide users with a list or range of options. Sometimes these options can be greyed out to let the user know that it is not available for use – and so prevent them for making mistakes. There are three kinds of menu: • **full screen** – something like a switchboard in a database • **pop ups** – that appear when a user begins to perform an action • **pull-down/drop-down** – often used to validate choices when entering data, or to carry out specific actions (e.g. printing)
Buttons	Buttons can be added to perform actions, run commands, or to move to other locations in a document. For example, command buttons can be used: • in a database to carry out actions such as search, sort or edit • in spreadsheets to allow users to recalculate, move to another worksheet, or begin a look-up • in documents and presentations to move to other pages, to show pictures or other text, or to show videos or play sound files. They can also open web pages or files.
Forms	Forms are often used to make it easier to enter or edit data in a spreadsheet or database. Instead of tabbing from cell to cell in a table in order to enter data, users are presented with a simple form that structures the way they work, and often presents them with **drop-down menus** and **validation codes** to prevent errors. Validation codes make sure that items such as post codes and dates of birth are entered in the required format.

Feature	How the customisation works
Form controls	Form controls enable the user to input data to a spreadsheet, and to provide information for other users.
	Form controls are often attached to single cells, unlike a form which can be set up to perform more than one operation.
	There are lots of different form controls. The most commonly used are: ● **buttons** – which are often linked to macros ● **labels** – which provide explanatory text for the user ● **option buttons** – which give users a set of options from which to make a choice ● **list box** – which provides a list of items from which the user may choose more than one item ● **check box** – where a user can toggle between on or off, checked or unchecked ● **combo box** – this is a text box with a drop down list. Usually the user can type in and then confirm an entry from the drop down list, or simply scroll down the list.
	Pre-validated entries such as those in list boxes or combo boxes prevent users from making other choices.

If there are options missing from form controls or drop-down menus, the users will not be able to do their tasks fully or without errors.

KEY POINT

An organisation needs to have people with the technical skills and knowledge to be able to maintain a highly customised environment: customised interfaces can fail to work if the software is upgraded.

Design considerations when customising software applications

When preparing for a customised work environment software developers need to think carefully about both the needs of the user and of the employer. The most common interface that a user will meet is a data entry screen that has been prepared to help users interface with a complex relational database.

Data entry screens are designed using forms that include labels with instructions and error messages, buttons, and other form controls that make data entry a straightforward process.

There are two main considerations in planning for effective and efficient data entry screens:
● **Consistency** – the screens should look as similar as possible so that the user knows where to look when they begin or continue their work. This means that buttons, messages and entry boxes should always be in the same place. If the data entry screen is designed to help users inputting data from paper-based sources it will be more efficient if the order of items is the same.
● **Relevance** – the data entry screens should only ask for relevant data – time will be wasted and users will become frustrated in their work if they are entering superfluous data. For example, there is no point in inputting data that

is held in another table within the database when entering only a **primary key** would be sufficient (see page 123). The screen must not be too busy – graphics and animations need to be kept to a minimum: not everyone wants to have a little animation in the corner of the screen reminding them what to do.

Transferring data between applications

All generic software packages allow users to import data from and export data to other applications. For the most part this can be done relatively easily from and to a range of different applications. There may be times when a user needs to merge data from one application with that of another: incorporating text from one document to another; importing text from a word processing document to presentation software; merging data from a spreadsheet with that of a database.

It may, of course, be possible to save the data in a format that is directly compatible with the import or export application. If that is not an option, the majority of software applications allows users to save the data in a portable format such as a **.csv data file** (comma separated values) or an unformatted or **rich text file** that can be imported / exported and reformatted within the receiving application.

PROGRESS CHECK

1. Many software applications have macro facilities. Describe what is meant by the term 'macro' and give an example of when the use of a macro would be appropriate.
2. How is it possible to transfer data from one application to another when the two applications are incompatible?

1. Macros are sequences of instructions stored within the application and activated by a programmed keystroke (like CTRL-ALT-F), clicking on a command button or icon, or selecting from a pull-down menu. Macros are used to automate tasks that are repeated often, or which are complex. This helps the user to work within an environment that has been customised to meet their working needs. A macro might be used to display a data entry form, reset any entries to zero or blank, keep or update generic information which is required for all entries (e.g. date of payment). Another macro on the same screen could be activated for saving that entry and beginning another.
2. Where two programs appear to be incompatible it may be appropriate to save the data in a portable format. For text this might be as an unformatted or rich text file; for numbers this might be as a comma separated values file. These files can then be exported to the other application, and then formatted as appropriate.

3.2 Developing software

LEARNING SUMMARY	**After studying this section you should be able to:** ● describe a range of approaches to software development ● identify the roles of the ICT developer and end-user ● explain why project management is an important element in software development

Why do organisations need to have software developed for them?

AQA **INFO 1, INFO 3**
OCR **G061, G062**
WJEC **IT1, IT3**
CCEA **A2 1, A2 2**

Generic applications may provide a number of solutions to the processes and problems that face organisations as they work to fulfil their requirements. However, there are some aspects of work that require the use of **task specific** or **bespoke** software (see page 57).

Task specific software is software that has been developed to perform one task, or a related group of tasks and activities. Examples include payroll software that calculates and manages the payment of employees; schools often have specific management information systems that manage data on pupil attendance, achievement and progress; kitchen designers have specific design software to develop layouts and provide estimates for customers. Task specific software applications can often be bought **off-the-shelf** and there is very little delay in installing and running the software after purchase.

> **KEY POINT**
>
> Bespoke software is an expensive option as it means that software is tailor-made for an organisation when no other suitable software has been found to fulfil the needs of the organisation.

Bespoke software can be developed by an **in-house** team of developers. This is useful in that internal communication systems mean that the in-house team will be able to report on their progress regularly and will understand the needs of the organisation. Where in-house expertise is lacking the job of producing the software can be **outsourced** to a company with the appropriate expertise. **Outsourcing** will require clear lines of communication, but may take longer as they get to know how the commissioning organisation works.

Software type	Advantages	Disadvantages
Task specific	• Specific software does what it says it will do. If it is a timetabling program in a school – then that is what you get. It meets the specific needs of the organisation. • There are often lots of other users – so user groups and training will provide help and guidance when needed.	• Flexibility is not often a feature of these programs – you may have to wait for an upgrade to get new features.
Bespoke	• Software can be designed to suit the way an organisation works – rather than changing work patterns to fit the software. • Because the end-user has a say in what the software will do, it meets their needs exactly. • The software can be designed to integrate specifically with other software (and the hardware) used by the organisation.	• Bespoke software is expensive as it requires teams of developers to produce the software. • Errors may not have an immediate impact on work, but may occur when a rarely used aspect of work is undertaken – this can disrupt work patterns and may mean that important deadlines are missed.

Approaching software development

AQA **INFO 1, INFO 3**
OCR **G061, G063**
WJEC **IT1, IT3**
CCEA **A2 1, A2 2**

Being able to link one area of your knowledge to another is very important. It shows that you have a grasp of the subject as a whole; not just selected parts of it.

Review Chapter 4 on the systems development life cycle for other approaches such as prototyping, as well as securing your understanding of the systems development life cycle itself.

It is important to think about **software development** as very much part of the same process as systems development. Much of the focus on systems is about the development of information systems built around databases. Here we are focusing on the development of all types of software.

There are many approaches to software development, each of which begins with the end-user specifying what is needed. In this chapter we will consider two approaches to software development:

- **the waterfall model**
- **Rapid Application Development (RAD)**

The waterfall model of software development

For the waterfall model of software development to work effectively the end-user has to specify exactly what it is they need. The waterfall model was first developed in 1970 and consists of seven stages. Each stage must be completed fully before moving onto the next.

- **Specification of requirements**: The specification sets out the nature and scope of the software. This stage should never be missed out, or skimped upon. If the specification is not clearly defined then the software solution will not be fit for purpose.
- **Design**: This is where the work on the software begins. All resources are specified, as are all the inputs and outputs required. The way the software processes data is also defined here (the software algorithm) and is perhaps the most important aspect of this stage.
- **Construction** (sometimes referred to as implementation): During this stage the algorithm is coded. This coding needs to be tested and validated regularly to ensure that the output is well designed software that meets the specification and fulfils the design.
- **Integration**: Often coding and construction are carried out by a number of programmers. This stage sees their work integrated. There is also a review of how the software will perform for the end-user, and a review of how the software will integrate with the end-user's existing systems.
- **Testing and debugging** (also known as validation): Here the software is tested to see that it matches the specification and design fully and that it runs as it should, responding to inputs **appropriately** and producing the expected outputs.
- **Installation**: At this point the software is handed over to the end-user. Further testing will take place to ensure that the software is fully compatible with the end-user's systems.
- **Maintenance and review**: This is a very long stage of the waterfall model in that the designers and programmers may have to provide constant support to resolve issues that arise as the software is run over an extended period of time. Errors may arise that were not detected earlier. These need to be resolved, and support will be offered for this.

Rapid Application Development (RAD)

RAD is an approach to software development that, unlike the waterfall model, develops prototypes quickly without much planning. The planning takes place at the same time as the development of the software allowing much more flexibility (especially as user requirements may change during the prototyping).

In RAD, the development process begins with a review of requirements and the development of initial data and operational models. It is important to get an early picture of how the organisation works and how it uses and produces data. The requirements that are generated from this process are verified by prototyping software solutions – reviewing these solutions constantly against the requirements and making changes where necessary in order to come up with a software solution that fully meets the needs of the end-user.

Advantages and disadvantages of these models

Model	Advantages	Disadvantages
Waterfall model	• Linear models (where one step follows another) are easy to work with. • Demands on resources are low as only one stage is implemented at a time. • Because documentation is produced at every stage it is easy to deal with changes in team membership – and to understand what happened at each stage. • The outcome is usually reliable as it is tested at every stage.	• If the design is wrong then the final product will not be fit for purpose. • End-users may request changes in design as the process moves forward – this can cause complications. • Undetected errors, or small changes, could cause problems later on – and these may be difficult to resolve. • Once the specification leaves the end-user they do not see the final result until the end of the project: the product may not be what they really wanted.
Rapid Application Development	• Outcomes are delivered quickly. • Alterations can be made to meet the changing requirements of the end-user.	• Speed of delivery may result in lower levels of functionality and performance. • Communication breakdown can lead to confusion and poor implementation.

User and technical documentation

AQA **INFO 1, INFO 3**
OCR **G061, G063**
WJEC **IT1, IT3**
CCEA **A2 1, A2 2**

Users will expect a range of documentation to support them as they implement new software. Whether that software is generic, specific or bespoke the need for support documentation remains the same. Even with generic and off-the-shelf software that come with manuals and online guidance and help, the need to produce organisational specific help sheets is important – and this is especially the case when the software has been customised to meet business needs.

Documentation tends to fall into two categories:
• **user documentation**
• **technical documentation**

User documentation

Comprehensive user documentation will contain the following:
• **Contents page** – this should include the page numbers of each section so that users can find what they are looking for quickly.
• **Introduction** – this should explain the purpose of the guide and describe what the software is intended to do.

- **Hardware requirements** – this is an important section – especially for off-the-shelf software. It is where users can check, for example, to see whether their hardware has enough memory to run the software.
- **Software requirements** – it is important to be able to check which Operating Systems are compatible with the new software.
- **Instructions** – this forms a substantial part of the guide. There should be guidance on how to install the system, and instructions on how to carry out all the functions that the software has been designed for.
- **Glossary of terms** – this should include all the technical terms used in the guide and should explain what they mean so that the average user can understand them.
- **Troubleshooting** – this should provide users with a list of the error messages that may be presented. With each error there should be a fix.
- **Index** – not everyone can work out what they need to look for from the contents page. An index based around technical terms and functions should be included.

No matter how good the user documentation is, there is likely to be a need for the development of **help sheets**. These can be developed in-house or can be purchased.

> **KEY POINT**
>
> Help sheets are small documents that help the user with specific tasks or activities by taking them through the activity step-by-step.

Technical documentation

Technical documentation is intended for those people who will maintain and support the running of the software. It should contain at least eight sections:
- Contents page
- Introduction
- The system design specification
- The diagrams used to define the system
- The data dictionary (see page 90)
- Configuration and settings – providing details of settings, coding, validation codes, macros, etc
- Screen layout and user interface designs
- Any test plans

Detail is important in technical documentation – if errors or problems arise the detail helps technical staff to refer back to the original source, or the original thinking, to ensure that they can work out why the problem has occurred and then make decisions about how they can resolve it.

Project management

AQA **INFO 1, INFO 3**
OCR **G061, G063**
WJEC **IT1, IT3**
CCEA **A2 1, A2 2**

Whichever model of software development that an organisation chooses to apply, there needs to be an overview of:

- how the development is going
- whether it is on schedule
- whether it will come in on budget
- if it will meet its objectives as defined in the specification of requirements.

This overview is likely to be overseen by a **project manager** who will act as an interface between the end-user and the developer.

These are important considerations – and organisations purchasing or developing software are likely to ask themselves these questions to ensure that the software meets the needs of the organisation and will contribute to the successful operation of the organisation's day-to-day and long-term objectives.

The effective management of software development can be facilitated by the use of Computer Aided Software Engineering or **CASE** tools.

> **KEY POINT**
>
> CASE tools are automated software tools that provide assistance to software developers by structuring their approach to their work.

The use of CASE tools reduces the amount of time spent in developing software and in doing so reduces the cost of producing software.

Upper CASE tools support the initial planning and structuring phase of software development using such tools as:

Entity relationship and data flow diagrams can be found on pages 91–94.

- entity relationship diagrams
- data flow diagrams
- decision trees and tables
- structure charts

Lower CASE tools support activities like:

- physical design
- construction
- testing and debugging
- integration
- maintenance

You should be able to see how the CASE tools link with the models of development (see the waterfall model and RAD on page 68–69).

Particular examples of CASE tools include:

- tools for creating diagrams
- computer display and report generators
- analysis tools that help check for poorly developed specifications
- data dictionary generators
- documentation generators
- code generators

CASE tools can be selected and combined by developers to meet their needs. They can be grouped into eight areas of work:

CASE group	What it enables the developer to do
Business planning and modelling	• Get a full understanding of the commissioning organisation. • Begin to see whether the specification requirements actually meet the needs of the organisation. • Develop the software algorithms.
Analysis and design	• Plan the design of the software against identified needs.
User interface development	• Plan a range of interfaces between end-user and software.
Programming	• Generate code to construct the software in accordance with the defined algorithms. • Produce code quickly and without errors.
Verification and validation	• Test the software with a range of data to check input and output processes. • User test the interface.
Maintenance and reverse engineering	• Respond to change requests. • Follow up on errors in design and coding. • Prepare for upgrades.
Configuration management	• Identify the functional and physical attributes of the software. • Track changes as they occur so that the software matches the initial and amended specifications.
Project management	• Define the project plan for the development. • Generate GANTT charts to model, monitor and evaluate the plan. • Undertake critical path analysis to identify stretch points within the lifetime of the software development project.

PROGRESS CHECK

1 Software can be developed using the waterfall model or by using Rapid Application Development.

(a) Describe the main features of the waterfall model.

(b) Give two disadvantages of the waterfall model.

(c) Describe two reasons why an end-user may prefer Rapid Application Development.

1. (a) The waterfall model has a number of separate stages ranging from specification of requirements, through design, construction, testing, installation and review. Each stage has to be completed before progressing to the next. There are, however, opportunities to revisit stages if errors occur. Every stage has a particular outcome that can be tested and documented. (b) The end-user in the waterfall model does not see the final product until the installation stage. Because the model is so reliant on the specification stage, if there are errors or misconceptions at this stage the outcomes of all the other stages may not be fit for purpose. (c) Rapid Application Development is useful for end-users as it allows them to develop their requirements as the project progresses – as they see things happen they can identify other attributes they would like to see in the software. It is also much quicker in reaching a final outcome.

3.3 Ensuring that software applications are fit for purpose

LEARNING SUMMARY	After studying this section you should be able to: • identify the key processes of software testing

Testing and maintenance

AQA **INFO 1, INFO 3**
OCR **G061, G063**
WJEC **IT1, IT3**
CCEA **A2 1, A2 2**

Testing software quality

Many levels of testing and review are built into the software development process. For example, each stage of the waterfall model of development has testing built into it.

> Note the relationship to the waterfall model of software development.

Application testing is carried out by the developer to test the software against the system requirements. It will include the testing of each of the modules that go to make up the software, and will then go through the process of **integration testing** to ensure that individual software modules are combined and tested as a group to see that they work together as they should.

> Acceptance testing will use a range of test data to ensure that all components work.

Acceptance testing is an important stage for ensuring that the software product matches the specification of requirements. It works on two levels:
• Software developers check that their code is working correctly.
• End-users check to see if the system is doing the right things.

Acceptance testing can in many respects take place at any stage to ensure that things are working well. Generally the process of acceptance testing by the customer would take place:
• regularly if the development process follows RAD
• towards the end of the project if the development process follows the waterfall model.

As the software product nears the end of its development a process of **alpha testing** begins. During this stage end-users trial the software with the developers: they work through simulated tasks and activities that replicate the normal work processes and look for flaws, or suggest modifications to ensure that the product is fit for purpose.

This stage is followed by **beta testing**. Here, versions of the software are released to a limited audience so that it can be tested in a variety of situations. Once again the purpose is to ensure that the product has as few bugs as possible. With large scale software products (such as new Operating Systems or generic suites) beta versions are offered for public access so that feedback can be gained from as large and as varied a source as possible.

Software maintenance

Once the software has been accepted or purchased by the end-user then a process of **software maintenance** begins. Users of generic software most often come across software maintenance when they are asked to download **software patches** to correct errors that have emerged, or when changes to other software (such as the Operating System) have had a negative effect on the performance of the software being used.

There are four types of software maintenance:

For more information on maintenance see page 217.

Type	Description
Corrective	Corrective maintenance happens as an outcome of error reporting by customers. It leads to diagnosis by the developer team and correction should the error report prove to be valid.
Adaptive	Adaptive maintenance responds to changes in the environment, such as changes to other software or to hardware. The adaptations modify the software so that it can interface properly with the changed environment.
Perfective	Perfective maintenance is a response to requests to enhance the software capabilities.
Reverse engineering (or preventative maintenance)	Reverse engineering is a process of going back through the development cycle (up the waterfall) to review the source code to identify aspects of the software that are under-developed or poorly documented. It can be used, among other things, for: • security auditing • cracking protection • removing access restrictions

The process of software maintenance

Software maintenance follows a number of specific steps. When a need for change or further development is identified the software developer will generate or respond to a software problem report and work with a team (including a project manager) to:
• identify the scale of the problem
• scope the modifications required
• prioritise the request (is it urgent or not).

The project manager will identify deadlines and resource allocation. It will require an updating of all associated records to support further maintenance should it be necessary in the future.

PROGRESS CHECK

1. Which type of maintenance is a response to requests to enhance the capabilities of software?
2. What is beta testing?
3. What is alpha testing?

1. Perfective maintenance
2. Beta testing is when software is released to a limited audience to test that it works in different situations.
3. Alpha testing is when end-users trial the software with the developers to ensure that the product is fit for purpose.

Sample questions and model answers

1. The head office of a fast food company uses word processing and publishing software to produce documents to be sent out to its employees. Define each of the following functions of the software and give an example of how each could be used by the fast food company.

(a) templates (2)

(b) style sheets (2)

(c) macros (2)

Keep the definition simple.

The focus here is on the house style and how it can be set up.

Provide examples of what the fast food company could use templates for.

Again, give a simple definition – it identifies that style sheets are a feature of desktop publishing.

Giving examples will help to ensure that you get the full marks available.

Note that the example is specific to word processing; a different example would be appropriate for desktop publishing. An example of a spreadsheet macro would not be appropriate in this instance.

(a) Templates are ready-made outlines of pages that set the format for word-processed documents.

The organisation could use a template to establish their house style and will set up things like the font, font size, margin width and header and footer content. It is likely that the fast food company will have their logo in the header of every document template.

Templates could be set up for such things as meeting reports, faxes, internal memos, and letters.

(b) Style sheets are templates for desktop publishing. They enable documents like brochures and flyers to have a consistent style by establishing the layout and format of the pages.

The company could use style sheets to ensure that colours remain consistent (to maintain the company image) and that page numbers, page layout, and features common to every publication (like the strap line) remain the same.

(c) Macros automate tasks that are undertaken regularly - by recording the steps that are taken to complete a task and assigning the macro to a button, a user could then simply press 'the' button to complete the task again without having to repeat the steps. In word processing the fast food company could, for example, use a macro to print out address labels for all its northern outlets.

2. Software maintenance is a feature of the software development process. Explain what is meant by:

(a) application testing (3)

(b) acceptance testing (3)

Keep your answer clear and simple.

Build on your answer by giving an example.

(a) Application testing is carried out by the developer throughout the development process to test the software against the system requirements.

It tests each of the modules that go to make up the software, and will then go through the process of integration testing and will use a range of test data to ensure that all components work.

(b) Acceptance testing is carried out when the software is ready to be handed over to the end-user. It is intended to give the end-users confidence that the software meets their requirements. The end-user tests the application, modelling their work using scenarios and data that represent what they do day-to-day. The users report back on any issues that emerge from their testing before signing off the software ready for final release.

Practice examination questions

1 You have been asked to standardise the school handbooks. Describe, using examples, how you would do this and what improvements it would offer to the school. **(10)**

_____

_____

_____

_____

_____

_____

_____

_____

_____

_____

2 The database used by a hospital records administrator uses tailored data entry screens and forms. Identify and describe three design considerations that should be taken into account when designing the data entry screens and forms. **(9)**

_____

_____

_____

_____

_____

_____

_____

_____

_____

_____

4 The systems development life cycle (SDLC)

The following topics are covered in this chapter:

- The systems development life cycle (SDLC)
- Securing the development of a project

4.1 The systems development life cycle (SDLC)

LEARNING SUMMARY

After studying this section you should be able to:

- present an overview of the systems development life cycle
- describe the process of system investigation
- outline the tools and techniques used to analyse systems
- describe system design processes and procedures
- outline the process of system implementation
- review the maintenance requirements
- explain the criteria for evaluating a system

An overview of the systems development life cycle (SDLC)

AQA	INFO 1, INFO 3
OCR	G063
WJEC	IT3
CCEA	AS 1

As organisations grow and develop, or as they contract or change focus they need to review their information and data processing requirements. Modified or new information systems are needed to meet changing requirements. The development systems can, especially in large organisations, be expensive in their use of time, capital and human resources. This means that a formal and structured approach to systems development is beneficial because:

- lines of accountability can be established
- time scales can be set and the progress of the project measured against them
- costs can be planned and staged
- success criteria can be specified for each stage of the development
- outcomes can be measured at each stage
- it is possible to go back to a previous stage if success criteria and outcomes are not met.

The diagram below is a variant of the waterfall model explored in Chapter 3.

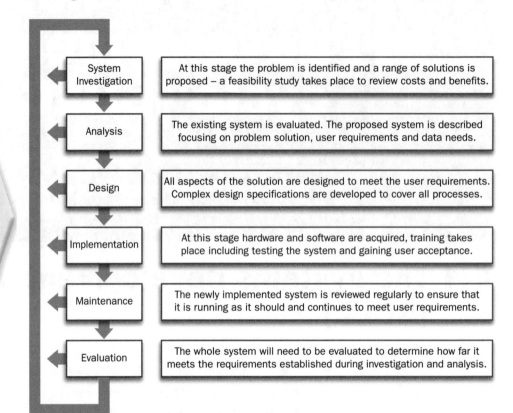

Note the direction of the arrows. It is possible to progress straight through – but at each stage the process can begin again to ensure that the development meets requirements.

System investigation

AQA   **INFO 1, INFO 3**
OCR   **G063**
WJEC **IT3**
CCEA **AS 1**

System investigation is the first stage in the SDLC. It begins with a **system request** which can be established as a result of responses to internal or external factors:

Internal factors	External factors
New development: the organisation may be launching a new product or service.	Competition: the organisation may be responding to a newly developing market that requires them to operate in a different way.
System failure: users may be unhappy about the scale of errors, or the slowness of the current system.	The economy: as the economic climate changes there may be a need to restructure the organisation.
Restructuring: a new sector within the organisation may have different information requirements from the rest of the organisation.	Legislation: each year brings new legislation that organisations need to respond to.

The system request is followed by the generation of a **feasibility report**. This involves looking at the system request from five different angles so that the feasibility of the project can be tested from the outset. These are:

Feasibility	Criteria for judgment
Schedule	How long will it take to deliver the proposed system? Can the system be delivered within the required time frame?
Technical	Does the organisation have the technical expertise in-house, or will the expertise have to be bought in? Does the organisation have the necessary equipment to implement the new system, or will new equipment have to be bought in? Will the new system be compatible with existing systems in other areas of the organisation?
Operational	Will the new system necessitate changes to the day-to-day work of the end-users? Will the organisation need to restructure as a consequence of this new system? Is the organisation prepared to deal with potential disruption to working patterns or to the organisational structure?
Legal	Is there a legal need to develop a new system? Has there been a change in legislation? Will there be a conflict between the proposed system and current legislation?
Economic	Is the project affordable? Will it contribute to the profitability of the organisation? Costs will occur in the areas of: human resources; training; new hardware; new software; consultant support; licensing agreements, etc.

> Acronyms like STOLE are useful ways of remembering important information.

> This could impact on the economic or operational feasibility as well.

> This could impact on the economic or technical feasibility as well.

> Being able to refer to specific legislation will be useful. See Chapter 13 for more detail.

If the feasibility report judges that the project does not meet any of the feasibility criteria it will not go ahead. Otherwise the next step is a **preliminary investigation**. This will result in a report to managers that will have four sections:

- A description of the problem – an analysis into the scope and nature of the problem with a description of how the proposed system would resolve any issues that end-users have with the current system. This section should outline potential issues that could emerge if the proposed system gets the go-ahead.
- Scope and constraints – the report will identify the scope of the project – will it be limited to one area or to many areas of the organisation? The relationship with other systems in the organisation should be explored in this section, as should a discussion about the cost limitations and the expected time frame for the development and implementation of the system.
- Costs – this section explores the total cost of the proposed system. As well as a consideration of the financial costs incurred by the project the report should review the impact on human resources, the amount of time spent, and the opportunity costs.
- Benefits – any new system should offer the organisation some perceived benefits and these should be explored fully in this section: what will the organisation be able to do now that it couldn't before? What can they do better? How does this improvement in facility measure up against the costs incurred? Is the organisation more profitable as a consequence?

Systems analysis

AQA **INFO 1, INFO 3**
OCR **G063**
WJEC **IT3**
CCEA **AS 1**

Systems analysis is a process that builds on the user requirements and develops a detailed specification for the new system.

> **KEY POINT**
>
> The most important aspect of systems analysis is about meeting the needs of the end-user. It is all about what the client wants, not what the analyst thinks they want.

Essentially there are three stages of the analysis phase of the SDLC:
- Clarifying what the end-user wants from the system.
- Establishing the data parameters for the new system.
- Developing the specification for the new system.

Clarifying user wants

Getting the right information at this stage is the key to a successful project: more information is always better than less.

Successful systems analysis begins with three key questions:
- What do we need to know about issues the end-user is facing?
- Who will need to provide further information about the issues?
- What tools and techniques will be used to obtain this information?

With these questions in mind the systems analyst needs to arrive at a series of further questions to gather as much relevant information as possible.

Issues	Informants	Tools and techniques
<ul><li>What does the current system do?</li><li>What issues are there with the current system that the new system will resolve?</li><li>What data will the new system deal with?</li><li>Are the data collection processes going to be different for the new system?</li><li>What are the input procedures that work for the organisation?</li><li>What outputs are required from the new system?</li><li>Are there existing systems that will interact with the new system?</li></ul>	Internal sources of information: <ul><li>users of the system</li><li>management</li><li>existing documentation</li><li>policies and procedures</li><li>technical support</li></ul> External sources of information: <ul><li>clients</li><li>customers</li><li>suppliers</li><li>consultancy</li><li>competitors</li><li>legislation – national and European</li><li>trading standards</li></ul>	<ul><li>Observation of current working arrangements – how do people interact with the existing system?</li><li>Structured interviews using pre-defined questions</li><li>Forums – open ended discussion to determine how people feel about the old system and what they want from the new system</li><li>Going through existing documentation to highlight current practice</li><li>Questionnaires</li><li>Review of outputs from the system – do they meet requirements?</li><li>Review of other systems – is there another organisation that has a similar system?</li></ul>

Establishing the data parameters

Systems use data to provide operational and evaluative information to end-users. Therefore, systems analysts need to describe in detail the data that is input to the system, the way that data flows through the system, and the data storage requirements.

There is a wide range of techniques available to the analyst:

For more information on data flow diagrams see pages 91–92.

- **Data flow diagrams** (**DFD**): these are diagrammatic representations of the relationship between the systems that manage the functions of an organisation and the way that data moves around the organisation. There are four elements within a data flow diagram. They are:
  - **Entities** – an entity refers to an item that has data attached to it. The entity 'student' will only hold data about students.
  - **Processes** – these are the things the system will do in order to organise data into formats suitable for the user. In a timetabling system one process could be the allocation of teachers to classes.
  - **Data flow** – from the source of the data following the direction of flow to the destination of the data.
  - **Data storage** – the location where data is held such as a student data table or a classroom data table.

Examples of how data flow diagrams work are useful in showing your understanding of how systems can be broken down into smaller components. You can work through some examples later in this chapter.

- **Process coding** – for each process a logical description is generated in a structured format. For example, in a school registration system: For each PUPIL in YEAR_GROUP if ABSENCE is <=5% then print PUPIL
- **Decision tables** – these are tabular representations of the way decisions about a process can change according to different conditions.

In this example, we can see that a class is allocated to a teacher when both teacher and class are free at the same time. This is the case in test 1. In test 2 the teacher is free, but the class is not – that means that the class remains unallocated. Note how the tests check each possible combination to determine whether a teacher can be allocated to a class.

ALLOCATE CLASS to TEACHER				
CONDITION	1	2	3	4
Teacher free	Y	Y	N	N
Class free	Y	N	Y	N
Allocate class	✓			
Don't allocate		✗	✗	✗

Developing the specification

The focus of this area of analysis is on producing a report and developing a detailed specification to pass forward to the design stage of the SDLC.

The report should contain:

- a detailed evaluation of the strengths and weaknesses of the current system
- a description of what the organisation wants to get from the new system
- a description of the end-user requirements that the new system will fulfil
- a description of how the new system will meet the requirements asked of it.

The specification outlines the aims, objectives and success criteria for the system. It should also define and justify each of the features of the system so that the designers can work effectively to develop a system that works, and also so that the end-users can verify that the user requirements have been understood and described effectively.

KEY POINT

A detailed specification allows the end-user to make sure that the systems analyst has understood the requirements. It means that the analysis will help to provide them with a system that meets their needs.

Example

An independent fashion clothing store has decided that it needs an online presence complete with an Internet shopping facility. This needs to link with their stock control system and the customer database and distribution system.

The systems analyst took a question-based approach to the development of the user requirements for the new system. For the Internet shopping aspect of the system the analyst decided, with the store owner, that the system needed to do the following:

Requirement	Reason
Store and display details of each item for sale	So that customers can see the products that are available
Display the price of each item	So that customers can make a judgment about the item
Allow the customer to select parameters	So that customers can get the size and colour that is right for them
Present items in relevant groups	So that customers wanting a 'type' of clothing (such as underwear) can get to the most appropriate range of clothing quickly
Collect and store customer details	To ensure that customers who purchase items receive them (details passed on to the distribution system) and that the store can contact the customer in future with details of special offers and sales that might interest them (link to customer database)

This, of course, represents only a small part of the system specification. Getting detail like this is very important – a successful specification has detail about everything.

Design

AQA **INFO 1, INFO 3**
OCR **G063**
WJEC **IT3**
CCEA **AS 1**

During the **design phase** the solution to the problem begins to be developed. The designers take the problem and begin to work towards a solution.

> **KEY POINT**
>
> The system design phase is possibly the most critical factor affecting the quality of the solution, and has a major impact on the later phases, particularly testing and maintenance.

The output of the design phase is the design document: it sets out the plan for the solution to the problem and is used later during implementation, testing and maintenance.

There are two sub-phases within the design phase:

- **system design** (or **top-level design**)
- **logical design** (or **detailed design**).

System design	Logical design
The focus is on identifying the modules that will make up the solution to the problem.	The focus is on designing the logic for each of the modules.
The attention is on what components are needed.	The attention is on how the components can be implemented.
Aims to identify the modules that should be in the system, the specifications of these modules and how they interact with each other to fulfil the requirements.	The internal logic of each of the modules specified in system design is decided.
At the end of system design all the major data structures, file formats, output formats, as well as the major modules in the system and their specifications are decided.	The details of the data structures and algorithmic design of each of the modules is specified.

It would be unusual for this stage to be undertaken by just one designer. More often it will be carried out by a team of designers. In any case it is clear that a large system cannot be looked at as a whole. Even the fashion store example on page 82 has a number of interrelated systems working together to produce an integrated solution.

System designers can choose to allocate aspects of the solution design using two approaches: **problem partitioning** and **abstraction**.

> Make sure that you show that you understand that any one system rarely acts independently of other systems.

Problem partitioning	Abstraction
Breaks the system into smaller systems.	Concentrates on how the smaller systems interact with each other.
The design looks at one part of the system at a time.	Presents an overview of how the system behaves without going into the detail.
Uses the Level 0 and Level 1 data flow diagrams to identify and then develop the smaller systems (see pages 91–92).	Abstraction would look at the system by using the context or top level data flow diagram.

KEY POINT

The designer is able to concentrate on one part at a time – they do not need to be concerned with the details of other components.

Like every other phase in the SLDC the design phase ends with verification of the design: the process will not continue forward if the design is not verified.

Implementation

AQA **INFO 1, INFO 3**
OCR **G063**
WJEC **IT3**
CCEA **AS 1**

Implementation begins when the system has passed through the design phase and is then:

- built according to the specification
- tested to ensure that it works
- installed.

Stage	Explanation
Construction	Construction is based on the system and logical designs developed from the specification. Each component will be developed in a standard programming language with associated documentation, data tables and consolidation of links between components.
	Construction may also include the acquisition of new hardware and software.
Testing	Thorough testing is extremely important. Testing takes three forms:
	- alpha testing – by the developers
	- beta testing – by a selection of users
	- acceptance testing – by the users once the system has been installed.
Installation	Installation can include:
	- installing new hardware and software
	- training
	- data preparation including the **conversion** of files from the old to the new system, or the creation of new files.

Review the section on software testing in Chapter 3.

Construction takes place when the system is built following the design that was specified in the design stage. Construction often includes:

- programming code needed to produce the working solution using the design specification as a template
- customising and modifying software to meet the needs of the end-user
- developing the framework needed for databases
- ensuring that a working system is produced to meet end-user requirements.

For the fashion store's Internet shopping facility (described in the example on page 82), the programmers and web-developers would produce a working system that draws upon a well organised and grouped database of items for sale, displays them effectively on a web page, and collects payment and delivery details from customers – storing these in another database that could be used for marketing purposes in the future.

Testing is best implemented by using the specification to develop a detailed **test plan**. Because the specification describes the user requirements in full, the testing phase can review the outcomes of each system operation and identify repairs, rewrites or rebuilds that will resolve any issues that impair the effective working of the system.

As all systems deal with data it is important that the testing process uses test data that has been designed to present the system with challenges: if the processes work according to plan, the system will be seen as successful in meeting the needs of the end-user.

Test data should ensure that:

- inputs to the system are valid
- outputs from the system are accurate
- outputs are presented clearly
- the solution meets the requirements established by the end-user
- the system is usable by the end-user and intended audience.

There are three types of test data:

Type of test data	Explanation	Examples
Normal test data	Data that follows expected formats and types and produces the outcomes that the system has been designed for.	• Are the correct reports generated? • Is the outcome as expected?
Erroneous test data	Data that contains typographical or format errors that could be entered by an operator in error.	• Does an error message appear? • Is the notification visual and audible? • Does the error message relate to the actual error? • Is there a suggested alteration? • Is the operator taken back to the entry screen?
Extreme test data	Data that contains errors that are not likely to be made – but which push the limits of all operations.	• How does the system respond? • Are the entries recognised as improper? • What advice is the operator given? • Is an error report produced?

Conversion refers specifically to the change from one system to another. It can take place in four ways:

Conversion type	Description	Advantage	Disadvantage
Direct changeover	This is when the old system shuts down and the new system is implemented immediately.	It means that things are up and running very quickly.	Normal operations could be severely disrupted if things do not go according to plan.
Parallel conversion (or parallel running)	The old and new systems run alongside each other for a set period of time.	If errors arise in the new system the running of the old system means that work continues.	The duplication of effort could have a negative impact on employees.
Pilot conversion (or pilot implementation)	The new system is used in one area of the organisation before scaling up to full implementation across the whole organisation.	Any errors impact on only a small part of the organisation. It can be seen as an extension of beta testing.	It could be time consuming and delay the implementation of the full system – and this could impact on the economic feasibility of the system.
Phased conversion (or phased implementation)	There are two types of phased conversion: when individual modules of the system are implemented over time – allowing older modules to run in the meantime or when, for example, some orders are processed on the new system while the rest are processed on the old.	Allows for error testing and provides a buffer for the organisation should things go wrong with the new system.	It can mean that more staff are involved – increasing the cost of implementation. It might also mean that training has to be phased – again duplicating effort.

Maintenance

AQA **INFO 1, INFO 3**
OCR **G063**
WJEC **IT3**
CCEA **AS 1**

Maintenance takes place to ensure that the system continues to run effectively. There are likely to be a number of approaches to, and needs for maintenance.

Software upgrades may conflict with the existing hardware and may require some reconfiguration (for software maintenance see Chapter 3).

Evaluation

AQA **INFO 1, INFO 3**
OCR **G063**
WJEC **IT3**
CCEA **AS 1**

An **evaluation** of the system is the final phase of the SLDC. That being said, you can see from the SLDC diagram on page 78 that the process of systems development is iterative. For example, one outcome of the evaluation may be that changes in the environment in which the organisation is operating give rise to new requirements, and so the cycle begins again.

As with all other stages of the SDLC the evaluation will use the specification of user requirements to structure the evaluation report. An evaluation report is likely to contain the following elements:

Element	Evaluation
A measurement of performance against the user requirements and objectives	• Does the system fulfil all requirements or just some of them?
A review of user satisfaction	• Are the users happy with the system? • Has it been designed for ease of operation? • Are problems resolved quickly?
A review of compatibility	• Is the system compatible with other areas of work?
A review of reliability	• Does the system fall down at times of heavy use? • Is the software reliable? • Is the hardware reliable?
A review of performance	• Does the system run as efficiently as it should? • Does it run as quickly as the user expected it to? • Are there any times when things slow down?
A review of output	• Is the output of the right quality? • Is it accurate? • Is it complete? • Can it be directed to the right people? • Does it transfer easily to other systems within the organisation?

Note the link with compatibility here.

PROGRESS CHECK

1. Name the stages of the systems development life cycle and explain why it is described as a cycle.
2. What is the role of the systems analyst in the development of a solution to an identified problem?
3. **(a)** Describe the purpose of conversion in the implementation phase of the systems development life cycle.
   (b) Name **two** types of conversion.

1. There are six stages in the systems development life cycle. They are: investigation; analysis; design; implementation; maintenance and evaluation. The outcomes of each stage provide the starting point for the next stage. These outcomes are tested and validated. If the outcomes are found to be faulty or incomplete the process returns to the beginning of the stage. This can happen at the end of any of the six stages – the process loops until the outcomes are verified.

2. The systems analyst leads the development of the process and is involved in all stages. The analyst will liaise with the client, review their needs and lead on the development of the feasibility study and the specification. The development of the detailed specification will support the programming team and enable the analyst to play a key role in measuring the performance of the developed system against the user requirements during alpha testing.

3. **(a)** Conversion takes place when the data files and working methodologies are transferred from the old system to the new system. Files such as customer records may need to be stored in a new format in order to be processed by the new system; staff may need to work in different ways. **(b)** Any two from: Direct changeover; Parallel conversion; Pilot conversion; Phased conversion.

4.2 Securing the development of a project

LEARNING SUMMARY

After studying this section you should be able to:

- describe how alternative project development methodologies offer different approaches to systems development
- describe and explain how analytical tools are used throughout the systems development life cycle
- explain how critical path analysis and Gantt charts are used in project management

Project development methodologies

AQA **INFO 1, INFO 3**
OCR **G063**
WJEC **IT3**
CCEA **AS 1**

Systems are developed by people in a variety of roles using a range of techniques and tools to aid their work, and to provide a structure to the process that they are working through. You have seen in the review of the systems development life cycle, and in the review of software development in Chapter 3, that a high level of detail is required in order to secure the development of a successful project that fulfils the requirements laid out in the specification and that contributes to increasing efficiency for the organisation.

> **KEY POINT**
>
> Project development methodologies are used to define and represent systems. Users and developers should be able to identify how data flows through the system and also identify the key operations that the system will fulfil.

Prototyping

The SDLC can lead to a relatively linear approach to the development of a system, and like the waterfall model could mean that the end-user does not really get to see how the proposed system is working until the project is drawing to a close.

Prototyping allows for modifications to the design as the project proceeds and encourages the development team and the commissioning organisation (including managers, technicians and operators) to learn about the requirements of the system as the development runs its course.

The development of any system relies heavily on the accuracy of the specification of requirements. Skilled analysts are able to draw from their investigations a detailed review of what it is the user wants from the new system. This will in part be based on their analysis of the old system and their use of interviews, questionnaires, research and observations. However, users often find it difficult to be as clear as they might because they may not:

- fully realise the possibilities open to them
- have a clear idea about how the final system will function.

This may mean that the system specification is internally flawed from the outset, and that despite all the testing, verification and evaluation it will never fully meet the requirements of the organisation.

In prototyping, a model of the new system is constructed in order to evaluate it before going on to the full development. This may mean that small elements of the total system are 'mocked up' so that end-users can experience how the system works and suggest improvements or make other recommendations before moving on to the next stage.

In the fashion store example on page 82 a prototype would present the store owner with a mock-up of the 'shopping page' attached to a limited database so that they could test out how a customer would make a choice from the items for sale. At this point the store owner would be able to offer rapid feedback about how they felt development was going.

> **KEY POINT**
>
> In prototyping, the specification of requirements is seen as a fluid document – user involvement throughout the project will mean that the specification of requirements will change.

Prototyping looks something like this:

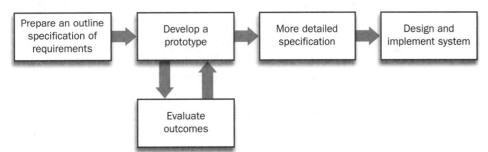

There are two main forms of prototyping:
- **Throw-away prototyping** – called this because once the early development has achieved its purpose they are discarded and the 'real' system is developed. Detailed approaches to throw-away prototyping are:
  - **piloting** (where the prototype is used to test the feasibility of the design)
  - **modelling** (where a module is built to test the understanding of the user's requirements)
- **Evolutionary prototyping** – each prototype that is developed and evaluated represents another step towards the final solution. The cycle of prototype development and evaluation leads to refinements and improvements.

Benefits of prototyping include:
- Early identification of misunderstandings between systems analysts, developers and end-users.
- User requirements can be checked for completeness or inconsistencies.
- Missing or inaccurate functions will be detected early.
- It enables management to check feasibility at an earlier stage.
- A prototype can be used to train users (and thereby fast-track implementation) before the final system is ready.

It is good to focus on benefits – but remember that where there are benefits there will be drawbacks.

A key drawback of prototyping is that it may not change systems radically enough to fulfil all the feasibilities because when users are involved they might stay within their comfort zone.

Rapid Application Development

Rapid Application Development (**RAD**) is a feature of software and systems (including hardware) development. It draws heavily on prototyping as a methodology. It enables products to be developed more quickly, whilst maintaining quality by:

- sharing the development of the specification of requirements with focus groups or workshops of end-users
- prototyping paying special attention to user testing
- re-using old components that are known to work, and that will continue to meet user requirements
- placing less formality on the process of reviews and other communications. However, less formality might mean that aspects that require development are not challenged rigorously enough.

Using analytical tools in systems development

AQA	**INFO 1, INFO 3**
OCR	**G063**
WJEC	**IT3**
CCEA	**AS 1**

There are many tools that analysts and developers can use to help them when defining the detail of system processes, inputs, outputs and storage requirements. The key tools you need to be familiar with are:

- data dictionaries
- data flow diagrams
- entity relationship diagrams
- state transition diagrams.

Data dictionaries

The **data dictionary** is a file that details the content, structure and format of (the **metadata** about) data sets to be used within a system. These details will include:

- the data tables or **entities** included in the system
- the names of these entities
- relationships between entities

Entries and attributes are covered in more detail on page 93

- the data characteristics of each field/data item – also referred to as an **attribute** (length, data type, special format)
- value restrictions of attributes (e.g. input masks, >=9)
- a description of each attribute (e.g. rooms available for letting in a hotel)
- the names of programs/processes that use the data and a description of what that use is (is the data being read, or is it being altered?)
- in large organisations that use the same database different departments often use alternative names for the same things – systems analysts need to record these as **synonyms** within the data dictionary so that these alternative names are not confused when the new system is developed.

The example below is a data dictionary entry for the room_number attribute within a school timetabling system.

Attribute name	room_number
Synonyms	None
Data type	alphanumeric
Format	aa0-000
Description of the attribute	Building (2 alpha), floor (single numeric) and number of room (3 numerics)
Attribute length	7 characters
Entity names	TEACHING_ROOMS ICT_FACILITIES CLASS_ALLOCATION TIMETABLE

Data flow diagrams

We've already seen how data flow diagrams are used by systems analysts to describe the functions of an existing system and to map out the design and specification of a proposed system.

There are three levels of data flow diagrams:
- the **context diagram** (or top-level diagram)
- the **level 0 diagram**
- the **level 1 diagram**

The movement from context through the level 0 and then to the level 1 is all about moving from the generic or overall system, through to the specifics of each process within each sector of the system.

The following examples use a school timetabling system to show how data flow diagrams could be constructed.

Context diagrams show:
- the whole system as a single process
- no data storage
- inputs and data sources (as external entities)
- outputs and destinations (as external entities).

Context diagram

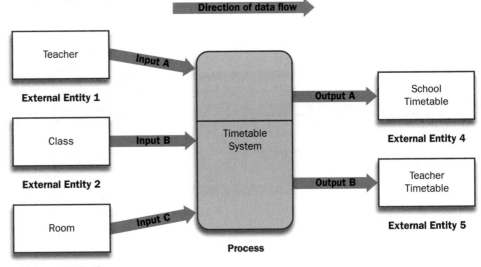

The level 0 diagram focuses in on the timetable system and defines what it does in more detail. As we zoom in more processes will appear. These new processes are numbered: the numbering system helps us to track the development of the system and to see the relationship between the whole system (in the context diagram) and the components of the system described in detail in the level 1 diagram.

Level 0 diagram

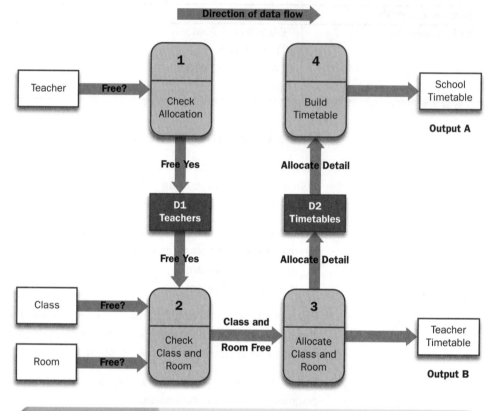

KEY POINT

Note how the data flow diagrams zoom in on the detail as we move from context to level 0 and then on to level 1.

Level 1 diagram

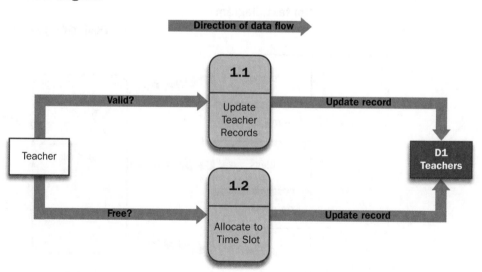

Entity relationship diagrams

An **entity relationship diagram** (**ERD**) is a graphical representation of system elements and the associations that they have between them. The elements that make up a system are referred to as **entities**. An entity can be anything about which data is held. It could include places, objects, customers, stores, motor vehicles, students, or teachers. Each entity has associated **attributes**. An attribute provides extra detail about an entity. For example:

Entity	Attributes
Cinema	Location Code
	Post Code
	Telephone number
	Number of screens

The **relationship** is the association that tells us about the interaction between the entities. To show the relationship between the two entities we need to be able to see:
- the **degree** or **cardinality** of the relationship
- the name of the relationship.

There are three levels of degree or cardinality:
- one-to-one
- one-to-many
- many-to-many

Let's consider an entity relationship diagram for a cinema that has a number of screens, with each screen staffed by a number of employees and having a number of seats that need to be filled by customers.

The entities within this system are: Cinema; Customer; Cinema Seat; Employee; Screen.

For more information on entity relationship modelling see pages 129–132.

We need to decide what the relationships are between these entities.

Each customer fills one seat in a cinema to see a film. This is a **one-to-one** relationship.

Each cinema may have many screens. This is a **one-to-many** relationship.

Many staff will work in the cinema to check tickets and show customers to their seats. They will do this for all screens. This is a **many-to-many** relationship.

93

In the example cinema system we can see that there is one cinema that is made up of many screens. Each screen holds many seats. Each seat can hold one customer at a time. The cinema has many employees.

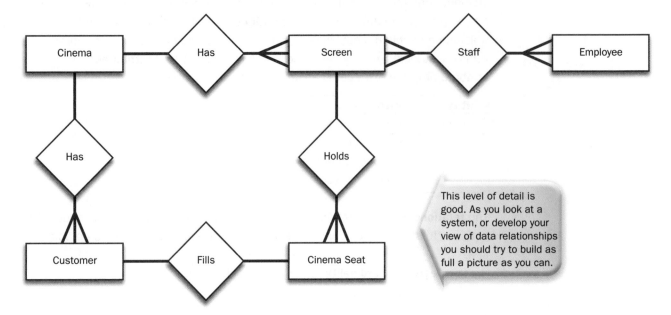

> This level of detail is good. As you look at a system, or develop your view of data relationships you should try to build as full a picture as you can.

State transition diagrams

A **state transition diagram** (**STD**) highlights how the system deals with specific data at specific times: it describes *what* is happening *when*. State transition diagrams are largely used to define and develop **real-time systems** (i.e. systems that process data and provide an immediate response). Examples of real-time systems include:

- telephone switching systems
- password response systems
- ATMs (cash machines)

If we look at a typical ATM, for example, the system is idle until a customer inserts their bank card. The customer's PIN is requested, entered and validated. Once validated the customer is presented with a number of options – one of which might be to distribute cash. In the diagram below the boxes represent the **state** and the arrows represent **state changes** or **transitions**. You can see that once a process begins it can move on to another process or return to idle.

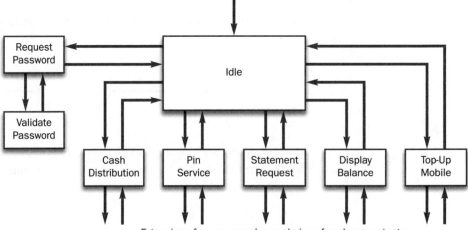

Extension of processes above: choice of cash amount, etc.

Project management tools

AQA INFO 1, INFO 3
OCR G061, G062
WJEC IT1, IT3
CCEA A2 1, A2 2

Project management is the process of organising the people, equipment and other resources to achieve objectives outlined in the specification. It requires that a project is broken down into tasks, and that these tasks take place in sequence (setting out when they begin) and a specific time for completion (outlining the length of time available to complete a project and setting an end date).

There are several tools available to aid the project management process. Perhaps the most important tools are:
- **Gantt charts**
- **Critical Path Analysis**

KEY POINT

The SDLC is all about getting the structures right, and having a structured methodology. These tools support that by providing graphical representations of the structure. They also provide monitoring opportunities to keep things on track.

Gantt charts

Gantt charts are useful tools for planning and scheduling projects. They enable project managers to:
- plan how long a project should take
- determine the order in which activities need to take place
- review what should have been achieved by agreed deadlines
- see the relationship between one activity and another
- allocate staffing and resourcing across and between activities.

ID	Activity	Predecessor	Duration	January 1							January 8							January 15						
				S	M	T	W	T	F	S	S	M	T	W	T	F	S	S	M	T	W	T	F	S
	Investigation																							
1	Start																							
2	Review Hardware	1	3 days																						
3	Review Software	1	3 days																						
4	Scope System	2, 3	7 days																						
5	Prepare DFD	4	5 days																						
6	Identity Problems	5	2 days																						

As you can see there are some tasks that can be done concurrently (Tasks 2 and 3). Some cannot start until their predecessor is complete (Tasks 4 and 6), while others can begin before the end of its predecessor based on the work completed to date (Task 5). Note that because Saturday and Sunday are not normal work days the scope of the bars is longer because they cut across the weekend.

The primary focus of the Gantt chart is to develop the schedule of work; it does not differentiate between the size of the work elements: having the preparation of the DFD running behind schedule may be much more significant than an over-run of the hardware and software reviews.

Critical Path Analysis

Critical Path Analysis (**CPA**) is an extension of the methodology applied in Gantt charts. Like the Gantt chart, CPA:

- identifies the individual activities within a larger project
- sets out the order in which they take place
- shows which activities can only start once others have been completed
- shows activities that can be run at the same time
- shows when resources are needed (like the purchase of new hardware)
- sets out the duration of each activity.

With all this in place the **critical path** can be identified. The critical path is the route through the project that allows for no slack: it shows the minimum time in which the whole project can be completed.

> **KEY POINT**
>
> CPA is a complex approach to the management of a project through the SDLC. It is important to build the CPA in stages to ensure that it accurately represents the stages of the project.

From the Gantt chart example on page 95, we can see that the project has a number of steps. In CPA each step is represented by a **node**. We know the duration of activities so a simple network diagram might look like this:

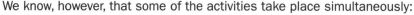

We know, however, that some of the activities take place simultaneously:

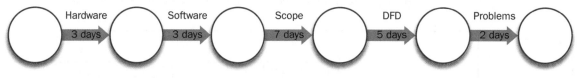

We also know that there is an overlap between scoping and developing the data flow diagram and we need to account for this. We can begin to sort this out by branching again:

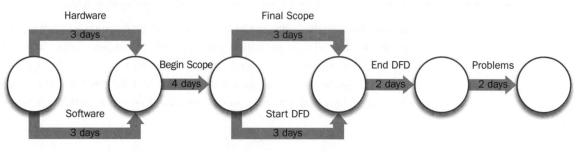

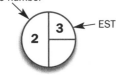

node number

Each node contains structured information. The first will be the node number (in the largest sector of the node), followed by the **earliest start time** (**EST**).

In the first node the EST is always zero. As we move through the following nodes the EST is calculated by adding the EST of the previous activity to the duration of the previous activity. Where the activities are of different durations we always take the highest figure.

So the CPA now looks like this:

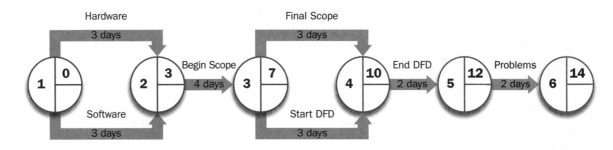

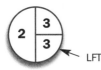

The final area of the node describes the **latest finishing time** (**LFT**). This is calculated by taking the EST of the final node: in our case this is 14. We then work back subtracting the duration of the previous activity from the LFT.

And so we arrive at the final CPA:

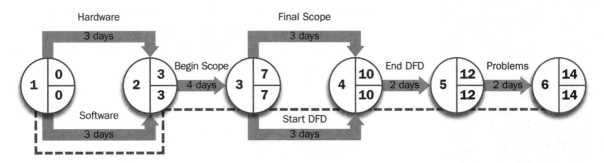

All nodes on the critical path should have an equal EST and LFT. That is the case with the example above. The critical path is identified with a red dotted line.

Sample questions and model answers

1. Name and describe two stages in the ICT systems development life cycle. **(6)**

The first stage of the systems development life cycle is the investigation phase. This phase determines the feasibility of the project by looking at the schedule, technical, operational, legal and economic implications of the project. One outcome of this stage would be a decision about whether the development of a system would be feasible when costs are measured against perceived benefits. Another stage in the development process is the analysis stage. Here a systems analyst reviews the current system and gathers user requirements from which to begin to establish the specification. The analyst will use tools such as questionnaires and observations to gather the user requirements, and will detail the system by using a data flow diagram to ensure that the analysis presents a full and accurate picture of the existing system.

2. Prototyping is a tool that is used during the systems development life cycle.
   (a) Name and describe two types of prototyping. **(6)**
   (b) Give three benefits of prototyping. **(3)**
   (c) Describe two drawbacks of prototyping. **(4)**

(a) There are two types of prototyping. The first is evolutionary prototyping where the prototype is developed in stages. Each stage is tested and validated by the end-user. Improvements are made, and lead to the development of the final system. With throwaway prototyping the prototype is used to determine the system requirements. Once these have been established the prototype is discarded.

(b) Prototyping allows for:
   (i) an early identification of misunderstandings between systems analysts, developers and end-users
   (ii) a check on user requirements for completeness or inconsistencies
   (iii) management to check feasibility at an earlier stage

(c) Prototyping is a less formal approach to systems development. This may mean that less structured documentation may be produced. This could complicate maintenance should errors occur in the future. In evolutionary prototyping, because the requirements of the user may change with each iteration of the prototype the original objectives of the project may not be finalised.

3. Describe two project management tools that can be used to facilitate systems development. **(6)**

Gantt charts are useful in project management as they support the planning and scheduling of staff, time and resources against elements of the overall project. They enable project managers to gain a quick overview of the structure of a project, and allow them to monitor the progress of a project against time related milestones. Critical Path Analysis (CPA) develops the process of breaking a project down into smaller components and shows where activities are dependent upon the completion of others and also shows where activities can be run concurrently. Each element of the CPA shows the duration of activities and can identify when resources are needed.

Practice examination questions

1 Implementation and maintenance are two of the stages in the development of an information system.

(a) Identify three activities that take place during implementation. **(3)**

_____

_____

_____

(b) Identify three activities that take place during maintenance. **(3)**

_____

_____

_____

2 A systems analyst has looked at the data required by a booking system and has found that the following rules apply:

(i) any person or group can make a number of bookings

(ii) a booking is for one room only (either the Conference Hall or the smaller Meeting Room)

(iii) a booking may require many items of audio visual equipment

(iv) each item of audio visual equipment belongs to one room.

Complete the entity relationship diagram below to show these relationships. Label all relationships. **(8)**

5 Spreadsheet modelling

The following topics are covered in this chapter:

- Spreadsheet basics
- Refining modelling functions
- Applications of spreadsheet modelling

5.1 Spreadsheet basics

LEARNING SUMMARY

After studying this section you should be able to:

- describe the characteristics of spreadsheet modelling software
- demonstrate and explain how variables, formulae, functions and rules are used to develop models
- describe and explain the relationship between worksheets, workbooks, rows, columns, cells and ranges
- identify and explain the role of referencing in spreadsheet modelling

The characteristics of modelling software

AQA **INFO 4**
OCR **G061**
WJEC **IT1**
CCEA **AS 1, AS 2**

Spreadsheet modelling focuses on the way we use data to answer 'what-if' questions. Spreadsheet software allows users to create worksheets that represent numerical and other data in rows and columns. Generally spreadsheets are used for developing solutions to business and organisational problems such as:

- budgeting
- developing cash flow forecasts
- producing profit and loss statements
- recording student performance data
- maintaining detailed records

Spreadsheet features

Spreadsheets offer a range of facilities that support the development of solutions from the analysis of numerical data. These facilities include the ability to:

- format cells, rows and columns so that data is presented effectively
- move data contents around without changing the format or the relationship with other data in the spreadsheet
- insert, move or delete cells, rows and columns
- use functions that simplify arithmetical and numerical calculations
- apply 'what-if' hypotheses to test the data
- apply simple data functions to sort, filter and analyse data according to its characteristics (e.g. all MALE students UNDER 19 studying ICT)
- present data in tables, reports, graphs and charts
- support the development of macros to automate regularly repeated procedures

> You need to know about and be able to describe the key features of the software you use to solve problems.

- create templates which are pre-populated with formats and formulae to support easy and co-ordinated data entry
- support multi-dimensional worksheets within workbooks so that data from one sheet can be used to support calculations in another.

The functionality of modelling software falls, broadly, into three categories:
- data entry
- data analysis
- displaying and reporting results

> **KEY POINT**
>
> Using these three basic functions of spreadsheet modelling software enables users to organise data effectively, identify trends within that data, and begin to understand and evaluate the background to the data within the model.

Data entry

Effective data analysis and reporting cannot exist without accurate data entry. The entry of data into spreadsheets can be simply typed in as a **data list**, though this method may be cumbersome if there is a lot of data to be entered. This can be resolved if the data can be imported from **external sources**. **Data forms** can also be used to simplify and co-ordinate the process of inputting data into specific cells within the spreadsheet.

Type of data entry	Description
Data lists	A data list is a group of values that have a clear pattern and relationship – a shopping list would be a good example. In a spreadsheet, data items are grouped and consolidated so that they make sense to the reader. | Item	Wanted	Price Per Item	Cost per purchase
---	---	---	---
Butter	2	0.98	£1.96
6 Eggs	1	1.20	£1.20	
External data	Most spreadsheet modelling programs allow data to be imported by: - copying and pasting the data - importing structured text data directly into the spreadsheet file - importing data from other programs in the form of a .csv file - importing large quantities of filtered data from database files.
Data forms	The manual input of data can be simplified by using data forms. These consist of a dialogue box with fields into which users can input data which conforms to specific data values, ranges and formats (e.g. enter start date, no more than 30 days in the past or the future, in the format dd/mm/yy).

Data analysis

When data is analysed, tools are used to compare data values. The analysis can be as simple as adding up a list of numbers, or sorting a list in alphabetical order. More complex comparisons can be made by applying **formulae** and **functions**, developing **macros** or using one of the pre-programmed analysis tools that are supplied with the spreadsheet software.

Tools	Description
Formulae	Formulae are used to analyse data values taken from single or multiple cells. Formulae can combine cell references, mathematical operators, or built-in functions.
Functions	A function is a pre-defined process that, when included in a formula, carries out specific calculations. Most spreadsheet programs have over 200 functions for different types of calculations (see page 105 for examples of functions).
Macros	Macros are used to repeat processes such as hiding columns, inserting rows, or carrying out a series of calculations. They save time by enabling repeated processes to be carried out (see page 115).
Pivot tables	Pivot tables are used to summarise data by combining values from different fields. You can, for example, analyse the grades achieved by male students taught by a particular teacher. Pivot tables are dynamic: if you change fields and apply other filtering options the output will change immediately.
Analysis tools	Most spreadsheet software provides analysis tools that can be applied such as conditional formatting, filtering and data validation.

Displaying and reporting results

The analysis tools available in spreadsheet software packages provide detailed numerical summaries of the data being analysed. They can also be used to create a range of graphical representations of the data.

Graphical representation	Description
Charts	Charts provide a visual representation of the data values in the spreadsheet. Charts can be embedded within the spreadsheet containing the data, or can be presented on a separate chart sheet within the workbook. There are usually chart types available to suit the nature of the data being analysed. Charts can be customised further by changing titles, fonts, legends, and labels.
Pivot charts	Pivot charts combine all the functionality of general charts with the dynamic capability of pivot tables.

Developing spreadsheet models

AQA **INFO 1, INFO 3**
OCR **G061**
WJEC **IT1**
CCEA **AS 1, AS 2**

It is important that you are very clear about the difference between a simple spreadsheet and a spreadsheet model that allows you to explore hypothetical questions about the data that you have. Models generally have **inputs** and **outputs**: changing elements of the input data should have a direct impact on the output. These changes should be planned for within the development of the model – so that assumptions and hypotheses can be explored.

A model will generally include a variety of data types, variables, formulae, functions and rules.

Data types

Data types refer to the nature of the value that is stored in a cell. When data is input it is automatically structured according to its type: text, numerical or formula.

Data type	Description
Text	Cells containing text are usually used to define the data that is next to them. These cells are said to contain labels which identify the cells, columns and rows that contain numerical values or the outputs from formulaic calculations.
Numerical	Cells containing numerical values display their data in different formats: • number (with or without decimal places) • percentage • currency • time • date and time
Formula	Formulae can be created within any cell of a worksheet to evaluate the data values stored elsewhere. They can carry out simple or complex calculations, and must be preceded by an appropriate symbol so that the spreadsheet program recognises the entry as a formula (e.g. =SUM(A1:A10))

Variables

Knowing the difference between constants and variables is extremely important.

Numerical data in a spreadsheet is known as a **constant**. The number 10 is always the number 10, just in the same way that 1066 will always be the year in which the Battle of Hastings took place. For spreadsheet models to work effectively and efficiently it is better that we work with **variables**, i.e. values that change to meet the conditions required by the spreadsheet model.

For example, a catering wholesaler shows its prices without VAT, which is calculated at checkout. A spreadsheet is used to calculate bills and present receipts.

	A	B	C	D	E	F	G
1	Item	Price	Number Purchased	Purchase Price	VAT	Price Charged	VAT Rate
2	9" white plate	1.29	6	=6*1.29	=(6*1.29)*20%	=6*1.29+((6*1.29)*20%)	20%

The calculations in the example above work – but they are all expressed as constants. If the price of the plate changes, or if the VAT rate changes, then the formulae would have to be written out in full again to calculate the correct price charged to the customer.

With variables this is much easier as the formulae work with the data value that is in the cell. For the formula to work it does not matter if the price of the plate is changed from £1.29 to £9.99: the formula will still give the correct answer.

There are two ways of doing this: by using the cell reference, or by allocating a name to a cell or range of cells.

Formulae using variables (cell references)

	A	B	C	D	E	F	G
1	Item	Price	Number Purchased	Purchase Price	VAT	Price Charged	VAT Rate
2	9" white plate	1.29	6	=B2*C2	=D2*G2	=D2+E2	20%

Formulae using variables (names)

	A	B	C	D	E	F	G
1	Item	Price	Number Purchased	Purchase Price	VAT	Price Charged	VAT Rate
2	9" white plate	1.29	6	=Price*Number_Purchased	=Purchase_Price*VATRate	=Purchase_Price+VAT	20%

Setting up the names is pretty straightforward. You should note that they are the same as the column labels. The name can be defined for either a single cell or a range of cells.

Look how it works for another item added to the list of purchases in the spreadsheet:

Formulae using variables (cell references)

	A	B	C	D	E	F	G
1	Item	Price	Number Purchased	Purchase Price	VAT	Price Charged	VAT Rate
2	9" white plate	1.29	6	=B2*C2	=D2*$G$2	=D2+E2	20%
3	Saucer white	0.69	6	=B3*C3	=D3*$G$2	=D3+E3	

Formulae using variables (names)

	A	B	C	D	E	F	G
1	Item	Price	Number Purchased	Purchase Price	VAT	Price Charged	VAT Rate
2	9" white plate	1.29	6	=Price*Number_Purchased	=Purchase_Price*VATRate	=Purchase_Price+VAT	20%
3	Saucer white	0.69	6	=Price*Number_Purchased	=Purchase_Price*VATRate	=Purchase_Price+VAT	

In each of the examples above the formulae in columns D, E and F contain references that produce results based on their relative position within the model. Because the formulae in row 3 are referring to the price and number of the saucer the cell references reflect that. This is known as **relative cell referencing**.

In column E there is a combination of cell references. An efficient model that uses one tax rate will only have the tax rate stored once. It would be a waste of time and effort to have the tax rate referenced many times, and if it changed it would need to be changed many times. As it is set up as a single cell within the spreadsheet it is important that it is referenced accurately. We can do this by fixing the column and row position of the cell either by naming the cell (in this case VATRate) or by inserting $ in the cell reference ($G$2). This is known as **absolute cell referencing**.

> **KEY POINT**
>
> The distinction between relative and absolute cell referencing is an important one.

Formulae, functions and rules

There is a wide variety of features and functions available within spreadsheet modelling software. As you will know from your work, and the brief review above, formulae are used to calculate and analyse the outcome of calculations within a spreadsheet model.

As a minimum you should be familiar with, and be able to describe and use, some very basic functions. These are:

Function	Purpose	Example
SUM	Adds the defined range of cells and places the total in the selected cell.	=SUM(A1:A10)
AVERAGE	Calculates the mean average of the defined range of cells.	=AVERAGE(A1:A10)
COUNT	Counts the number of numerical values in the defined range of cells. If a cell in the range contains a non-numerical value it is ignored.	=COUNT(A1:A10)
MAX	Finds the maximum value in the defined range of cells.	=MAX(A1:A10)
MIN	Finds the minimum value in the defined range of cells.	=MIN(A1:A10)

Note that the formulae in the table above have exactly the same format:

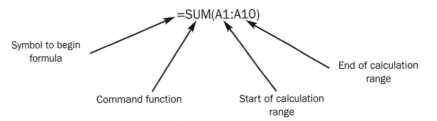

Symbol to begin formula

Command function

Start of calculation range

End of calculation range

=SUM(A1:A10)

Other functions you should be familiar with include:

Function	Purpose	Example
RAND	Returns a value between 0 and 1	=RAND()
RANDBETWEEN	Returns a random number between the numbers specified.	=RANDBETWEEN(1,100)
ROUND	Rounds a number to the specified number of digits (and follows mathematical rules for rounding).	=ROUND(C3,0)
ROUNDUP	Rounds a number up to the specified number of digits.	=ROUNDUP(C3,0)
ROUNDDOWN	Rounds a number down to the specified number of digits.	=ROUNDDOWN(C3,0)
TODAY	Returns the current date.	=TODAY()
NOW	Returns the current date and time.	=NOW()

Conditional formulae present very useful opportunities to begin to answer 'what-if' questions within a spreadsheet model or to define how data should be calculated, changed or formatted if conditions are met.

In its very simplest form the conditional formula looks like this:

=IF(A2>70,'PASS','FAIL')

Here the cell will display PASS if the mark recorded in A2 is larger than 70, and FAIL if it is less than or equal to 70.

The formula can be refined if 70 is the pass mark:

=IF(A2>=70,'PASS','FAIL')

Sometimes multiple conditions have to be met. These are commonly referred to as **nested IF** function statements.

For example, in a marking system students are awarded grades according to the following **rules** (rules define the tests that are applied to the data within the scope of the model). In this example, Steven's mark falls between 60 and 70 and is therefore allocated a C.

	A	B	C	D	E	F
1	Mark	Grade		Steven	65	C
2	90	A*		Jo	29	Fail
3	80	A		Ishmael	59	D
4	70	B		Gok	73	B
5	60	C		Sofia	80	A
6	50	D		Katie	92	A*
7	40	E				
8	30	F				
9	<30	Fail				

The formula is constructed like this:

=IF(E1>=90,'A*',IF(E1>=80,'A',IF(E1>=70,'B',IF(E1>=60,'C',IF(E1>=50,'D',IF(E1>=40,'E',IF(E1>=30,'F','Fail')))))))

IF condition 1 is met THEN 'A*'
IF condition 2 is met THEN 'A'
IF condition 3 is met THEN 'B'
IF condition 4 is met THEN 'C'
IF condition 5 is met THEN 'D'
IF condition 6 is met THEN 'E'
IF condition 7 is met THEN 'F' OTHERWISE FAIL

Steven	65	C
Jo	29	Fail
Ishmael	59	D
Gok	73	B
Sofia	80	A
Katie	92	A*

This nested 'IF' example is constructed from the highest numerical value within the rules table to the lowest, and contains the maximum number of nests that can be applied, i.e. seven.

The teacher using this mark book model could also apply **conditional formatting** rules so that every student getting above 70 would be shown as green, those between 50 and 70 would be amber and those below 50 would be red.

With a larger set of data other functions can be applied to ensure that the data can be analysed effectively. If a student administrator is asked for the subject grade for a student in a group a **LOOKUP** function can be used to find the required data.

With VLOOKUP the data is looked for according to the ROW (which is in numerical or alphabetical order) in which it appears according to the following criteria:

=VLOOKUP(value in the first column, the range in which the data is held, the column from which the displayed data is to be drawn).

	A	B	C	D
1	StudentID	Student	Mark	Grade
2	1	Steven	65	C
3	2	Jo	29	Fail
4	3	Ishmael	59	D
5	4	Gok	73	B
6	5	Sofia	80	A
7	6	Katie	92	A*

In the mark book model we have to include a student ID number in ascending numerical order.

The administrator is looking for the results for Jo. They input the student ID and are presented with the results for the correct student.

The formula looks like this: =VLOOKUP(L2,A1:D7,4)

The cell in which the request ID is input

The data range included in the search

The number of the column in which the Grade data is held

There are times when it is not possible to look within a sorted list. Under these circumstances a normal LOOKUP function would not be appropriate. In the case of the mark book example, if the administrator did not have access to student IDs then they would still be able to locate Jo's result.

	A	B	C
1	Student	Mark	Grade
2	Steven	65	C
3	Jo	29	Fail
4	Ishmael	59	D
5	Gok	73	B
6	Sofia	80	A
7	Katie	92	A*

The administrator in this example types in the name of the student they are looking for. The formula to produce the result looks like this:

=INDEX(A1:C7,MATCH(L2,A1:A7,0),3)

The whole data range included in the search

The cell in which the request name is input

The column range in which the value will be found

Must be an exact match

The number of the column in which the Grade data is held

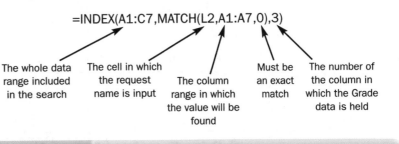

PROGRESS CHECK

1　Why are conditional formulae important in spreadsheet modelling?

1　Any suitable answer, e.g. Conditional formulae allow us to ask "what-if" questions and provide validated responses that make data analysis easier. The use of text and cell formatting are useful and important elements of conditional formulae.

5.2 Refining modelling functions

LEARNING SUMMARY

After studying this section you should be able to:

- identify and describe a range of facilities for data entry
- explain the purpose of data validation techniques within a spreadsheet model
- understand and explain the concept of workbooks
- define 3D referencing
- explain the process and purpose of database functions within a spreadsheet
- explain why macros are useful in developing automated routines
- consider the range of display and formatting options available

Data entry and validation

AQA	INFO 1, INFO 4
OCR	G061, G063
WJEC	IT1
CCEA	AS 1, AS 2

There are many options available to users and developers of spreadsheet models when it comes to entering data for processing. Data can be entered simply, or it can be structured within defined parameters, and can be validated to ensure that it:

- fits within required ranges (such as a list of local towns)
- matches locally defined formats (where, for example, dates are in UK format rather than US format).

Data entry and validation can be supported by using **dialogue boxes** to collect information from the users in a **form**. Dialogue boxes allow spreadsheet designers to work within specific parameters, and so make the process of data entry efficient and effective.

> You should include a range of effective tools and functions in your spreadsheet data modelling work. You should also include a range of error trapping functions.

Combo boxes

Combo boxes allow users to click on an item from a list, which can then automatically insert values from the list. Look at the example of a list of office supplies below to see how it works:

	A	B
1	Item	Price
2	A4 Paper	£ 1.25
3	A5 Notepad	£ 0.40
4	HB Pencils	£ 0.99
5	Black gel pens	£ 1.30
6	Red gel pens	£ 1.30

In this list the cell range from A2 to A6 has been named using the heading in the top row: Item. The range B2:B6 is named Price. A combo box has been set up on a Price Enquiry worksheet. The data is stored on a Data worksheet.

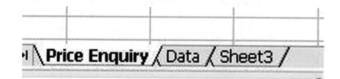

The combo box displays the data from the list of items. As a user selects from the list of items the price associated with it is displayed. It takes its reference from the cell link (cell C1 on the Data worksheet) that is defined in the settings, which was established when the parameters for the combo box were set up.

Item Required	HB Pencils					▼
Price	£ 0.99					

The formula for presenting the price data looks like this:

=INDEX(Price,'Data'$C$1)

Spinners

Spinners allow the users to specify a value by clicking on one of the arrow buttons to increase or decrease the value. This type of feature is often seen on booking forms: how many tickets do you require; how many persons per room; how many items?

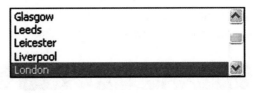

The spinner here is set with a minimum of 1 guest and a maximum of 4: the designer sets the parameters within which the user will operate to ensure that the data entry is valid.

List boxes

List boxes present a list of items from which a user can select an item or a number of items. This can then be confirmed.

| Glasgow |
| Leeds |
| Leicester |
| Liverpool |
| London |

Note the scroll bar at the side, and how the highlighted city has been confirmed.

You have selected: **London**   =INDEX(Cities,A13)

The designer here has cleared the gridlines and hidden the cell link from the list box control by formatting the text as white to match the background. Once again, parameters are defined and data entry is validated as the user has selected from the pre-defined range.

Data validation

There are options that can be applied to cells, rather than to defined boxes. Designers can restrict the type and format of data entered into cells by using **data validation** and so specify the contents of cells to conform to specifications.

Validation	Explanation
Any value	... why would you bother since cells already allow any value?
Whole number	Can set a minimum and maximum value for the whole number (e.g. for youth club membership – ages between 13 and 18). Can set a specific number against which arithmetical operators can be applied (e.g. greater than 19, less than 65).
Decimal	Sets a decimal value to be tested (fixed price, prices between...)
List	Provides an in cell drop down list of external data (like the list of cities) or typed into the properties box (red, blue, green, orange).
Date	Allows the designer to set start and end dates, applying the arithmetical operators in the decision making (before, after, between, not between).
Time	Allows the designer to set start and end times, applying the arithmetical operators in the decision making (before, after, between, not between).
Text length	Sets the number of characters that can be entered within the cell.

> **KEY POINT**
>
> For each of these types of validation, the designer can set up a message to inform the user about the parameters for data entry, and can also provide an error message should the user make a mistake.

Examples might include validating the:
- minimum and maximum length of a password
- list of cities that can be visited
- membership number of six digits only
- the length of a tweet.

Workbooks

AQA **INFO 1, INFO 4**
OCR **G061, G063**
WJEC **IT1**
CCEA **AS 1, AS 2**

Workbooks contain a number of different **worksheets**. In many spreadsheet programs the user is presented with a workbook automatically, even though they may very well only use one worksheet within the workbook.

Workbooks are useful in that they allow different aspects of data to be stored on different worksheets. You have seen some examples of how this works in the combo box description.

We can look in more detail at another example, based on a personal income and expenditure model.

Note how the workbook includes a worksheet for each month of the year, and an 'Annual Summary' front sheet.

| 28 |
| 29 |

|◄ ◄ ► ►|\ **Annual Summary** ⟨ January ⟨ February ⟨ March ⟨ April ⟨ May ⟨ June ⟨ July ⟨ August ⟨ September ⟨ October ⟨ Noveml |◄

	A	B	C	D
1		Income	Expenditure	To Savings
2	January			
3	February			
4	March			
5	April			
6	May			
7	June			
8	July			
9	August			
10	September			
11	October			
12	November			
13	December			
14				
15	**Savings Pot**	£		-
16				
17	**Target**	£		5,000.00
18				
19	**How far to go?**	-£		5,000.00
20				

The 'Annual Summary' front sheet is set up so that the final outcomes from each month are recorded, and a summary of how much the user is saving towards their target of £5000 is presented.

January income will be extracted from the January worksheet: ='January'!$F$1 and expenditure also from: ='January'!$B$33

3D referencing

The summary sheet can be simplified by using **3D references**. A 3D reference allows us to reference several worksheets that have the same structure. For this example, each month follows the same pattern and the cells on each worksheet contain the same type of data.

F1		▼	*fx*	3000		
	A	B	C	D	E	F
1		Expenditure	Balance		Income	3000
2	01/01/2010	5	2995		To Savings	401
3	02/01/2010	1200	1795			
4	03/01/2010	200	1595			
5	04/01/2010	10	1585			
6	05/01/2010	5	1580			
7	06/01/2010	9	1571			
8	07/01/2010	100	1471			
9	08/01/2010	60	1411			
10	09/01/2010	35	1376			
11	10/01/2010	75	1301			
12	11/01/2010	10	1291			
13	12/01/2010	10	1281			
14	13/01/2010	10	1271			
15	14/01/2010	10	1261			
16	15/01/2010	35	1226			
17	16/01/2010	100	1126			
18	17/01/2010	100	1026			
19	18/01/2010	50	976			
20	19/01/2010	10	966			
21	20/01/2010	10	956			
22	21/01/2010	75	881			
23	22/01/2010	100	781			
24	23/01/2010	100	681			
25	24/01/2010	30	651			
26	25/01/2010	25	626			
27	26/01/2010	25	601			
28	27/01/2010	25	576			
29	28/01/2010	10	566			
30	29/01/2010	50	516			
31	30/01/2010	45	471			
32	31/01/2010	70	401			
33	Total	2599				

|◄ ◄ ► ►|\ Summary \ **January** ⟨ February /

So each sheet is made up of monthly income (in F1), a record of daily expenditure in column B, and a balance to be carried over into savings in F2.

A 3D reference will allow us to calculate the savings value quickly and efficiently:

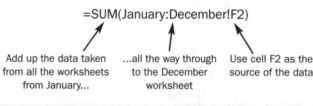

	A	B	C	D	E	F
1						
2			Savings Pot	£		4,237.00
3						
4			Target	£		5,000.00
5						
6			How far to go?	-£		763.00
7						

D2 — fx =SUM(January:December!F2)

The formula for calculating the annual savings relies on the fact that the amount of savings is in the same place on each worksheet:

$$=SUM(January:December!F2)$$

Add up the data taken from all the worksheets from January...

...all the way through to the December worksheet

Use cell F2 as the source of the data

Database functions

AQA   **INFO 1, INFO 4**
OCR   **G061, G063**
WJEC **IT1**
CCEA **AS 1, AS 2**

In order to use spreadsheet functions as a database the fields and records of a table need to be structured so that:

- data fields are set up in adjacent columns
- records are held in each row of the table
- column labels are defined in the first row of the table.

Because spreadsheet software organises data in rows and columns we can apply a number of database functions in very much the same way that we work with **flat file database** tables (see pages 126–127).

The stationery file we looked at earlier is laid out with column/category headings and can be reviewed in the same way as a database.

We can of course add further items to the data file by simply typing in additional data at the bottom of the data table.

Data forms

Data forms help to structure the data entry. Here the user has highlighted the original data table (A1:C6) and has begun to add data using a data form.

	A	B	C	D	E	F	G	H
1	Stock number	Item	Price					
2	A4P1	A4 Paper	£1.25	Sheet1				✕
3	A5N1	A5 Notepad	£0.40	Stock number:	A4P2			New Record
4	HBP1	HB Pencils	£0.99	Item:	A4 Paper Yellow			New
5	GLP1	Black gel pens	£1.30					
6	GLP2	Red gel pens	£1.30	Price:	1.45			Delete
7	A3P1	A3 Paper	£2.25					
8								Restore
9								
10								Find Prev
11								
12								Find Next
13								Criteria
14								
15								Close
16								
17								
18								

Note here how we focus on the benefits for the user of data validation.

A3 paper has already been added to row 7 and A4 Yellow paper is ready to be added to row 8. It is easier to add new records using a form as it means that the user cannot make the mistake of entering data into the wrong row or column.

With a data table in place the data form can be used to search for items within the data set. Here the user is looking for 'paper' and wants to find the items in stock that meet those criteria.

By typing in * Paper the data form will display the record for A4P1, A4P2 and A3P1 by clicking on the Find Next button.

	A	B	C	D	E	F	G	H
1	Stock number	Item	Price					
2	A4P1	A4 Paper	£1.25					
3	A5N1	A5 Notepad	£0.40					
4	HBP1	HB Pencils	£0.99					
5	GLP1	Black gel pens	£1.30					
6	GLP2	Red gel pens	£1.30					
7	A3P1	A3 Paper	£2.25					
8	A4P2	A4 Paper Yellow	£1.45					

Sheet1

Stock number: [ ]
Item: [* Paper]
Price: [ ]

Criteria
New
Clear
Restore
Find Prev
Find Next
Form
Close

Data queries

As data files get larger it becomes more difficult to maintain an overview of all that data. Searching for records in large data files would take a very long time if we just used the data form. Most spreadsheet applications allow users to simulate a **database query** by specifying the criteria by which we want to look at the data we have (see pages 136–138). Using the column headings we can use an **AutoFilter** function that use aspects of the data to allow users to select from a drop-down list.

In this example there are 150 records of sales areas and their attached sales representatives. AutoFilter allows the user to filter on all fields, some of which will return only one record (for a council), and others that will return a number of records (for a sales representative).

	Reference Number	Council Name	Sales Region	Sales Representative
1				
2	301	Barking and Dagenham	Lon1	Sort Ascending
3	302	Barnet	Lon1	Sort Descending
4	370	Barnsley	Y&H	(All)
5	800	Bath and North East Somerset	SW	(Top 10...)
6	820	Bedfordshire	East	(Custom...)
7	303	Bexley	Lon2	Angela Andrews / Brian Bartok
8	330	Birmingham	EWM	Carl Carruthers
9	889	Blackburn with Darwen	NW	Danutza Danilov
10	890	Blackpool	NW	Eric Enderby / Fatima Faruk
11	350	Bolton	NW	George Grundy
12	837	Bournemouth	SW	Henrietta Harvey
13	867	Bracknell Forest	SE	Junior Jones / Henrietta Harvey
14	380	Bradford	Y&H	Brian Bartok
15	304	Brent	Lon1	Angela Andrews
16	846	Brighton and Hove	SE	Henrietta Harvey
17	801	Bristol City of	SW	Carl Carruthers

Note that the AutoFilter allows users to sort the data. This could be important if the database needs to be sorted by reference number, rather than by council name.

It is also possible to sort data using the Sort function available within the spreadsheet program.

Here a choice is made to sort by reference number, and then by council name. This produces a data file that begins at 202 and goes through to 938, with council names in ascending alphabetical order. Note how the alphabetical order begins again when we get to the 300s. It will change again at 400, then again at 500 and so on until we reach the 900s.

	A Reference Number	B Council Name	C Sales Region	D Sales Representative
2	202	Camden	Lon1	Angela Andrews
3	203	Greenwich	Lon2	Eric Enderby
4	204	Hackney	Lon1	Angela Andrews
5	205	Hammersmith and Fulham	Lon2	Eric Enderby
6	206	Islington	Lon1	Angela Andrews
7	207	Kensington and Chelsea	Lon1	Angela Andrews
8	208	Lambeth	Lon2	Eric Enderby
9	209	Lewisham	Lon2	Eric Enderby
10	210	Southwark	Lon2	Eric Enderby
11	211	Tower Hamlets	Lon1	Angela Andrews
12	212	Wandsworth	Lon2	Eric Enderby
13	213	Westminster	Lon1	Angela Andrews
14	301	Barking and Dagenham	Lon1	Angela Andrews
15	302	Barnet	Lon1	Angela Andrews
16	303	Bexley	Lon2	Eric Enderby
17	304	Brent	Lon1	Angela Andrews
18	305	Bromley	Lon2	Eric Enderby
19	306	Croydon	Lon2	Eric Enderby

Data lists can be searched using the **LOOKUP** and **reference functions**. According to the arrangement of the data you can use three different lookup functions:

LOOKUP function	Description
VLOOKUP	Searches the first column of a data array and returns the value of the row in which the search criteria was found.
HLOOKUP	Searches the first row of a data array and returns the value of the column in which the search criteria was found.
LOOKUP	Searches the values of an array.

Lists that are arranged as a database table can be searched using the VLOOKUP function. As we have discussed before the data must have a numerical key that is sorted in ascending order. In order to search the sales representative data we can enter the reference number and be presented with the name of the council, the sales region and the name of the sales representative.

Enter reference number:	304

Council	Brent
Region	Lon1
Sales Representative	Angela Andrews

The formulae for accessing the data are:

Council:	=VLOOKUP($E$7,'LA List'!$A$2:$D$150,2)
Region:	=VLOOKUP($E$7,'LA List'!$A$2:$D$150,3)
Sales Representative:	=VLOOKUP($E$7,'LA List'!$A$2:$D$150,4)

Searching can also be done using keyboard commands, or using menu commands such as Find, or Find and Replace.

Macros

AQA	**INFO 1, INFO 4**
OCR	**G061, G063**
WJEC	**IT1**
CCEA	**AS 1, AS 2**

Macros can be used to increase the efficiency of all spreadsheet files. A macro is a set of instructions that is used to automate a task or procedure. They enable designers to set up validated, secure and efficient routines that a user would have to repeat a number of times: this helps the user to save time.

Straightforward macros are recorded using **Visual Basic** (VB). It is not necessary to know how to code in VB, and you do not need to know how to use the VB Editor to create and run successful macros. If your spreadsheet program has one, a **macro recorder** translates your actions into code that can then be applied many times.

Once you have created a macro you can modify it or delete it. This is very important: because the macro recorder records each action and mouse click that you make you should always plan out your macro in advance.

> **KEY POINT**
>
> Plan what you want to do, test it out to see if it works and then write down each movement – one step at a time – so that you can repeat the process accurately when it comes to recording the macro. It will save time and frustration!

Formatting and display options

AQA	**INFO 1, INFO 4**
OCR	**G061, G063**
WJEC	**IT1**
CCEA	**AS 1, AS 2**

A designer of a spreadsheet model has to take the needs of the audience into consideration when planning a data model that has to be used by others. You will need to consider issues like:

- the font you use
- font size and colour
- use of colour to highlight
- white space
- page layout
- print layout
- what you want the user to see and change
- the use of form controls and protection.

Fonts

As with word processing the choice of font can have an impact on the user. For some worksheets, especially those that the user may not see, the choice and size of font may well be irrelevant. The presentation of data in a data entry form is quite another matter. Let's remind ourselves about an example that we have seen before in this chapter.

Here the designer has increased the size of the font to ensure that the summary is immediately clear. The message conveyed by the red font is also clear: there is some way to go before the target of £5000 is reached.

D2		f_x =SUM(January:DecemberlF2)			
	A	B	C	D	E	F
1						
2			Savings Pot	£		4,237.00
3						
4			Target	£		5,000.00
5						
6			How far to go?	-£		763.00
7						
8						

There are other considerations about fonts. Very often you will see spreadsheets filled with colour – but with no consideration about the font colour. This is important as it impacts negatively on:

- readability
- the need to hide background data you do not really need users to see.

With each of the following colour choices it can, for some users, be difficult to read the text:

Red	Blue	Orange	Green

As a general rule of thumb with dark colours use a light coloured font; with light or pastel colours use a darker font. Always think about colour contrast. Remember though: pink and yellow together is not a good look!

The following colours work much better: you can see what is in each of the cells more clearly.

Red	Blue	Orange	Green

In the employee attendance tracker on the next page you can see how the designer has planned for the use of colour to highlight key features of the data sheet. In this instance there was a discussion about colours that the user could recognise as being distinct and different. The turquoise blocks show where the employee is having their two days off (DO), green indicates holidays (H) and blue indicates where the employee has been absent (AB). A data form collects this data, with additional data requested to provide additional detail for the absence.

Behind each block of colour is either some text (providing data about the employee) or numerical (providing data about absences) data. The conditional formatting has ensured that the font is the same colour as the fill colour: the user just needs to see the colour block and the numerical data in the summary. The red for sickness may well be a flag that there needs to be a review of the employee's sickness record.

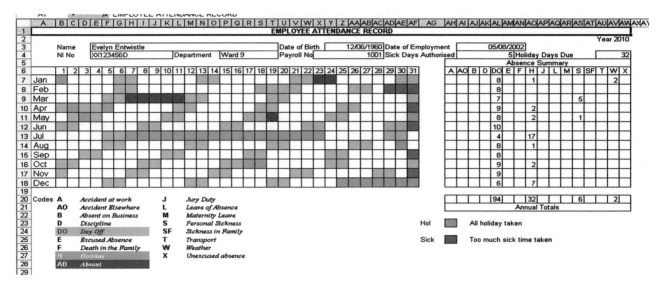

Page and print layouts

Note how the gridlines have been removed to ensure that the white space is used to frame the separate blocks of data within the spreadsheet.

When planning a spreadsheet model it is important to consider how the spreadsheet will look on the screen and when it is printed out.

For screen layout the designer needs to consider whether or not the data sheet fits easily onto the screen. It is best to consider a user interface that fits onto one screen without the need for scrolling across or down. This can be challenging with large data files but we need to ask: what does the user need to see?

It may be that in general the user only needs to see the outcomes of a search, or to input a small sub-set of data. This means that the screen they see can be specifically designed to meet their needs.

Print layout needs careful consideration. We do sometimes need to have a printout of a complete data set. Questions to ask here are:
- Should it be printed landscape or portrait?
- Will it be readable if it is printed out on one sheet of paper?
- Will the column headers be carried over to the next page if it goes onto a further printed page?
- Will the definition be clear if the worksheet is printed out in black and white?

PROGRESS CHECK

1. Why is it important that data in a spreadsheet model is presented clearly?
2. What is a macro and why is it used?

1. Any suitable answers, e.g. Clearly presented data is easy to see and helps the user to make judgments. Spreadsheet models are about testing hypotheses. Display and formatting functions can be used to facilitate analysis.
2. A macro is a set of instructions that is used to automate a task or procedure. It is used to save the user time.

5.3 Applications of spreadsheet modelling

LEARNING SUMMARY	After studying this section you should be able to:
	• recognise and describe how spreadsheet models can be applied to meet the needs of a variety of audiences
	• identify and explain the advantages and disadvantages of spreadsheet modelling

Spreadsheet applications

AQA **INFO 1, INFO 4**
OCR **G061, G063**
WJEC **IT1**
CCEA **AS 1, AS 2**

We have already seen that spreadsheets can be used for a variety of modelling purposes. Successful applications do pay careful attention to the user interface: but a bright and shiny façade is useless if there is no real data processing going on in the background. Spreadsheet models should ensure that data follows the input–process–output principles.

Input	Process	Output
Should be something that is input regularly (daily, weekly or monthly) so that the processing appears meaningful.	The processes could include: adding-up; summarising; PivotTable; filtered; GoalSeek; averaged; looked-up; indexed, etc.	Outputs could include: a report; a tailored printout; a series of charts.

Budgeting applications

Spreadsheet models are often used to develop business plans, or to identify how much to charge for tickets to the school disco. Budgeting models can be as simple or as complex as you like. If we followed a business plan through from start to completion the application would need to include at least four inter-related outputs:

- The opening balance sheet to show the assets and liabilities available to a business at its beginning.
- A profit and loss account to show the relationship between income and expenditure.
- A cash flow statement that shows how much hard cash is available to the business at any one time.
- A final balance sheet that presents a picture of assets and liabilities at the end of a period of trading.

Examples are always useful – they show that you know how your knowledge can be applied.

Spreadsheets are useful tools in preparing budgets as they enable designers to plan for links between worksheets, as data outputs from one sheet provide essential data for another.

Expense claim forms

Business employees who travel for their work often have to claim expenses, and apply certain parameters to their claims (amount per mile based on the type of fuel used and the size of the engine). They may also be able to claim for hotel stays, meals and other items such as postage and public transport. Organisations may want to maintain central records based on all individual claims so that they can calculate the impact of all employee claims.

Invoicing and sales

Small businesses often use spreadsheets to manage their invoicing and sales, enabling them to print out invoices and receipts, and to develop a database from which detailed summaries can be produced.

Student attendance and assessment monitoring

We have already seen details of a small student assessment tracking system. These can be developed so that projections of potential grades (based on completed assessments) can be made, and built around the parameters defined by the awarding body. Attendance data can also be kept – presenting a picture of achievement and attendance, and generating letters to students and their parents through mail-merging.

The benefits of spreadsheet modelling

AQA	**INFO 1, INFO 4**
OCR	**G061, G063**
WJEC	**IT1**
CCEA	**AS 1, AS 2**

Being able to develop a spreadsheet model to test scenarios is useful for all kinds of business, scientific, engineering, and personal financial problems.

Advantages

A key advantage of spreadsheets is that they are so common when dealing with financial and statistical data. This means that there is a shared understanding about the type of issues that can be managed using spreadsheets and that others may have developed solutions that can be refined and developed further; this takes away some of the development time. Spreadsheets calculate much more quickly than can be achieved in manual data processing, and they can also present data very dynamically. The production of charts, tables and reports can be done efficiently to aid decision-making, and to test out a range of 'what-if' scenarios. There is plenty of capacity to develop historical data that can be used to produce longitudinal data (i.e. data that has been collected over a period of time). For example, student assessment data where data about performance in core subjects has been collected from Year 7 to Year 11.

Disadvantages

Many of the disadvantages related to the use of spreadsheets are those that we would face generally in our use of computers. We can always be worried about the security of data, viruses and hacking but there are systems and procedures that can be put in place to ensure that work is as safe as it can be. The designers of spreadsheet models, just as they would in systems and software development, have to be mindful of the needs of the user. Some users may find it very difficult to adapt to working with a spreadsheet: this may lead to errors in data entry or to increased frustration as the data error trapping and data validation require alternative inputs. It goes without saying that the development of complex spreadsheet models requires both designers and users to have a secure understanding of how the model works, and how to develop it further. This involves being able to unpick the meaning and structure of complex formulae: for some people this can be very challenging.

> **PROGRESS CHECK**
>
> **1** What types of problems are spreadsheet models useful for?
>
> 1. Any suitable answer, e.g. Spreadsheets can be used for a variety of data models. They are best applied when numerical data needs to be processed and analysed. Budgets, expense claims, sales and invoicing applications and attendance models are all useful applications of spreadsheet data models.

Sample questions and model answers

1. Spreadsheet packages can be used to solve many different problems.

   Describe a problem that you have solved using a spreadsheet and explain how the functionality of the spreadsheet helped you to solve that problem. **(6)**

This is a good start: the description is clear, and it is a real problem that is suitable for the development of a spreadsheet solution.

I live in the country and have milk delivered every other day. Our milkman has over 600 customers and was recording all deliveries and payments by hand, and was relying on customers being at home to present them with their bill. He has a computer and was thinking about developing a sales and invoicing system. I offered to do it for him.

This answer is detailed: it refers to functions and processing tools as well as describing advantages and considerations for the user.

In developing the solution I set up one worksheet as a database of all the customers - giving each customer a unique customer number so that I could develop a quick search and invoicing facility using VLOOKUP. This data was used in other worksheets - such as the sales and delivery sheet, and as a basis for mail-merging to produce the personalised invoices. It was important that as a new user I allowed the milkman to be able to input sales using a form control. Each delivery is input for each customer, as is each payment. This adds detail to each customer's record and allows me to calculate the bills by adding up the numbers of bottles of milk and multiplying by the cost per bottle, which is stored as a named cell to ensure that it works right across the workbook.

2. A school uses ICT software to monitor student attendance.

   Describe two activities for which the spreadsheet component would be the most suitable. **(4)**

The answer responds to the issue of attendance and highlights key issues – numerical and graphical.

Spreadsheets can be used to perform calculations such as total/average/best attendances. A more sophisticated use could be that of using conditions or look up tables so that students with poor attendance could be highlighted. Spreadsheets can also be used to produce charts or graphs that show summaries or trends in attendance.

3. Explain why conditional formatting would enable a school attendance officer to review student data quickly. **(2)**

An explanation is given and expanded on to gain full marks.

If a trigger level of student attendance was set (e.g. at 95%), below which a student was deemed to be absent too much, a condition which coloured the cell red would enable the attendance officer to see quickly all the students that were absent too often.

Practice examination questions

1 Describe the purpose or function of two different formulae that you have used in a spreadsheet. **(4)**

_____

_____

_____

_____

_____

2 Describe one method of how you have simplified data entry in a spreadsheet stating the advantages of using such techniques for entering data. **(4)**

_____

_____

_____

_____

_____

3 Describe two methods of data validation and error trapping you have used in a spreadsheet. **(4)**

_____

_____

_____

_____

_____

4 Describe the purpose or function of two other different processes you have used in a spreadsheet. **(4)**

_____

_____

_____

_____

_____

6 Database systems

The following topics are covered in this chapter:

- **Understanding and using databases**
- **Database design**
- **Interrogating and managing databases**
- **The use of distributed databases**
- **The safety and security of systems and data**

6.1 Understanding and using databases

LEARNING SUMMARY

After studying this section you should be able to:

- identify the key components of a database
- describe the relationship between different components of a database
- explain how primary and foreign keys can be used to create relationships between different tables

The components of a database

AQA **INFO 1**
OCR **G061**
WJEC **IT1, IT3**
CCEA **AS 1, A2 1**

> **KEY POINT**
>
> A **database** is an organised collection of data (information) that can be used for one or more purposes.

Although paper-based databases are still in regular use (e.g. the card index systems), most databases are created electronically by using either proprietary or customised software. Before looking at how databases are designed and how they work, it is important to become familiar with the components of a database and the key terms that are used when referring to them.

Tables

Databases display stored **data files** in a tabular format, with the **records** arranged in rows and the **fields** arranged as columns. The amount of data stored in any single table is dependent upon the type of data being stored and can vary considerably (from just a few records in a small database to many millions of records in a large company database).

Records

Records are made up of a series of fields, each of which contains a single item of data. A complete set of records is referred to as a **file** (in programming language, records are also referred to as **tuples**). For example, a personnel file is likely to contain information about a company's employees, and include fields containing information such as first name, last name, gender, date of birth, employee number, National Insurance number, etc.

Fields

Each record is made up of lots of individual items of information, and a field is a space in the record that has been allocated for the collection of one of those individual items (e.g. a person's date of birth). When data is first gathered it is important to ensure that it is collected in a way that will allow similar items of information to be processed and interrogated in a consistent manner. Consequently, if a database is to store people's names, fields need to be allocated to the recording of this information. Keeping individual items in separate fields allows for much more effective interrogation and reporting to take place. All fields are allocated a **field name** (which is used to identify the type of data it contains), and **attributes** (which indicate the type of data they will contain).

In some cases, rather than an operator entering data into a field, the data is generated as the result of a function or calculation involving other fields. This type of field is called a **calculated field**.

For more information on attributes see pages 125–126.

Key fields

AQA **INFO 1**
OCR **G061**
WJEC **IT1, IT3**
CCEA **AS 1, A2 1**

Key fields contain information that is unique to a particular record. They enable individual records to be identified through the use of **primary keys** and enable the establishment of relationships between records in different tables through the use of **foreign keys**.

Primary keys

A primary key (sometimes referred to as a **unique key**) is a unique label (usually in the form of a number or code) that is used to identify a specific record as being different from all other records (even if they contain similar information). Each database table can only have one primary key. For example, a database might contain information about people, several of whom have the same name (e.g. Brian Jones). However, because the primary key for each person is unique, the database can clearly identify the records for each Brian Jones as being distinctly different from each of the others. Fields containing primary keys are often appended with the label 'ID' in order to indicate that the content for each record is unique (e.g. ProductID, CustomerID, LocationID).

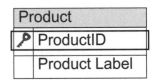

Once a field has been formatted as a primary key it may not be left empty, and the database will only accept new records if a new unique identifier has been entered. Primary key fields can be set to accept user generated identifiers, or can be set to generate them automatically.

A primary key that is set on a single field is referred to as a **simple primary key**. However, it is possible for the primary key to be made up of data from more than one field (providing this combination results in a unique identifier). In cases where this occurs, it is known as a **composite primary key** (also known as a **compound primary key**).

Foreign keys

A foreign key is a label that is used to identify a key field in another table (usually the primary key). Consequently, the use of a foreign key establishes a relationship between records in two or more different tables (i.e. it provides a cross-reference between the two tables). Unlike the primary key, tables will accept records even if the foreign key field is left empty. Also, unlike the primary key, the contents of a foreign key field do not have to be unique. This is because some information (e.g. client details) may be used on a number of occasions.

For example, the image below shows the relationship between two tables from the database of a freight haulage company. The first table shows client details (with ClientID set as the primary key), and the second table shows work undertaken (with OrderID set as the primary key). In the second table the field ClientID is a foreign key. In this case clients (in the form of the ClientID) can appear more than once because the haulage company carries out regular work for them.

ClientID	Client Name	Contact Name	Contact Phone
DG0027	D C Graham & Co	Mrs S Patel	0192664936
DP0025	Devonshire Pies	Mr N Bardy	0178203980
KH0023	K Hardman Ltd	Mr K Hardman	0192664092
ML0026	Martins Ltd	Mrs L Carter	0178277315

OrderID	ClientID	Pick Up Date	Destination
GH017	KH0023	05/03/2011	Norwich
GH018	DG0027	06/03/2011	Manchester
GH019	VS0024	06/03/2011	Dorchester
GH020	DP0025	06/03/2011	Manchester
GH021	KH0023	07/03/2011	Coventry
GH022	ML0026	07/03/2011	Wolverhampton

Secondary keys

Secondary keys are used to identify fields that need to be included in an **index** (see below). There is no limit to the number of secondary keys that can be set.

Data

AQA **INFO 1**
OCR **G061**
WJEC **IT1, IT3**
CCEA **AS 1, A2 1**

Indexes

In the same way that an index in a text book helps you to find pages containing the information that you are looking for, an index helps a database to find and sort records faster. By using secondary keys it is possible to identify chosen fields so that, rather than scanning through all records one by one until a required item of information is found, the database can go directly to the required location. This means it works much faster than if an index were not used.

Duplicate data

For more information on flat file databases see pages 126–127.

Data that appears more than once in a table is referred to as **duplicate data**. In a **flat file database** (i.e. a single table database) it is quite likely that the duplication of data will occur (e.g. in the table below, multiple jobs are carried out

For more information on normalisation see pages 132–135.

for a single client). Clearly it makes sense to avoid duplicating data because it requires more storage space, takes longer to search and increases the chance of errors occurring. Duplication can be significantly reduced by good database design (e.g. by creating relationships so that data that is likely to be duplicated is drawn together from separate tables, and by effective use of **normalisation**).

JobID	ClientID	Client Name	Contact Name	Job Date
10021	JC003	JD Clothing Ltd	Mrs J Devish	07/02/2011
10022	HH026	Harman Hair Salon	Mrs M Pike	08/02/2011
10023	PC008	Plumbing Centre	Mr K Jones	09/02/2011
10024	JC003	JD Clothing Ltd	Mrs J Devish	10/02/2011
10025	KK011	Kwik-Korner-Mart	Mrs V McDonald	11/02/2011

Referential integrity

For more information on relational databases see pages 127–128.

When working with **relational databases** (i.e. multiple tables), adding, changing or deleting an item of data in one table may well have a significant impact on the data in other tables. **Referential integrity** uses the relationships that have been created through the use of primary and foreign keys to **cascade** any changes (e.g. automatically change the data in Table A to match the data being entered in Table B). It ensures that no **orphan** records are created (i.e. records of data that no longer have connections to other data) and prevents accidental deletion of data that is related to data in another table.

Data independence

All data contained within a database structure is completely independent from the program that processes that data. This means that changes can be made to the content and format of data without the need to make changes to the computer program that processes it (because this is managed automatically by the database management system).

Entities

Databases are made up of one or more related tables, each of which contains information about a separate group of things/objects/people. Each of these groups is referred to as an **entity**. For example, amongst other things, a hospital needs to manage information about doctors, nursing staff, ancillary staff, patients, appointments and bed allocation. Whilst all of these are related in some way (e.g. the patients are seen by a particular doctor), because each of them requires different types of information to be stored, they can clearly be identified as being separate entities.

> **KEY POINT**
>
> In a database, each entity is represented by a separate table.

Attributes

When used in the context of a database the term **attribute** refers to a property or characteristic of an entity. For example, in a database of second-hand cars, examples of attributes associated with the Client field would include: Registration number, Make, Model, Engine size, Colour and Date of registration.

Attributes can also have properties assigned to them. For example, the attributes applied to second-hand cars could include:

- Registration number (alphanumeric – the car's unique identifier)
- Make (text)
- Model (foreign field with an integer identifier – this draws information from a separate table that includes specific details about models)
- Engine size (integer)
- Colour (text)
- Date of registration (date)

Relationships

A **relationship** is a link between different entities. For example, there is a direct link between a doctor and his/her patients. Therefore a hospital database might include tables containing details of each of the following entities: doctors, patients and appointments. You will find out more about relationships in the next topic.

PROGRESS CHECK

1. Describe the purpose of a foreign key.
2. What is the main benefit of adding an index to a database?
3. Why is it a good idea to avoid the use of duplicate data when designing a database?

3 Duplicate data requires more storage space, takes longer to search and increases the chance of errors occurring.
2 An index helps the database to find and sort records faster.
1 A foreign key is used to establish a relationship between records in two or more different tables.

6.2 Database design

LEARNING SUMMARY

After studying this section you should be able to:

- describe the difference between flat file and relational databases
- identify and establish relationships
- explain the purpose of normalisation
- describe the purpose of a data dictionary

The characteristics of an effective database

AQA **INFO 1**
OCR **G061**
WJEC **IT1, IT3**
CCEA **AS 1, A2 1**

Flat file databases

In a flat file database all of the data is stored in a single table. Flat file databases work perfectly adequately and for people creating databases for the first time it is a straightforward approach to take.

However, once you start to look at the type of data that is to be stored, the shortcomings of this type of database structure soon become apparent.

For example, the flat file structure shown here has been designed for use by a vehicle repair and servicing workshop. It contains information about the customer, the vehicle and the servicing. Whilst this initially seems fairly logical, it soon becomes clear that all of the data needs to be entered every time a service takes place. So even though a customer's name, address and phone number has already been entered into the database, it needs to be entered again every time their vehicle is serviced. Not only does this take extra time (in both entering and interrogating the data), it leaves open the possibility that some data could be entered differently on subsequent occasions and

Field Name	Data Type
🔑 CustomerID	AutoNumber
FirstName	Text
LastName	Text
Address1	Text
Address2	Text
Postcode	Text
PhoneNum	Text
RegistrationNum	Text
Make	Text
Model	Text
Engine Size	Number
Milage	Number
ServiceDate	Date/Time
ServicePrice	Currency

lead to inaccurate results from searches (e.g. if a customer's name is entered as Smith at the second service, when it should be Smyth, a search would show that they have only had one service and not two). Because customers often return to the same company for their repairs and servicing year after year, a flat file database would generate a considerable amount of duplicate data. In order to develop a more effective database, it makes sense to divide the data into separate entities and identify the relationships between those entities.

Relational databases

A relational database uses data that is stored in separate, but related, files (tables). Whilst creating a relational database is a more complex process than creating a flat file database, the advantages of doing so soon become apparent. For example, the tables shown here contain similar information to that contained in the flat file database illustrated above. However, in this case the data has been separated into three different entities (as illustrated by the three tables). The first table only contains the information about the vehicles themselves. The second table contains details about the servicing and the third table contains details about the customer.

Vehicle Table
Registration_Number
Make
Model
Diesel/Petrol
Engine_Size
Mileage_At_Last_Service

Service Table
Service_ID
Customer_ID
Registration_Number
Date_Of_Service
Time_Of_Service

Customer Table
Customer_ID
Title
First_Name
Last_Name
Address_1
Address_2
Postcode
Phone_Number

The two key relationships identified in this example are those between the service table and the customer table (with the relationship identified as the Customer ID), and between the service table and the vehicle table (with the relationship identified as the vehicle's Registration Number).

The first time a customer books a service all three tables will need to be completed. However, for each additional service only the service table will need to be completed, because it will automatically draw down all of the details about the customer and the vehicle from the other two tables. This results in a high level of **data consistency** because all of the attributes for each entity are stored in a single file (table). Less data needs to be entered each time a service is booked and data doesn't need to be duplicated. This eliminates **redundant data** and avoids errors occurring.

This also results in a high level of **data integrity** because information can be updated and edited by making changes to just one table. For example, by changing someone's details in the customer table, all references to that person in other tables will automatically reflect the changes. Likewise, because well-designed relational databases include such a high degree of referential integrity, data in any of the individual tables can be modified independently without affecting the data in the other tables. For example, if a customer changes their address it does not affect the information held about their vehicle.

An item of software that can handle relational databases is known as a **relational database management system** (or **RDBMS**). As the full set of data is only assembled at the point of retrieval (i.e. when a query or report is generated), relational databases are also classified as **dynamic** database management systems.

Hierarchical databases

Hierarchical databases are relational databases that organise data into a tree-like structure. The structure uses a 'parent/child relationship' where each parent can have many children but each child only has one parent, as described further in the following section on entity relationship modelling.

Selecting appropriate data types

You will find more information on data types in Chapter 1 (including the advantages and disadvantages of each data type).

Once the contents of an entity has been identified (e.g. the fields and field names), it is important to identify what type of data each of the fields will contain and to consider which is the most appropriate data type for that data. When working with databases the main data types are:

- Boolean – used for logical values (e.g. yes/no).
- Date/Time – used for storing various formats of dates and time as a single calculable number.
- Integer – used for whole numbers (i.e. those that do not include decimal points or fractions).
- Real – used for numbers that include decimal points and fractions.
- Text/String – used for text, a combination of text and numbers (alphanumeric) or numbers.

It is important to remember that when working with databases, the software often presents the user with options which may, at first, not seem to be exactly what is required. Information about gender is a typical example of how a clear understanding of data types can result in the design of a much more effective database table. Although we normally think of Boolean data as representing yes/no, it is actually a logical data type that can have one of two values. Therefore, if the result required needs to be displayed as either 'male' or 'female', it can also be regarded as a logical Boolean field.

Although the default data type in the example shown here appears only as Yes/No, by making changes to the Field Properties (shown below the main table structure) a much greater degree of control can be achieved.

> The way in which data types and attributes are formatted differs according to the brand and version of software that you are using.

By selecting 'Text Box' in the **Lookup tab**, the **Format** in the **General tab** can be manually changed to display the required customised text (in this case 'Male' or 'Female').

In a similar way, the data type 'Number' is used for both integer and real data, and the more detailed level of control (e.g. setting the data as integer) is managed through the General tab in the Field Properties.

Field Name	Data Type
Contact_ID	AutoNumber
First_Name	Text
Last_Name	Text
Gender	Yes/No
Phone_Number	Text
Appointment_Number	Number
Appointment_Time	Date/Time
Fee	Currency

Field Properties — General | Lookup
Format: "Male";"Female"
Caption:
Default Value: 0

Quality of data

As described in Chapter 1, the quality and usefulness of information generated from a database is dependent upon the quality of the data that the database contains. It is important to remember that if a database contains information that is faulty, incomplete or nonsensical, any output from that database will be completely worthless. Remember the phrase 'garbage in, garbage out' (**GIGO**), and try to ensure that the data you use is of the highest quality. Factors such as the age, completeness, level of detail, presentation and relevance of data will all affect the quality of the outcome of any interrogations (e.g. searches and queries).

Entity relationship modelling

AQA **INFO 1**
OCR **G061**
WJEC **IT3**
CCEA **A2 1**

As we have already established, the design of a relational database is based upon identifying relationships between different entities. Although there may be multiple relationships between all the tables in a database, it is important to start by establishing individual relationships between pairs of tables. When doing this, there are three types of relationships to consider: **one-to-one**, **one-to-many** and **many-to-many**.

Perhaps the easiest way to think about this is to think about members of a family (e.g. the relationships within a family of two parents and three children). The mother has a one-to-one relationship with the father, and he has a one-to-one relationship with her (i.e. the wife only has one husband and the husband only has one wife). However, the mother has three children so she has a one-to-many relationship with them (as does the father). The children have several cousins so, as a group, the children have a many-to-many relationship with their cousins. It is these types of relationships that need to be identified and applied to the entities (tables) within a relational database, by creating an **entity relationship model** (an **ERM**).

> For more information about entity relationships and how they are applied see pages 93–94.

In order to help people understand how a particular ERM will work, database designers present their clients with an **entity relationship diagram** (an **ERD**), which is a graphical representation of the relationships involved. In an ERD, the entities are shown as shapes and the relationships are shown as lines that connect the shapes.

One-to-one relationships

One-to-one relationships occur when only one record in the first entity (table) is related to just one record in another entity. Examples of one-to-one relationships include:

- Husband to wife: A husband only has one wife, and the wife has only one husband.
- Employee to National Insurance (NI) number: Each person is allocated a unique NI number, which they keep throughout their life no matter which company they work for. This means that a NI number can only apply to one person.
- Book to ISBN: When published, each book is allocated a unique International Standard Book Number. So an ISBN applies to only one book.

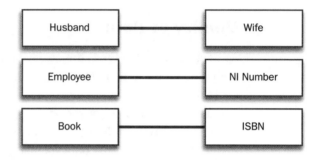

One-to-many relationships

One-to-many relationships are the most common type of relationships used within relational databases. They occur when a record in one entity is related to a number of records in another entity. Examples of one-to-many relationships include:

- Publisher to publications: A single publisher produces many publications, but each publication is produced by only one publisher.
- Pilot to aircraft: A pilot is able to fly many different aircraft, but each aircraft can only be flown by one pilot at a time.
- Mother to children: A mother can have a number of children, but each child only has one mother.

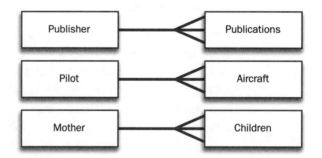

Many-to-many

Many-to-many relationships occur when more than one record in the first entity is related to more than one record in another entity. Examples of many-to-many relationships include:

- Students to teachers: Each individual student is likely to be taught by many teachers. Likewise, each individual teacher will be involved in teaching many students.
- Buses to drivers: At a bus company it is likely that each individual bus will be driven by a number of different drivers, and that each individual driver will drive a number of different buses.

- Hotels to tourists: In a typical holiday resort there will be many hotels offering rooms to tourists, and there will be many tourists looking for hotels.

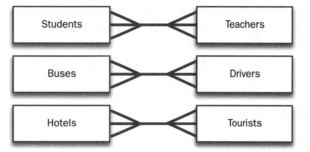

Whilst most database software can cope with many-to-many relationships they are extremely complex so, where possible, it makes sense to look at the data in a different way. For example, whilst an entity as a whole may have a many-to-many relationship with another entity, the individual records within that entity can be designed to have a one-to-many relationship. Therefore, rather than thinking of a group of students and a group of teachers, a table containing details of students could contain records where the primary key establishes a one-to-many relationship with a foreign key in a table containing details of teachers.

Identifying and establishing relationships

A significant part of designing a relational database is identifying the various entities into which the data can be divided and planning how the data will be broken down and allocated to each of those entities. This involves thinking about the entities, the attributes and the entity relationships. However, by the time a database designer reaches the stage of establishing these relationships, they are usually fairly familiar with the type of data that needs to be stored and interrogated. Indeed, the more familiar a designer is with the data, the easier it is to establish clear relationships between the various tables that will be used to store the data for each entity.

The database being designed will rely on being able to match values in both of the tables involved in a relationship. Although relationships do not have to include a primary key, because it is the unique identifier within a table it is common practice to define relationships as being between primary and foreign keys (remembering that a foreign key is, in effect, a primary key field that has been added to a related table). When producing diagrams to illustrate relationships, a primary key is usually used to represent the 'one' side of a relationship and a foreign key is usually used to represent the 'many' side of a relationship.

> It is important to remember that it is much easier to sort out problems on paper at the modelling stage than it is to do so once construction of a database is underway.

Time invested at the planning stage, by creating an effective entity relationship model and illustrating the relationships between entities in a graphical format as entity relationship diagrams, will pay significant dividends once formal construction of the database begins. In summary, when designing a database for any given scenario it is important to do the following:

- Identify the entities that contribute to the scenario, and use a separate table to represent each of these entities.
- Within each table, identify the attributes (fields), a suitable primary key and appropriate foreign keys.
- Having established the contents of each table, identify the relationships as being either one-to-one, one-to-many or many-to-many. And, for those relationships identified as many-to-many, try to restructure them as one-to-many

Normalisation

AQA **INFO 1**
OCR **G061**
WJEC **IT3**
CCEA **A2 1**

> **KEY POINT**
>
> Normalisation is a systematic approach to ensure that a database structure is fit for purpose and free of any undesirable characteristics and anomalies.

For the purpose of AS/A2 GCE ICT syllabuses it is only necessary to focus on the first three normalised forms.

Normalisation is carried out by applying sets of rules, which are known as **Normal Forms** (usually numbered from 1 to 5 as 1NF, 2NF, etc. with data that is in an un-normalised form being listed as UNF or 0NF).

Normalisation also involves taking the data through a process of **atomisation**, which means reaching a stage where the data is in a form that it cannot be broken down any further. For example, a field called 'Address' could contain the data '38 Ash Green Road London EC3 9GW', but in this format it would require quite complex queries to display sub-sets of the address (e.g. similar postcodes). Consequently, it makes sense to break the address down further into its **atomic form**. However, it is important to remember that **atomic data** does not have to be in the form of single words. For example, 'Ash Green Road' does not need to be broken down into three separate fields, because it is an entity in its own right.

In order to illustrate the atomisation of data and the application of successive levels of normalisation, we will take a close look at an extract from a database being designed to keep records for group classes at a health club.

Client ID	First Name	Last Name	Class ID	Class Name	Class Time	Trainer ID	Trainer Name
4278	John	Thompson	PIL	Pilates	Mon 2 PM	JGA	John Gardner
			KBX	Kickboxing	Fri 10 AM	JGA	John Gardner
4295	Wendy	Wolfe	AQU	Aqua Aerobics	Tue 10 AM	SHA	Sarah Harper
			STP	Step Class	Tue 2 PM	SHO	Sally Hood
			JAD	Jazz Dance	Wed 10 AM	SHA	Sarah Harper
4296	Ann	Hall	STP	Step Class	Tue 2 PM	SHO	Sally Hood
			JAD	Jazz Dance	Wed 10 AM	SHA	Sarah Harper
			KBX	Kickboxing	Fri 10 AM	JGA	John Gardner

Un-normalised form

Tables that contain one or more repeating groups of data are said to be in an **un-normalised form** (**UNF** or **0NF**). In its un-normalised form, details of the classes are repeated for each client.

First normal form

The primary rule for the first normal form (1NF) is that there should be **no repeating attributes** or groups of attributes. In this example, to avoid the repetitive entry of details for each class the client attends, data is split into two separate entities; the first contains details of the clients and the second contains details of the classes.

Client

Client ID	First Name	Last Name	Class ID
4278	John	Thompson	PIL
4278	John	Thompson	KBX
4295	Wendy	Wolfe	AQU
4295	Wendy	Wolfe	STP
4295	Wendy	Wolfe	JAD
4296	Ann	Hall	STP
4296	Ann	Hall	JAD
4296	Ann	Hall	KBX

Class

Class ID	Class Name	Class Time	Trainer ID	Trainer Name
PIL	Pilates	Mon 2 PM	JGA	John Gardner
AQU	Aqua Aerobics	Tue 10 AM	SHA	Sarah Harper
STP	Step Class	Tue 2 PM	SHO	Sally Hood
JAD	Jazz Dance	Wed 10 AM	SHA	Sarah Harper
KBX	Kickboxing	Fri 10 AM	JGA	John Gardner

Although the data is now in the first normal form, there is still a degree of **data redundancy** as the clients' names are still being repeated unnecessarily.

Second normal form

The primary rule for the second normal form (2NF) is that there should be **no partial key dependencies, and the data should already be in 1NF**. In this case the First Name and Last Name fields are fully dependent on the Client ID because each client has a unique ID (so if a second person called Wendy Wolfe joined the club they would be identified as being a different person by having a different Client ID). However, the First Name and Last Name fields are not uniquely dependent on the Class ID because each class can be attended by a number of different clients. Therefore there is **partial dependency** on the client table shown in the 1NF example.

Class

Class ID	Class Name	Class Time	Trainer ID	Trainer Name
PIL	Pilates	Mon 2 PM	JGA	John Gardner
AQU	Aqua Aerobics	Tue 10 AM	SHA	Sarah Harper
STP	Step Class	Tue 2 PM	SHO	Sally Hood
JAD	Jazz Dance	Wed 10 AM	SHA	Sarah Harper
KBX	Kickboxing	Fri 10 AM	JGA	John Gardner

Sign-ups

Client ID	Class ID
4278	PIL
4278	KBX
4295	AQU
4295	STP
4295	JAD
4296	STP
4296	JAD
4296	KBX

Client

Client ID	First Name	Last Name
4278	John	Thompson
4295	Wendy	Wolfe
4296	Ann	Hall

The 1NF illustration shows a many-to-many relationship. However, as previously explained, it is best to avoid this type of relationship when creating relational databases. In order to do this, a third entity (the sign-ups table) can be created, to link the clients with the classes.

Third normal form

The primary rule for the third normal form (3NF) is that there should be **no non-key dependencies, and the data should already be in 2NF.**

In the 2NF example of the class table, the Trainer Name is fully dependent on the Trainer ID, but not on the Class ID (because the health centre could decide to allocate a different trainer to the class). Therefore, the trainer's name could easily be removed from the class table and placed into a fourth table containing specific details of trainers (which has also atomised the data further by breaking the name down into First Name and Last Name. The data is now in the third normal form.

Sign-ups

Client ID	Class ID
4278	PIL
4278	KBX
4295	AQU
4295	STP
4295	JAD
4296	STP
4296	JAD
4296	KBX

Class

Class ID	Class Name	Class Time	Trainer ID
PIL	Pilates	Mon 2 PM	JGA
AQU	Aqua Aerobics	Tue 10 AM	SHA
STP	Step Class	Tue 2 PM	SHO
JAD	Jazz Dance	Wed 10 AM	SHA
KBX	Kickboxing	Fri 10 AM	JGA

Client

Client ID	First Name	Last Name
4278	John	Thompson
4295	Wendy	Wolfe
4296	Ann	Hall

Trainer

Trainer ID	First Name	Last Name
JGA	John	Gardner
SHA	Sarah	Harper
SHO	Sally	Hood

The advantages and disadvantages of normalisation

Advantages of normalisation	Disadvantages of normalisation
Data is stored efficiently because atomisation not only reduces the quantity of data stored, it also makes it possible to combine the data in many different ways.	It takes longer to design and create a normalised database than an un-normalised database.
The structure of a normalised database is incredibly flexible, so changes can be made with minimum disruption and without the need to carry out a major redesign of the structure.	Normalised databases generally include many more tables than un-normalised databases.
The database is easy to maintain because each item of data is stored only once, so when a single item is updated it is automatically reflected across the whole database.	The more tables that there are, the more relationships that need to be identified.
The elimination of duplicate and redundant data reduces the quantity of data that needs to be stored and results in far greater levels of referential and data integrity.	The more tables included in a database, the longer it takes to run a query.

Data dictionaries

AQA **INFO 1**
OCR **G061**
WJEC **IT3**
CCEA **A2 1**

A **data dictionary** is a file that contains a description of all the data items contained in a database. The data dictionary does not contain any of the database's actual data; it is simply a catalogue of information about the data (e.g. it is 'data about data', otherwise known as **Metadata**), which enables the data to be accessed by the database management system. Most database management systems keep the data dictionary hidden from view, in order to prevent users from accidentally changing its contents (which would have a catastrophic effect on the database).

The data dictionary contains information about the data such as: table names, field names, field lengths, data types, default values, validation rules, primary and foreign keys, relationships, indices and access rights. It also contains more general information about the database (e.g. who is permitted to access the database, what parts of the data each user is allowed to see, what parts of the data each user is allowed to edit).

PROGRESS CHECK

1. Describe the difference between a flat file database and a relational database.
2. Identify the relationship between the following:
   (a) landlord and tenant
   (b) Prime Minister and country.
3. What is the rule for data in the second normal form?

3. The data should already be in 1NF, and there should be no partial key dependencies.
2. (a) one-to-many – a landlord may have many tenants, but a tenant is likely to have only one landlord (b) one-to-one – each country only has one Prime Minister, and a person can only be Prime Minister of one country.
1. A flat file database contains all the data in a single table, while a relational database groups data into distinct entities (each of which is represented by a separate table) and uses relationships to draw together relevant data from each of the tables.

135

6.3 Interrogating and managing databases

LEARNING SUMMARY	After studying this section you should be able to:
	• describe how to create a dynamic parameter query
	• explain how to ensure that reports are fit for purpose
	• identify the key aspects of managing database systems

Queries

AQA **INFO 1**
OCR **G061**
WJEC **IT3**
CCEA **AS 1, A2 1**

The main function of a database is to store and organise data in a way that it can be used to generate information as a result of systematic interrogation. The interrogation of a database is carried out through the construction of **queries**. Whilst it can take a little while to plan a query, once created they can generate results (in some cases thousands of records) in just a few seconds.

> When naming queries, it is important to use names that clearly describe the content of the query. In this way you will easily be able to identify the query you want to use from the list that is presented to you.

When designing a query, the software will present an interface that allows you to give the query a name and to select the fields required. However, unless you include **parameters** in the query (**search criteria**), when the query is run it will generate a table showing the chosen fields for every record. A parameter is a value that is used by a query to select records. The introduction of parameters automatically reduces the number of records that will be displayed. For example, if searching for daily sales figures, introducing a range of dates as a parameter within the 'Date' field would ensure that the query displays only those records that fall within the specified range.

Parameters commonly used within search criteria		
Parameter	**Symbol**	**Use**
Equal	=	Shows an exact match
Less than	<	Shows all values less than the one given
Less than or equal to	<=	Shows the value given and all values less than the one given
Greater than	>	Shows all values greater than the one given
Greater than or equal to	>=	Shows the value given and all values greater than the one given
Between	> AND <	Shows all values within the given range not including the two values given
Between	BETWEEN	Shows all values within the given range inclusive of the two values given
Not	<>	Shows all values other than the value given
Or	OR	Shows either value

In addition to the more commonly used parameters, **wildcards** can be used to add even greater flexibility to searches. A question mark is used as a wild card symbol for a single digit and an asterisk is used as a wild card symbol for a string of digits. Wildcards can be used either individually or in combinations. For example: G* searches for any string that starts with a 'G' (e.g. all people whose last name begins with the letter 'G' – Gilbert, Green, Grey, etc); *ENT searches for any string that ends with 'ENT' (e.g. event, recent, commitment, etc), and BL??D* searches for all strings that start with 'BL' and that have 'D' as their fifth letter (e.g. blond, blending, blandest, blundered, etc).

Simple queries

Simple queries are queries that include just **one parameter**. The search shown here is designed to identify heavy packages. As only three fields need to be shown, only the required 'Show' boxes have been ticked. This will result in displaying all records showing the contents of the 'ContractID', 'Weight_Kg' and 'NextDay' fields for all packages that weigh 10 kg or over.

Field:	ContractID	Name	Weight_Kg	NextDay
Table:	Customer	Customer	Customer	Customer
Sort:				
Show:	☑	☐	☑	☑
Criteria:			>=10	

Complex queries

Complex queries are queries that include **two or more parameters**. The search shown here is designed to identify heavy packages that have been sent by two particular customers (Smith and Jones). This will result in displaying only the records showing the contents of the 'Name' and 'Weight_Kg' fields for all packages weighing 10 kg or over that were sent by either of the two customers.

Field:	ContractID	Name	Weight_Kg	NextDay
Table:	Customer	Customer	Customer	Customer
Sort:				
Show:	☐	☑	☑	☐
Criteria:		"Smith"	>=10	
or		"Jones"	>=10	

Static and dynamic parameter queries

The two examples shown above are typical examples of **static parameter queries**. The parameters (the search criteria) have been entered into the query design table in a fixed format (e.g. each time the query is run it will show the results for Smith and Jones). However, it is likely that the company will regularly want to run similar queries (e.g. to identify all the heavy parcels sent by a particular customer).

Rather than creating a different query for each customer, it is much more efficient to design a single **dynamic parameter query** where the name of the customer could be changed each time it is run. By entering a message instead of 'fixed' criteria the user will be presented with a request to enter the required data each

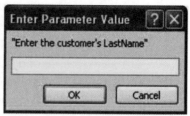

time the query is run (e.g. 'Enter the customer's LastName'). In this case, it means that just one query has been designed to perform the task, but the query can be used to find the same type of information for all customers.

Data mining and data warehousing

AQA **INFO 1**
WJEC **IT3**
CCEA **AS 1**

Data mining is the process of searching through data in order to identify hidden patterns. Rather than use standard query techniques, sophisticated search capabilities and statistical algorithms are used in order to identify new links and patterns in large data sets.

This can result in:
- finding out things that were not previously known
- looking for patterns to establish how one event (or set of actions) is associated with another
- discovering patterns that can be of help in predicting future behaviour.

Data mining techniques are regularly used by commercial organisations to extract useful information from websites about customer behaviour and shopping patterns.

Data warehousing is the process by which data is extracted from a range of different databases and reassembled into a new structure in order to facilitate effective interrogation. The result of this process is known as a **data warehouse**.

Consequently, a data warehouse facilitates analysis of data on a much larger scale than that undertaken by an individual database (e.g. to present a coherent picture of international trading conditions for a particular product at a given point in time).

During the process of data warehousing the data gathered from each of the source databases is 'cleaned' (superfluous data is removed), 'transformed' (reorganised into a common structure), and then 'catalogued' (indexed). The resulting data warehouse is then able to be used for data mining, analytical processing, business intelligence, market research, and to aid decision-making processes.

Reports

AQA **INFO 1**
OCR **G061**
WJEC **IT3**
CCEA **AS 1, A2 1**

Another key function of a database is to present information in a way that can be clearly understood by those viewing it. Databases do this by generating **reports**, which can be customised to meet the needs of users. Although reports can be presented on screen, they are generally produced in hardcopy format (i.e. printouts).

Reports can present information taken directly from entity tables or, more commonly, present a summary of information generated as the result of the query. In either case, the control over what appears on the report lies in the hands of the designer. In some cases the whole contents of the query might need to appear, whilst in other cases only selected information might need to be shown. Similarly, in some cases two or more different reports might need to be generated from the same query in order to meet the needs of individual users (e.g. the two reports shown here are generated from the same query, but the second report has been designed in a way to make it clearer for the van driver).

Packages to Derby and Manchester

Pick Up Point	Dep Date	Destination	Contract ID	Packages
Derby				
	22/07/2010	Manchester	76311	2
	07/10/2010	Manchester	76344	5

Delivery Schedule

Destination	Dep Date	Pick Up Point	Packages	Description
Derby				
	18/04/2010	Leeds	1	Bicycle
	07/10/2010	Manchester	1	Bricks

There are many different types of reports, but operational and summary reports are frequently required within most organisations:

- **Operational reports** provide users with a snapshot of the current situation.
- **Summary reports** usually present common information for a defined period (e.g. freight movements during the past month).

It is important that reports meet the needs of the people who will read them, i.e. that they are **fit for purpose**. The designer needs to make sure that they are accurate, clear, complete, relevant, and that they are presented in a logical format that will be meaningful to the user/audience.

Database Management Systems (DBMS)

AQA **INFO 1**
WJEC **IT3**
CCEA **A2 1**

A **database management system** (**DBMS**) is software that uses a systematic approach to cataloguing, interrogating and retrieving information. It manages incoming data, organises it, and provides an interface that enables the data to be modified and interrogated by both human users and by other software (e.g. a management information system).

Data frequently needs to be passed between different organisations, and because there are so many different proprietary database management systems available (e.g. Access® , dBase® , Oracle®), it is important that the DBMSs can communicate with each other. Consequently, most DBMSs include an **Open Database Connectivity** (**ODBC**) driver which is independent of the actual database system. The ODBC can be used to interrogate data from a database, regardless of brand or platform, by acting in the same way as a language interpreter (e.g. someone who translates French into English), and presenting the data in a format that the application being used can understand.

Every DBMS includes four main components:

- A **modelling language** that defines the structure of each of the databases managed by the DBMS (e.g. relational, hierarchical, object and network models).
- A **data structure** (e.g. tables, fields, records) that facilitates the management of large amounts of data.

- A **database query language** and report writer that allows the interrogation of data generation of output depending upon the level of access permitted to individual users.
- A **transaction mechanism** that maintains the integrity of the data in the database.

A DBMS provides users with user-friendly interfaces through which they can:

- enter new data
- update existing data
- interrogate the data (e.g. carry out a query)
- generate a hard copy of the outcome of a query in a format that can be easily interpreted.

Database administration

AQA **INFO 1**
OCR **G061**
WJEC **IT1, IT3**
CCEA **A2 1**

After a database has been designed, tested and put into operation, it will require regular maintenance in order to ensure that it runs effectively and that users are able to access up-to-date information.

In most cases a **database administrator** would be appointed. In the case of larger organisations this is likely to be a full-time role, whilst in smaller organisations this work would be taken on as a sub-set of a wider role (e.g. network manager) or contracted out to a third-party (e.g. managed remotely by an independent commercial organisation).

As part of their role, a database administrator would:

- ensure that the database is always available
- update and maintain the system
- implement and manage a disaster recovery scheme (e.g. make backups and archive data)
- monitor usage of the database
- train operators to use the system effectively
- manage potential threats to the integrity of the data.

PROGRESS CHECK

 Explain the purpose of a dynamic parameter query.

2 List at least four examples of parameters that can be used to search data.

3 Describe three roles carried out by a database administrator.

1 A dynamic parameter query allows an operator to enter a variable (e.g. a client's name) and then run a pre-prepared query (e.g. to display the client's account details). It saves the operator having to design a new query every time they want to carry out the same type of search.

2 Amongst the most common parameters used are 'equal to', 'less than', 'greater than', 'less than or equal to', 'greater than or equal to', 'not equal to', 'between' and 'or'.

3 Any three from: updating and maintaining the system, implementing and managing a disaster recovery scheme, monitoring usage and managing potential threats to the integrity of the data, training operators to use the system effectively.

6.4 The use of distributed databases

LEARNING SUMMARY	**After studying this section you should be able to:**
	● describe the three ways in which distributed database systems can be organised
	● describe the role of an expert system
	● explain how management information systems can be used to aid business practice.

Distributed database systems

AQA **INFO 1**
OCR **G063**
WJEC **IT1, IT3**
CCEA **A2 1**

Distributed databases are controlled by a central database management system (DBMS) but their storage devices are not all attached to the same computer. This means that data can be stored on a number of different computers, either located at the same location or dispersed over a number of different locations. Although the data is stored on multiple hard drives, the DBMS regularly synchronises the data held in the various locations and ensures that the data links together seamlessly, so that users get the impression that they are working with one single database.

Distributed database systems can be located on network servers, intranets and extranets, or they can even be located on the Internet. By distributing and replicating databases across a number of locations, organisations can ensure that end-users (e.g. their employees) benefit from the improved performance of the database.

There are three ways in which distributed database systems can be organised:
● A central database with local indexes
● A duplicated database
● A partitioned database

Central databases with local indexes

A **central database** is a database where all of the data is held in a single location. Even though it may be accessed by users working in a number of locations, a stand-alone central database cannot be referred to as a distributed database because it is simply a central database with **remote access**.

However, in order to increase the speed at which data on a central database can be searched and retrieved, **local indexes** can be created for each of the locations across the network. For example, a bank might store all its data on a single central database (located at its head office), and create a local index of accounts for each of its other locations (e.g. an index of account holders at the bank's branch in Stratford-upon-Avon). Each local index is stored on a local server (hence the label for this type of distributed database as being a central database with local indexes), and is used to identify the location of the required records on the centrally held database. This greatly accelerates the process of accessing information about account holders from the central database. Because the bulk of the data is stored in a central location, any updates (either by staff at the head office or by staff in the **remote locations**) are immediate and are therefore available to all users as soon as the new/updated data is entered.

Duplicated databases

A **duplicated database** (also referred to as a **replicated database**) is a database where all of the data from a central database is copied to each location. Although this requires more storage space in each of the locations, it does mean that data retrieval is much quicker because there is no delay in transferring data to and from a central server. However, data that is updated locally will not be available to users working at other locations until it has been uploaded to the central database, synchronised with updated data from all other locations and then redistributed across the whole network.

Partitioned databases

A **partitioned database** is a database where no individual computer stores all of the data, but instead, different parts of the data are stored on computers/servers located in different places (sites).

Partitioned databases organise data in either **horizontal** or **vertical** partitions.

Horizontal partitioning involves separating data according to individual records. For example, in the case of an airline, all information about individual flights could be stored at the airport from where the flight starts (e.g. information about flights starting the journey from Birmingham International would be stored on the Birmingham server, whilst information about flights starting from London Heathrow would be stored on the London server). Consequently, as can be seen from the illustration, because the same type of data is held in each location the database structure at each of those locations would look the same.

Flights (Birmingham Int)	**Flights** (London Heathrow)	**Flights** (Manchester Int)
Flight Number	Flight Number	Flight Number
Destination	Destination	Destination
Departure Date	Departure Date	Departure Date
Departure Time	Departure Time	Departure Time

Vertical partitioning involves separating data based upon individual fields. For example, a retail company might decide to hold all of the information about products in one location, all information about prices in another location and all information about suppliers in yet another location. In this case, as can be seen from the illustration, because a different type of data is held in each location the database structure at each of those locations looks quite different.

Products (Branch A)	**Prices** (Branch B)	**Suppliers** (Branch C)
Product ID	Product ID	Product ID
Description	Cost Price	Supplier ID
Classification	Retail Price	Supplier Name
Supplier ID	VAT Code	Address

Although different parts of the data are stored in different locations, users have access to the whole database and not just those parts stored in their own location. This means that data that is updated locally will be instantly available to users working at other locations.

Advantages and disadvantages of distributed database systems

	Central databases with local indexes	Duplicated databases	Partitioned databases
Data storage requirements	In addition to the space required on the central server, only needs enough storage space on local servers for the local index.	The same amount of storage space is required in each location because a complete copy of the data is stored on each site.	A smaller amount of storage space is required in each location because the data is 'shared' across a number of local servers.
Speed of data access	This option results in the slowest access to data, because all data needs to travel to and from the central location.	This option offers the fastest access to data, because a copy of the whole database is stored locally.	Because some data is accessed locally and some from other locations, access speeds within this option are generally inconsistent.
Quantity of network traffic	Because all data needs to travel to and from the central location, this option results in the highest level of network traffic.	Data only needs to travel across the network when the system is being updated/backed up.	Although not all of the data needs to travel to and from other locations, this option still results in a fairly high level of network traffic.
Level of data integrity	It is easier to maintain referential integrity when only working with one centralised set of data.	Referential integrity is more difficult to maintain when synchronising data from multiple locations.	Most key integrity issues are likely to be addressed within the locally stored partition(s).
Level of security	Because only one set of data is maintained centrally, security can be carefully controlled. However, multiple access points can make the system vulnerable.	Because multiple sets of data are held in multiple locations (with multiple access points), the system is vulnerable to being compromised.	Because only relevant data is stored locally, opportunities for the system to be compromised are reduced.
Backing up requirements	Regular backup is essential because all locations rely on the integrity of the one central system.	This option results in a high level of integrity because multiple copies of the backed up database are available in the event of a systems crash in one or more locations.	Because data is not replicated on more than one site, regular backup is essential in order to avoid complete loss of one or more partitions.

Distributed databases in action – the National Health Service

Each of us depends upon the quality and efficiency of the National Health Service to ensure that we (and our friends and families) can lead fit and healthy lifestyles. Whilst we spend most of our lives within a short distance of our own homes, we also travel to different parts of the country to visit friends and relatives, to carry out work, and to enjoy holidays and leisure pursuits. Consequently, it is essential that the information/data collected about each of us is held safely and made available to health professionals no matter where we might be in the country when that information is needed.

The National Health Service is responsible for the well-being of nearly 60 million people, so imagine the size and power required to design a database that could cope with that much information. Therefore, it can be of no surprise that, rather than use one single database, the National Health Service relies on the use of a range of interrelated distributed databases to gather, store and distribute information to health professionals both in this country and (when appropriate) in other countries throughout the world.

Within the National Health Service, amongst many other things, distributed databases are used to handle:
- electronic patient record keeping – combining and distributing data collected by local GPs, hospitals, dentists, etc.
- tracking test samples and results – blood tests, cholesterol tests, electrocardiogram (ECG) results, cervical smears, toxicology, etc.
- storage and distribution of image scanning – x-rays, computerised axial tomography (CAT) scans, magnetic resonance imaging (MRI) scans, etc.
- tracking the storage, distribution and use of medicines.

> There are other examples of distributed databases – examiners like to see current examples – keeping an eye on the press can be very important.

Expert systems

AQA	**INFO 1**
OCR	**G063**
WJEC	**IT1, IT3**
CCEA	**A2 1**

An **expert system** (often also referred to as a **knowledge-based system**) is a database that is used to aid the process of decision-making and recommend particular courses of action. In order to do this it contains knowledge and rules that have been agreed by human experts and which, in effect, enable the system to process information in a similar way to how human experts would (e.g. apply logic and sets of rules to the input data), and thus present results in a way that helps the user to solve a problem, make a decision or make a recommendation.

It is quite likely that you have already used an expert system in order to aid your own decision-making processes. For example, one type of expert system commonly used by young people is Kudos, the software used to help them identify the type of careers for which they are best suited. By gathering information about an individual's strengths, weaknesses and preferences the software can suggest a range of career pathways that might be of interest.

Banks use expert systems to help identify the most appropriate financial planning options for individuals. For example, if a client wants to put money aside for their future, the bank's expert system gathers information about their income and expenditure, explores their attitudes to financial risk, looks at their previous spending and saving patterns and then presents a series of options best suited to the needs of the client. It is at this point that the bank's financial adviser (the user) helps the client to use the information in order to make a suitable decision.

Not only is the information presented in a visual format on screen, the system also generates a printed report, which explains its recommendations in a format that the client can clearly understand (e.g. 'Although you have not invested regularly in the past you can see the benefit of this in the long term. You would like to make a regular commitment to grow your savings by investing on a monthly basis').

Another commonly used expert system is NHS Direct. This is an extremely sophisticated web-based expert system that enables users to enter details of their symptoms, explains why questions are being asked (e.g. 'This question is looking for common symptoms of meningitis or other serious conditions'), and concludes with making a recommendation (e.g. 'See your GP today') and giving further advice about how to deal with the situation that has been diagnosed.

An expert system consists of a **knowledge base** (i.e. knowledge gathered from human experts) and an **inference engine** (i.e. software that can apply the rules held in the knowledge base to make decisions as a result of the data entered by a user). Well-designed expert systems include features that:
- provide the user with an interface that enables them to enter data about the problem (e.g. respond to questions) in a clear and structured way
- provide the user with options to respond to questions in an appropriate way when they are unclear about their response (e.g. 'I'm not sure' or 'I don't know')
- provide the user with ongoing feedback (such as the example above, for NHS Direct)
- provide the user with advice/recommendations on either a specific course of action or a range of options to be considered
- provide the user with an explanation of why it has made those recommendations.

Advantages of expert systems	Limitations of expert systems
<ul><li>They can perform tasks much quicker than humans.</li><li>If well-designed, they are very accurate.</li><li>They use time in a more cost-effective way than highly paid human experts.</li><li>They combine knowledge from lots of experts (remember the old saying 'two heads are better than one').</li><li>Their recommendations are always impartial.</li><li>They can be used to aid decision-making when human experts are not available.</li></ul>	<ul><li>They can make mistakes (e.g. misdiagnose a problem) but do not learn from them.</li><li>The system's conclusions/recommendations still need to be interpreted by a user who can decide whether or not they make sense.</li><li>Users still need to consider special circumstances, which the system may not have been programmed to cope with.</li><li>Although the system will present reasons for its conclusions, the user cannot enter into dialogue with it (e.g. to ask further questions about the conclusions).</li><li>They work well when a problem can be clearly defined, but are less effective when it is more difficult to identify the symptoms of the problem.</li></ul>

Management information systems

AQA **INFO 1**
OCR **G063**
WJEC **IT1, IT3**
CCEA **A2 1**

In commercial and business settings, databases are used in a wide variety of ways that help organisations run effectively. However, on their own, databases cannot provide those organisations with the full range of information they require in order to be successful. Consequently, databases are frequently used as part of a more integrated approach to the management of organisations.

Management information systems (**MIS**) are designed to provide managers with all the information they need in order to run their organisations effectively. They are sometimes also referred to as **management information services**. MIS generally include software that helps in decision-making, data storage and interrogation (e.g. databases), personnel management and project management applications, and any other computerised procedures that help individuals to manage their organisations efficiently.

> Schools and colleges use management information systems – you could find some useful examples here.

Key functions of an effective MIS include maintaining, processing and distributing information about:
- personnel – staff records, qualifications, training undertaken, training needs, hours worked, salary/pay records, bank details, etc.
- finance – income, expenditure, sales, purchases, loans, debts, interest paid, staff pay/salaries, etc.
- stock control – goods in, goods out, location of goods, transfer of goods from one site to another, reordering levels, etc.

An MIS collects, stores, processes and disseminates information in a format suited to the specific needs of particular members of an organisation, in order to help them with decision-making, planning, control and monitoring at all three management levels:
- **operational** – decision-making on a day-to-day basis (e.g. automatically ordering items when stock levels are low)
- **tactical** – responding to market forces and the actions of competitors (e.g. increasing production in response to a high level of demand for a particular product)
- **strategic** – medium and long-term planning (e.g. investing in expensive automated equipment in order to reduce future overheads).

This can be illustrated by looking at the example of a car manufacturer. A line manager (working in an operational role) might need a daily report on the status of all the vehicles made, or still under construction, on their line. In contrast, the production manager (working in a tactical role) might want weekly construction reports in order to be able to move staff around to increase output levels on a particular line. Meanwhile, the sales manager (strategic) might want to analyse vehicle sales over the past few years in order to predict how many need to be made during the next few months.

MIS are frequently used to generate lists of all the items that fail to conform to a particular norm. These are known as **Exception Reports**. Examples include: employees with less than a 90% annual attendance rate, sales staff who fail to achieve their monthly targets, products with over a 5% return rate, etc.

Alongside their MIS, many organisations also use **decision support systems** (**DSS**). These are expert systems that are designed to support organisations with the process of making decisions. They allow managers to compile information from a range of sources (e.g. databases, knowledge bases, documents and market intelligence) and use the information to help solve problems and make decisions (e.g. comparing sales figures between one month and the next, projecting income based on predicted sales figures). DSS can include any application that processes data, and can be broken down into a number of broad categories, each of which aid decision-making. These include:

- communications driven DSS (e.g. email, web, video-conferencing)
- data driven DSS (e.g. databases, data warehouses)
- model driven DSS (e.g. spreadsheet models, forecasting).

PROGRESS CHECK

1. Describe a duplicated database.
2. List two ways in which a database can be partitioned.
3. What is an expert system?

1. A duplicated database is one where all the data from a central database is copied to each of the distributed locations.
2. A database can be partitioned using either horizontal or vertical partitioning.
3. An expert system is a database that is used to aid the process of decision-making and recommend particular courses of action.

6.5 The safety and security of systems and data

LEARNING SUMMARY	After studying this section you should be able to:
	• identify typical examples of internal and external threats to ICT systems and data
	• explain how viruses and malware can affect systems and data
	• describe key strategies for protecting data

Security

AQA   **INFO 1, INFO 2**
OCR   **G063**
WJEC **IT1, IT3**
CCEA **AS 1, A2 1**

KEY POINT

Having invested considerable resources in designing and populating databases, expert systems and management information systems, it is important to ensure that the data is kept safe in terms of access controls, and of both accidental and deliberate damage.

The more access points there are to any system, the more vulnerable that system is to unauthorised access. In the case of distributed databases, not only can problems arise as a result of the numerous access points (i.e. computer terminals within each of its various locations), there is also the potential for problems to arise as a result of data being regularly transmitted across the network.

Physical **unauthorised access to data** is normally managed through the allocation of passwords and access controls, which limit the amount of access an individual has based upon the needs of their role (e.g. read-only status, low-level read/write status, high-level read/write status). In some cases, access is also limited to specific workstations or sites (e.g. an individual's password will only work if it is entered into their normal workstation or will only work in a particular building).

High levels of data transmitted via telecommunications systems (i.e. network traffic) results in data being vulnerable to **interception** by unauthorised individuals (at which point it can be interfered with for the purpose of mischief or commercial gain). In order to make systems more secure, data is generally encrypted while it is in transit from one location to another, thus making it more difficult for unauthorised users to benefit from their intrusions.

ICT systems are vulnerable to threats from both **internal** and **external** sources:

Internal threats	External threats
• Loss of data/software as a result of staff misplacing/losing laptops • Staff misplacing/losing data (e.g. CDs, USB data sticks) • Deliberate damage/interference caused by disgruntled staff • Damage caused by inappropriate use of internal messaging and email • Failure of backup systems • Staff inadvertently opening fake antivirus scams • Theft of trade secrets • Financial fraud	• Phishing resulting from spoof and junk email • Viruses attached to incoming files • Intrusion and damage caused by hackers • Data gathered illegally by spyware • Interception of data whilst in transit • Malicious and unwanted emails (spam) • Theft

A number of different measures can be used to help protect ICT systems against both internal and external threats.

In terms of **hardware measures**, the first step is to ensure that the hardware is situated in a location where it is physically secure (e.g. in rooms or buildings that are locked when out of office hours or when no operators are present). Security can also be enhanced through the use of employee IDs and by issuing visitor passes. Individual computer terminals can be made more secure by the use of key locks, swipe cards and (a more recent development) biometric data such as fingerprint swipes and retina recognition.

In terms of **software measures**, it is important to use authorisation software which requires passwords to be used in order to access programs and which permits access level controls. Access rights (managed through allocation of passwords) can be used to define which aspects of the database can be accessed by individual users. For example, a low level user might not have the authority to change any of the data but they would be able to interrogate the data and create reports, whilst a medium level user might also be able to amend certain aspects of the data. Communication software can be used to ensure that an encryption key needs to be used in order for the receiver to be able to read/use any data that has been requested or transmitted across a network.

Security can be further enhanced by establishing appropriate **organisational procedures** such as virus checking all incoming and newly created documents and regularly backing up individual user documents and accounts in addition to the main system backups.

Over 80% of computer crime is committed by employees who plant viruses, and damage or interfere with data. Therefore, it is important for staff to be screened during the recruitment, induction and training process and for staff transactions to be regularly monitored. One way of reducing damage caused by staff is to ensure that key transactions are only activated once they have been approved by a second member of staff (i.e. sharing the responsibility for important actions). It is also important to ensure that members of staff are fully aware of the **legal implications** of misuse and interference with data.

Viruses and malware

AQA **INFO 1, INFO 2**
OCR **G061**
WJEC **IT1, IT3**
CCEA **AS 1, A2 1**

The term **computer virus** is one that is often used to cover a wide range of mischievous items designed to interfere with computers and their security. **Malware** is the term commonly given to malicious software that is designed to access a system without the operator/owner's knowledge or consent. **Viruses** are small items of malicious software that reproduce themselves within a system. You should be familiar with the following types of viruses and malware:

Type of malware/virus	Description
Adware	Small programs that automatically download and/or display adverts on a computer. Whilst a lot of adware is legitimate (i.e. the user has given consent for it to run), many adware packages appear without consent, and are thus considered to be malware.
File infectors	Viruses that infect executable files (e.g. EXE or COM files) and that are activated when the files are run.
Key loggers	Track a user's actions and are often used for legitimate purposes (e.g. in tests and in monitoring procedures). However, they are increasingly being used for malicious purposes (e.g. to discover logon procedures and passwords).
Logic bombs	Sit in the memory and only activate themselves (i.e. destroy data) when certain situations arise. Although they are not technically viruses (because they do not replicate), they tend to be grouped alongside viruses.
Macro viruses	Can be attached to macro-enabled documents in such a way as to be activated every time the document is opened. Macro viruses are one of the key reasons why it is important to be cautious when opening unsolicited attachments to emails.
Resident viruses	Permanently locate themselves in the RAM from where they can interfere with core operations as they are carried out by the system (e.g. corrupting files and programs as they are opened, closed, copied, renamed or moved).
Overwrite viruses	Delete some of the information contained in files, thus making them virtually useless.
Spyware	Collects information about users without their knowledge or permission, and transmits that data to third parties for illegitimate purposes.
Trojans	Usually infect a system by tricking the user into loading the file by appearing to do something good (e.g. 'click here for a free copy of...'), but actually then do damage.
Worms	Small programs that have the ability to self-replicate.

Use of passwords, firewalls, Internet security software and virus protection software can help protect against malicious damage of data resulting from hacking and malware, but they cannot guarantee 100% protection. Consequently it is important to have strategies for managing potential threats to security, and to develop and implement an effective **disaster recovery plan** that involves regularly backing up data to secure media.

Disaster recovery plan

AQA   **INFO 1, INFO 2**
OCR   **G061**
WJEC   **IT1, IT3**
CCEA   **AS 1, A2 1**

For more information on backing up data and backing up procedures see Chapter 1.

Disaster recovery is the process used to repair and/or replace the IT infrastructure of an organisation in the event of either a natural disaster (e.g. fire, flood, wind, earthquake, etc.) or a man-made disaster (e.g. hacking/malicious interference, theft, arson, chemical spillage, vehicle impact, terrorism, war, etc.). It is important to develop a plan that will help **minimise disruption** and enable the organisation to get back to normal working as quickly as possible. For any disaster recovery plan to work, it is essential to have a full backup copy of the system and data prior to the occurrence of the disaster. However, no matter how many precautions are put into place, no organisation can completely protect itself against the full range of potential disasters.

In developing a plan to cope with the after events of a disaster, organisations need to consider the potential threats (e.g. natural and man-made disasters) and the potential consequences of disasters to their business (e.g. loss of business, loss of client confidence). They need to understand how each level of their organisation would be affected in the event of different types of disasters and develop short and long-term recovery plans to enable them to get their business back to normal as quickly as possible.

A disaster recovery plan needs to include three key control measures:
- **Preventative measures** aimed at preventing problems from occurring.
- **Detective measures** aimed at finding problems at an early stage so that they can be dealt with before they become even bigger problems.
- **Corrective measures** aimed at restoring systems and putting right any problems that have occurred.

In addition to access controls (e.g. passwords, limited access, etc.), preventative and detective measures are generally dealt with by using commercial software such as Norton or McAfee. Common strategies are put in place so that data can be restored as part of the corrective measures. These strategies include:
- Making regular backups on **portable media** (CDs, tapes, external hard drives, etc.) and sending the media to an off-site storage facility. The backup media is then readily available to be restored to the main system.
- Making regular backups to **off-site storage media** facility (e.g. another branch of the organisation, another organisation with which it has mutual backup facilities, or a commercial media storage centre). The backup media is then readily available to be restored to the main system.
- Full **replication** of the data to other sites (e.g. distributed databases and other distributed systems). The data can be restored and synchronised directly with the main system.
- Using an **external disaster recovery provider** to provide services rather than using the organisation's own remote facilities.

PROGRESS CHECK

1. Define the term 'virus'.
2. List three key control measures that need to be included in a disaster recovery plan.

2 Preventative measures, detective measures, corrective measures.
1 Viruses are small items of malicious software that reproduce themselves within a system.

Sample questions and model answers

1. Explain what is meant by the terms 'key field' and 'composite key'. **(3)**

A key field contains a unique identifier that can be used to identify a record as being separate from all other records. Key fields often include `ID` as part of the field name. A composite key combines the contents of two or more fields to create a unique identifier.

2. Describe two security issues that apply to distributed databases. Suggest one method of overcoming each issue. **(4)**

As the computers are located on a number of sites it is important to ensure that only authorised users have access to the data. This can be achieved by issuing passwords to authorised users, and regularly updating those passwords in order to increase the level of ongoing security. Because data will regularly be transmitted between different sites, it is possible that some of the data may become corrupt or be tampered with during transmission. Therefore it is important that checks are put in place in order to ensure that the data that arrives is both accurate and secure.

3. List two internal and two external threats to ICT systems. **(4)**

Internal threats to ICT systems include loss of data/software as a result of staff losing laptops, CDs or data sticks; and deliberate damage caused by disgruntled staff. Other internal threats include damage caused by inappropriate use of internal messaging and failure to implement backup systems.

External threats to ICT systems include viruses that are attached to incoming files and intrusion from hackers. Other external threats include phishing, spyware, and interception of data whilst in transit.

4. Describe two advantages of using a relational database instead of a flat file database. **(4)**

A flat file database can contain redundant data. In a relational database there is a high level of data integrity because the redundant data has been eliminated. Relational databases also have a much higher degree of referential integrity than flat file databases, because single items of data that are changed in any table are automatically reflected across the whole database.

This type of question usually only carries one or two marks per explanation; do not waste time writing too much in your answer. Write one or two sentences to clearly explain the terms, and then move on.

This type of question takes a little more thinking about. To start with you need to decide what is meant by 'security issues', and then identify the way in which it can be addressed. There are, of course, numerous things that could be regarded as security issues in relation to ICT, but the question has been set in the context of 'distributed databases' so your answers need to be set in this context.

In this instance, there are numerous possible answers, so it is important that you select the answer that you feel most confident about. Try to include the correct technical terms for the example you are giving (e.g. 'data integrity', 'referential integrity'), but be sure that you put these into context. Remember, when asked to 'describe' something you need to say what it is and what it does.

Practice examination questions

1 Describe the difference between a simple query and a complex query. Give examples to illustrate your answer. **(4)**

_____

_____

_____

_____

2 Describe two different ways in which a distributed database could be stored in more than one physical location. **(4)**

(i) _____

_____

_____

_____

(ii) _____

_____

_____

_____

3 Describe two advantages of normalising a database. **(4)**

(i) _____

_____

_____

_____

(ii) _____

_____

_____

_____

7 Presenting and communicating information

The following topics are covered in this chapter:

- Developing effective text-based documents
- Presentation software
- Incorporating graphics and audio files
- Web authoring

7.1 Developing effective text-based documents

LEARNING SUMMARY

After studying this section you should be able to:

- describe the characteristics of documents
- analyse the effectiveness of documents
- describe how a document can be reformatted to meet needs
- describe the processes, and explain the purpose of, combining data from a range of applications to meet audience needs

The characteristics of documents

AQA INFO 1
OCR G061
WJEC IT1, IT2
CCEA AS 2

The key **purpose** of any document is to have an impact upon its intended **audience**. Regardless of the size, nature, format and content, the first glance at a document will either attract the audience or cause them to turn away. It is important to know about the key features of effective documents and other forms of presentation and written communication, and to apply those key features in your work. For many organisations getting the concepts of written communication right is central to their business ethos, and ultimately to their success.

What makes an effective document?

Surprising as it may seem there is clear guidance about the effectiveness of documents with a focus on 'professional quality'. The word processing software that you use will present you with a basic **template** in which to present your text.

This will have a set of pre-defined areas:

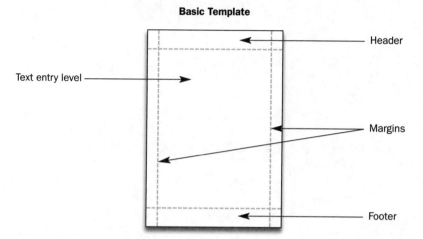

The first element of an effective document is the amount of **white space** that is provided. White space (sometimes referred to as **negative space**) is any area on a document that is free of text or graphics. White space is important as it frames the text (or graphic) and draws the eye towards it. If there is too much text or too many images on the page, it will look cluttered. Clutter makes it difficult to get across the message that the document is trying to convey.

Guidelines about **margins** are important in that they apply a sense of balance to the page. Planning to change margins needs to be carefully considered and you need to have a clear idea about why you want to do it.

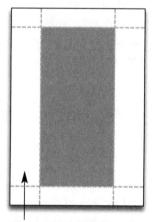

The margins in this document make the test block look rather too tall and thin on the page. It almost looks as though the writer is trying to fool us into thinking that there is more on the page than there actually is.

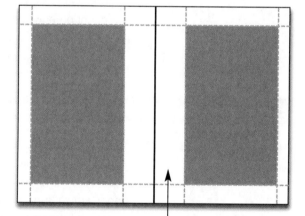

The margins in this document are different from the norm in that they are wider on one side than the other. The designer has thought about the purpose of the document: a two page spread like this needs a bit more space on the right of the left-hand page, and on the left of the right-hand page to accommodate the binding, staples or punched holes.

There are other areas of white space on a document that need to be looked at carefully. The key for effective presentation within a document is consistency:

- Do you have the same space between each paragraph?
- Are your indentations, tabs, bullets and numbers consistently displayed?

> **KEY POINT**
>
> After you have looked over your document for consistency you need to evaluate the balance between the white space and other elements on the page. If things are too tightly packed, the document will be difficult to read. If there is too much white space then it will look as though you are trying to pad things out.

The **header** and **footer** are important for the balance of the document but they are also very important document management tools as well. They provide signals and pointers to help the reader find their way through the document – or to provide them with a cue: is it the document they were looking for?

The header and footer help with the consistency of the document.

Header	Footer
<ul><li>Allows organisations space to personalise documents, e.g. a company logo on a letter.</li><li>In longer documents the title of the document provides an important cue.</li><li>Sometimes the name of the author appears in the header.</li></ul>	<ul><li>A useful place for page numbers.</li><li>Some organisations put in the name, location and version of the document into the footer: again an important cue should you want to revise the document in the future or if you need to check that you are using the most recent version.</li></ul>

Effective documents also have a limited number of **fonts**; generally the rule of thumb is that one is enough.

Choice of font is also an important consideration for the reader. Some organisations prefer to use a **serif font** (like Times New Roman) as the serif is said to contribute to the flow. Others insist on a **sans serif font** (like Arial or Verdana) because the additional elements that appear on the serif fonts can make the text more difficult to read for people with visual impairments or dyslexia. The only rule here is that you have to consider the needs of the audience and then make a judgment about whether or not your document is fit for purpose. If the document is for 'professional' purposes then you need to choose a font that meets that need. For an invitation to a Halloween party the font could, of course, be very different indeed.

> **KEY POINT**
>
> Advice from organisations like the British Dyslexia Institute can provide useful guidance when designing documents that can be read by as wide an audience as possible. Accessibility is an extremely important consideration when judging the effectiveness of a document.

You can, of course, change the size of the font: a larger sized font would be important for headings; a smaller size font for labelling diagrams or charts.

The choice and size of font can be as helpful or as distracting for the reader as too much or too little white space. The default font size in most word processing software is 12 point – chosen for ease of reading, and when we consider web authoring later on – it is a good font size for reading on the screen.

So far we have considered white space, use of the header and footer, font choice and size. We now need to consider the tools that are available to use to bring emphasis to words or elements on the page.

Words can be emphasised by using the bold, underline and italic variants of the font. They are good for emphasis – but again too much emphasis spoils the look of the document.

> Broadly speaking, for professional documents fancy borders, WordArt and multi-coloured fonts should not be used. They contribute to a lack of balance in a document and distract the reader from the content.

KEY POINT

Remember to focus on the needs of the reader not on your own personal preferences. There may also be specific organisational guidelines that you need to apply: step outside these and your document becomes immediately ineffective.

Finally, if we are considering effectiveness then it is important that spelling, punctuation and grammar are correct and consistent throughout the document. It is generally not acceptable to use contractions like 'you've' or 'don't'. The best thing to do, once you have produced a piece of text is to:

- see your piece of work as a draft document
- proofread it yourself
- get someone else to proofread it
- make necessary adjustments
- check it over again.

Sometimes the guidelines for setting up a document need to be adjusted to meet an individual's needs.

Example

An organisation requires all documents that go to board meetings to follow these guidelines:

- Paragraphs should be left justified, 1.5 line spaced and not indented.
- There should be a double 1.5 line space between paragraphs.
- The title page should include the author's name, title of document and date of meeting.
- The company logo should appear in the top right of the title page.
- The header of pages following the title page should contain author name left justified and meeting reference right justified.
- The footer of pages following the title page should contain file path left justified and page number (x of y) right justified.
- Main text font style is Times New Roman, size 12.
- Sub-headings are bold and size 14 (left justified).
- Main headings are bold and size 16 (left justified).
- Left and right margins are both to be 2.5cm.
- Bullets or numbering should be used to make points: bullet indented 1cm from the left margin; text 0.5cm from the bullet.
- New sections of reports should begin on new pages.

To facilitate the production of reports for the board a template was established that followed the rules. This was done by developing and applying a new style using commands from the Format menu. However, the requirement for Times New Roman was causing difficulties for one board member who had a visual impairment. This board member appreciated that the line spacing requirements were there to help board members make notes on the documents – but the increased amount of white space was making it difficult to follow the flow of the text. A new template was developed to include a sans-serif font, and to change the paragraphs to single line spacing. All other parameters remained the same.

Desktop publishing

AQA **INFO 1**
OCR **G061**
WJEC **IT1, IT2**
CCEA **AS 2**

Although text-based documents are largely produced using word processing software, more sophisticated text-based documents are produced with desktop publishing software.

Examples of such documents are:

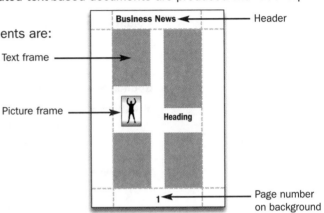

- newsletters
- invitations
- brochures
- business cards
- booklets
- flyers
- forms
- cards
- certificates

The terminology of desktop publishing is different from that used in word processing. However the principles of balance, white space, clutter and font characteristics all apply here.

Remember that too many elements on a page cause clutter.

Terminology	Description
Design element	A text frame, picture frame or other object placed on a page within the publication.
Object	An object is an element imported from another program, for example, a chart or table from a spreadsheet. The object can maintain its connection with the source program so that data can be edited from the publication (see page 158).
Text frame	Text is entered into a frame. The borders of the frame act like margins in word processing. Text frames are independent of each other – text does not flow automatically as it does in word processing. Frames can be layered so that a text frame could be placed over part of a picture frame.
Picture frame	Images are placed within picture frames – changing the size of the picture frame alters the size of the image. Frames can also be rotated or flipped.

Terminology	Description
Page layout	As in word processing the layout has an impact on the reader: good layouts help the reader to see clearly the message that is being conveyed. Page layout is determined by where you place the text and picture frames.
Foreground	Articles that include images, text and objects are placed in the foreground of the document. These are elements that are different on each page of the publication.
Background	Elements that need to be the same on each page of the publication are placed on the page background. Examples include: page numbers, strap lines, logos.
Margin	White space between the edge of the page and frames.
Columns and rows	Pages in desktop publishing are made up of columns and rows. The number of columns and rows can be specified by the designer when the document is created.
Boundaries and guides	These are non-printing lines that are shown on screen so that you can see where the margins, columns and rows, and frames are. They help to position elements on the page so that you can design the balance of the page as you work.
Workspace	This is the area around the page. It is a bit like your desk: you have the document you are working on but there is space around you for placing other things. It is possible to place text and images ready to drag them into place. Anything in the workspace is not seen in the published document until they become elements on the page.

Combining objects and data from other applications

AQA **INFO 1**
OCR **G061**
WJEC **IT1, IT2**
CCEA **AS 2**

Data from other applications is often combined with text-based documents to support the messages being conveyed. Within many text processing programs data or objects can be:

- **pasted**
- **inserted** (**embedded** or **imported**)
- **linked**
- **merged**

Pasting data from a spreadsheet or database into a text-based document will convert the data into an appropriate format. For example, copying a range of cells from a spreadsheet and pasting them into a text-based program will convert the active data in the spreadsheet into a table.

Pasting word processed text into a desktop publishing program places the text in a selected text frame. If the text frame is too small to accommodate all the text a new text frame will have to be created and linked to the other so that the text can flow from one to the other. In word processing the text would flow automatically onto a new page if that was needed.

When inserting or importing data there are a number of considerations to be made:

Consideration	Approach
Do you want the data that is imported to be integral to the text-based document?	The best approach here is to embed the object from another application by inserting it. A link to the source application is maintained. In most cases double clicking an embedded object will open the application in which it was created (so that the data can be edited) but the data is treated independently from the data in the source file.
Do you want updates to the data made in the source file to be reflected in the text file?	It is necessary to create a link between the two files. You can do this by selecting the data in the source file and pasting a link to that data in the text file. As with pasting, a table is created but this time any changes made to the data file will be reflected in the table linked to the data file. Sometimes this may have to be done manually by updating the link.
Do you want to include data from a large file – or include a large object such as a video or sound file?	**Hyperlinking** to the appropriate file or object is appropriate here. This keeps the size of the text-based document manageable, but allows access to other applications. This is useful when working on screen but not sensible if the document is only going to be seen in printed form.

Make a point of knowing about the examples you have in your portfolio of work. You may be asked to write about how you personalised a range of documents.

Merging data between applications, using mail merge, allows users to personalise documents such as:

- form letters
- school reports
- address labels
- envelopes
- invitations
- emails

It is also possible to produce documents such as directories, legal documents, inventories and catalogues.

The process involves merging a main document with a data source. In a letter to parents and carers informing them about an A-Level open evening the main document will contain the main body of text that will be constant in all the letters. It will also contain 'merge fields', which instruct the text program where to look for the data in the data source. The data source contains the information that changes in each letter – such as the name and address of each parent or carer. In a doctor's surgery or hospital, the data source could contain the name and address of the patient, the date, time and location of the appointment, and the name of the doctor.

You should note here that it is likely that the data will be held in some form of table, with each 'merge field' corresponding to a data field in the source data table. This source data can come from a table in:

- a text processing application
- a spreadsheet
- a flat file database (or a data table in a relational database).

It is possible to customise the merge further by using a feature such as
word field (found on the mail merge tool bar). These are additional commands
that allow the user to provide extra information that is not in the data source,
access an additional data source, or control the way in which the data is merged.

Word field	Description
Ask	Prompts the user for information during the mail merge process.
Fill-in	Again, this prompts the user for information that can be added to merged documents selected by the user. In a reporting system it could be an extra note of congratulations from the form tutor.
If... Then... Else...	This command sets conditions on the records that are to be printed. If the subject was equal to ICT then an invitation to a field trip could be printed, otherwise (else) details about a school-based event could be printed.
Merge Record #	Merge Record prints the number of each record selected on each merged document in order from 1 through to the number of records being merged.
Merge Sequence #	Merge Sequence prints the number of data records that were successfully merged with the main document.
Next Record	Allows two records from the data source to be merged into the same document.
Next Record If	Allows two records from the data source to be merged into the same document if a condition is met (if address fields are equal then insert the details of the next record).
Skip Record If	Misses out a record if a condition is met. It could skip all male patients if the mailing was intended for female patients only.

The advantages of mail merge are:
- It is possible to produce many personalised documents very quickly.
- All the documents are based on one main document so you only need to proofread one document. If that one is right – then you can be certain that they all are.
- You can be selective by using word fields to restrict the merge operation.

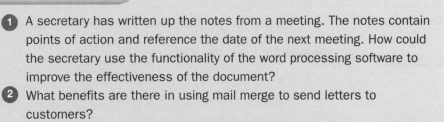

PROGRESS CHECK

1 A secretary has written up the notes from a meeting. The notes contain points of action and reference the date of the next meeting. How could the secretary use the functionality of the word processing software to improve the effectiveness of the document?

2 What benefits are there in using mail merge to send letters to customers?

1 Any suitable answer, e.g. The structure of the report could be enhanced by emboldening the heading for each section so that they stand out. The report could be produced in a sans serif font, size 12, to improve accessibility and increase the readability of the document. The points of action could also be emboldened to make them stand out. 2 It is much quicker to use mail merge than to write individual letters to each customer. Mail merge uses a standard letter as the template for all the personalised letters that are produced; this means that the author only has to proofread one letter to be certain that all the others are error free. Personalisation means that the data within the merged letters is pertinent to the recipient. Since the source for the merged data is often external it should have been through error checking, reducing the risk of generating further errors in the letters to be mailed.

7.2 Presentation software

LEARNING SUMMARY

After studying this section you should be able to:

- describe the features of presentation software
- compare and describe different modes of navigation in presentation software
- describe linear, non-linear and hierarchical presentation formats
- compare presentation methodologies and their effectiveness

The features of presentation software

AQA **INFO 1**
OCR **G061**
WJEC **IT1, IT2**
CCEA **AS 2**

Presentation or **multimedia** software allows users to combine text, graphics, sound and video in one presentation so that they can be presented directly to an audience. There are many variants of presentation software on the market – but they all offer a range of features that can be used to enhance a presentation.

Design features

Feature	Attribute
Consistent design	<ul><li>The use of templates for master title and presentation slides ensures that the presentation has consistency.</li><li>A presentation that uses a variety of slide designs looks unprofessional and confuses the message that is being conveyed.</li><li>Templates allow users to put key information (like slide numbers, dates, standard company information) into headers and footers.</li></ul>
Colour schemes	<ul><li>As with word processing and desktop publishing the template allows organisations to customise and personalise the presentation to reflect the corporate image using appropriate colours and fonts.</li></ul>
Background graphics	<ul><li>Like a watermark, background **graphics** can also be used to highlight a key feature of the presentation.</li><li>Inappropriate choice of graphics could distract from the presentation itself.</li></ul>

Feature	Attribute
Transitions	• Some thought should be given as to how to move from one slide to another during the presentation. • There are plenty of **slide transition** options available. • Once again the needs of the audience are paramount here – personal preference should not come into it, and the principle of 'keep it simple' is probably best. A straightforward 'appear' is often more effective than a side-sweep or checkerboard.
Animation effects	• Animation effects offer opportunities to focus on key points by controlling how text and images enter the field of vision, or how text and images are emphasised. This helps to control the audience's reaction to the presentation. • Rather than putting all the text or other objects on the screen, your presentation could have more impact if each point appears separately.
Images	• Static and moving images can be very powerful within a presentation. For example, in a fund-raising presentation a picture of a starving child tugs at the emotions more powerfully than a screen full of words. • In some circumstances the opportunity to show short clips of video and audio files can also give more weight to a presentation.
Hyperlinks	• Hyperlinks within presentations enable presenters to take the audience to other files, images, web pages, or live links. • Hyperlinks can also be attached to hot-spots on the screen.

Presentation features

Feature	Attribute
Preview	• Presenters have the opportunity to preview how slides build (especially if they have animation effects within them), and can make design changes if the impact of the presentation does not seem effective enough, or if the animations do not work as expected.
Re-ordering	• Slides can be dragged into a different sequence if the presenter feels that the message can be presented with more impact in a different order.
Speaker notes and handouts	• Sometimes the slides alone are not enough for a presenter to keep the audience focused on the message. • The opportunity to put in more detail in speaker notes keeps the structure of the delivery intact. • Speaker notes allow the presenter to keep the number of words on the screen to a minimum. • Handouts are useful tools: they keep the audience focused on what the presenter is saying, rather than copying what is on the screen.
Action buttons	• Action buttons allow the presenter some control over which slide is viewed next.
Hyperlinks	• Hyperlinks attached to a hot-spot allow the presenter control over the structure of the presentation to meet the needs of the audience.

Feature	Attribute
Timing	• It is possible to limit the amount of time that a slide is shown. This keeps the presenter on track and enables the presentation to be delivered in a specific time frame.
Narration	• It is possible for presentations to be delivered automatically (in kiosk mode) with a pre-recorded narration.
Automation	• With automation, presentations can be set to begin again once the presentation has finished. • Automatic **navigation** can be set so that the appearance of each point in the slide or each animation effect can be set to a specified amount of time. This is fine when the audience is not expected to interact. A question or comment from the audience, or if the presenter decides to talk a little longer on the previous point can throw the whole presentation out of sequence. If each point moves on 'too quickly' the audience could become disaffected with the presentation.

Advantages and disadvantages of multimedia presentations

AQA **INFO 1**
OCR **G061**
WJEC **IT1, IT2**
CCEA **AS 2**

Multimedia presentations offer both advantages and disadvantages to the developer and to the audience.

Advantages of multimedia presentations	Disadvantages of multimedia presentations
• Professional looking presentations. • Multimedia can grab and hold the audience's attention. • Presentations can be re-used. • Presentations can be set up to run with or without a presenter. • Presentations can be edited easily. • Presentations can be adapted to meet the needs of different audiences. • Presentations can have a variety of structures to meet different presentation needs.	• It is easy to get carried away by the technology and end up with an unprofessional looking presentation. • Projectors and screens are expensive to purchase and to maintain. • Audiences can respond negatively to a presentation – especially if it is the third or fourth presentation they have seen in a day.

Linear, non-linear and hierarchical presentations

AQA **INFO 1**
OCR **G061**
WJEC **IT1, IT2**
CCEA **AS 2**

Many presentations are **linear**, **non-linear** or **hierarchical**. They are useful in training situations where the presenter has a clear view about what needs to be covered.

Linear presentations

Linear presentations follow a rigid sequence from one slide to another.

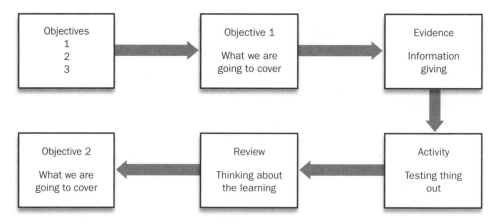

If the audience finds the activity challenging, or if they require more evidence the presenter may not have the information to hand.

The effectiveness of linear presentations is very dependent on the skill of the presenter and the design of the content.

Non-linear presentations

Non-linear presentations give a little more freedom to the presenter and to the audience. Rather than following a pre-determined path from one slide to another the presentation can include hot-spots and hyperlinks that connect with other pages so that the slides can be shown in any order.

Someone giving a presentation about a new medicine would have details about the new drug, and may be prepared to deal with questions about the side effects. These questions could come at any time during the presentation – the presenter could in these circumstances go to the side effects slide and then back to another slide to pick up the rest of the themes they wanted to explore.

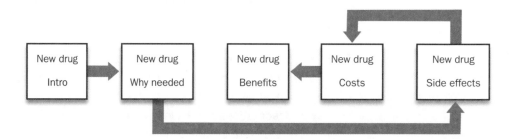

This non-linear approach is also useful if the presentation has been designed to be used by someone else such as in interactive presentations in museums and tourist centres where the presentation can follow the choices that the user wants to follow.

Hierarchical presentations

The hierarchical structure allows for a little more choice, usually from a menu. From the menu you select an option and follow the path for that option, eventually returning to the main menu.

The hierarchical structure can be useful in quizzes. Look at the example here and note how it branches:

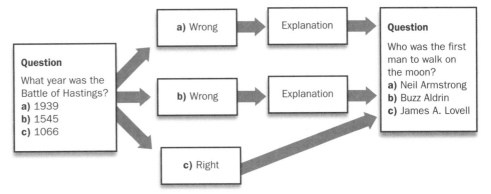

Hierarchical presentations are also useful in presenting different branches of information for a user to consider:

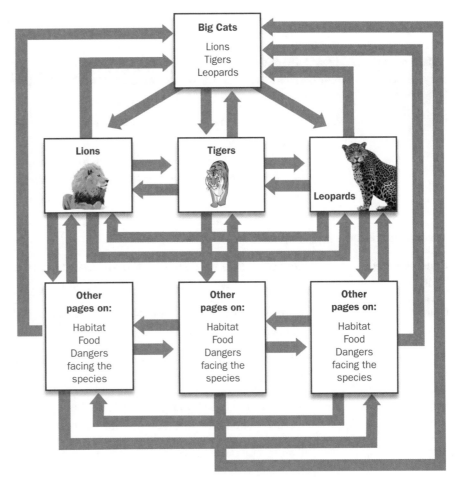

Hierarchical presentations offer a great deal of choice to the user – but they have to be set up very carefully. They can be confusing for some users because they can be so complex: following one menu to another menu and then to a third menu could make it difficult for a user to reflect on the path they have followed.

Other types of presentation media

AQA **INFO 1**
OCR **G061**
WJEC **IT1, IT2**
CCEA **AS 2**

In the past **overhead projectors** (OHPs) were used to give presentations (and they are still sometimes used today). Presentations were developed on overhead transparencies (**acetates**) by hand using indelible ink pens, or as photocopies or direct prints from a computer. They could be presented in colour or in black and white. Presenters had to place the slides onto the OHP in order to deliver the presentation to an audience.

Advantages of OHPs	Disadvantages of OHPs
• Cheap to produce. • An OHP is cheaper than a digital projector. • It is easy to miss out a few acetates if you need to.	• Slides have to be changed by hand. • Acetates can be damaged easily. • If you drop the acetates it is easy to get them out of order. • It is difficult to show information a bit at a time. • It cannot include audio visual files as multimedia presentations can: all the information has to be included on the acetate.

Considerations for an effective presentation

AQA **INFO 2**
OCR **G061**
WJEC **IT1, IT2**
CCEA **Unit AS 2**

The effectiveness of presentations is measured by their fitness for purpose. A presentation needs to consider the audience in a number of ways. These include the:

• nature of the audience: age, position, known or unknown by the presenter
• size of the audience: small room, large hall
• type of presentation: fun, informative, serious, stand-alone.

Key considerations	Explanation
Consistency	Do not change the nature of the slides within the presentation. Develop a master slide with a set colour scheme and stick to it.
Colour	Some colours work well, others do not. Black text, for example, on a blue background does not work well. As a general rule, use contrasting colours, i.e. dark text on a light background, light text on a dark background.
Font	The font needs to be large enough so that everyone in the room can see it clearly. Keep it uncluttered – do not try to say everything on screen.
Screen	Do not stand in the way of the screen – look at where your audience is going to be seated and make sure everyone can see the screen.
Presenter	Assume that your audience can read and do not read what is on the screen out loud to them: it is irritating!
Animations	Only use animations if absolutely necessary – they can be distracting. Remember that an effective presentation is not about showing all the technical wizardry that you have mastered. It is about getting the message across to the audience.

PROGRESS CHECK

1 A hospital administrator has been asked to update staff about a new patient record system. She has decided to use presentation software to help structure the update session. How can animation features help her to develop an effective presentation?

2 Describe the hierarchical presentation structure.

1 Any suitable answers e.g. Animation features will allow the administrator to show the key points to her audience as she wants to cover them. If she is focusing on a feature of the new record system she does not want her audience to be distracted by other features that may be listed on the slide. Bringing them up one by one at each mouse click will help her to keep control of the way the presentation is going. She can speed up or slow down according to her audience's reaction.

2 Hierarchical presentations are usually menu driven. From a main menu users can select a choice of topic to explore further, following the line of enquiry down through successive pages. At each level of the presentation there are likely to be opportunities to return to the main menu, to branch out to related topics, select new topics, or to keep progressing down the original line of enquiry till that reaches its end and and the user is returned to the main menu.

7.3 Incorporating graphics and audio files

LEARNING SUMMARY

After studying this section you should be able to:

- evaluate the use of clipart and thumbnail images
- describe the differences between vector and bitmap images
- evaluate the use of graphics libraries
- describe the process of incorporating sound and video in publications
- explain the advantages and disadvantages of audio and video files

The use of a variety of media within a publication can enhance the audience experience and support the dissemination of the message that the media is intended to convey. Graphics are a feature of both paper-based, web-based and multimedia presentations. Audio and video are more likely to appear as features in multimedia and web-based presentations.

Using clipart to enhance publications

AQA **INFO 1**
OCR **G061**
WJEC **IT1, IT2**
CCEA **AS 2**

Clipart often appears in publications and presentations as it provides quick and easy access to images. It comes bundled with many applications and can be purchased on CD or downloaded from the Internet. Much clipart is in the public domain and comes free of copyright for personal and educational use. If it is used for commercial purposes it may be subject to copyright.

Advantages of clipart	Disadvantages of clipart
<ul><li>Clipart is usually free at the point of use for personal and educational use.</li><li>Appropriate selections of images can enhance publications quickly.</li><li>You do not need skills in drawing or image manipulation to insert a graphic.</li><li>If organisations use clipart to develop their logo they may not have to pay for professional designers especially where clipart is copyright free or where copyright has been waived.</li></ul>	<ul><li>The most appropriate image may not be available.</li><li>It may take ages to find an appropriate image – and that can be a waste of time.</li><li>You may not get the quality of image you need – do you need a cartoon or a photograph?</li><li>It is easy to mistake a copyrighted image for one that is free to use: for organisations this could be an expensive mistake.</li><li>Because clipart is in the public domain it is highly likely that the images will have been seen already by your audience, which is boring!</li></ul>

Finding clipart

The majority of clipart collections come with a **browser** so that you can categorise the image that you are looking for: business, people, training, houses, etc. It is also possible to use **keywords** to facilitate the search and get nearer to the actual image that will be fit for purpose.

Keyword and category searches will present you with a series of **thumbnails**. Thumbnails are smaller than the image they represent, and are of lower resolution. Because they are smaller, users can see many images on the screen at the same time: this makes it easier to review suitability. However, because the resolution of these images is poor it is hard to make accurate judgments about how the actual image will look in the publication or presentation, or what the size of the image will be.

Types of images

AQA **INFO 1**
OCR **G061**
WJEC **IT1, IT2**
CCEA **AS 2**

There are two main types of images that can be used in publications and presentations:

- **bitmap** images
- **vector graphic** images

Bitmap images

Most of the images that appear on the web or that come from digital cameras or telephones are **raster graphics.** They are made up of a grid of pixels: the bitmap. Each pixel relates to a defined area of a picture, and contributes to file size. So, a picture that is 640 by 480 will have 307200 pixels; larger pictures obviously have more. A simple bitmap picture (with the file extension .BMP) will therefore be large as each pixel will be stored as one or more bits of data, but will be of high quality. These images are often used in print media because of this.

There are other file extensions that can be used. Saving an image file as a JPEG, GIF, or TIFF file uses a compression algorithm that maintains quality while significantly decreasing file size. For this reason these image extensions are used in electronic and multimedia presentations and publications. However the quality of JPEG images can degrade if they are opened and then repeatedly saved in JPEG format. This is not a problem if the image is not altered when included in a publication.

Extension	Meaning	Attributes	Approximate size of a 1600 x 1200 photograph from a digital camera
.BMP	Bitmap	Large file size	5.49 MB
.JPEG	Joint Photographic Experts Group	Access to a full range of colours	298 KB
.GIF	Graphics Interchange Format	Limited range of indexed colours available: 256	655 KB
.TIFF	Tagged Image File Format	Best for high resolution printing	269 KB

Editing bitmap images means that you have to change the properties of pixels in the whole graphic. Bitmaps are used mainly for photographs. In their original size bitmap images have high levels of detail and contrast. When they are resized the images can become pixellated and blurry. As you can see from the table above, bitmaps can be compressed into much smaller file sizes.

Vector graphic images

Unlike bitmap images, vector graphics are saved as geometric equations rather than allocating a bit for every pixel that goes to make up the picture.

Vector graphics are best used for the development of technical diagrams, cartoons and computer aided design. They are made up of lines, colours, curves and other geometrical shapes and attributes.

Each of the elements of a vector graphic is known as a **primitive**, and both simple and complex graphics are composed of these primitives. This means that the images are flexible and dynamic – they can be resized without degrading (i.e. they do not distort or blur).

Because vector graphics are made up of many primitives they can be quite complex with variations in colour, shade, layering, transparency, brightness, contrast or intensity.

KEY POINT

Specialist software is required for creating and editing vector graphic images. This can mean that they are not as portable as bitmap images – some systems may not support vector graphics that have been created in other software.

Graphics libraries

AQA **INFO 1**
OCR **G061**
WJEC **IT1, IT2**
CCEA **AS 2**

Graphics libraries provide standard symbols and images for use in industry standard applications. Examples of these include:

- kitchen design
- cartography (map-making)
- network design

Application	Description	Example images
Kitchen design	Symbols for cupboards, sinks and kitchen appliances used for planning and designing a kitchen. The same principles can apply to office, bathroom and stage design.	
Cartography	Maps use a set of common symbols to represent key features of the landscape. Although there are some national differences, around the world most maps use similar symbols for the same things.	PH = Public House P = Post Office = Church with Tower
Network design	Libraries of network design images contain industry standard symbols for the main components of a network. They aid the rapid construction of network diagrams by dragging and dropping the required symbols into place.	

The main advantage of graphics libraries is that they use industry standard images that will be recognised across the world.

The main disadvantage of graphics libraries is that images may not be up-to-date: it depends on the age of the software package and its ability to respond to the changes in design requirements over time.

Incorporating sound and video files

AQA **INFO 1**
OCR **G061**
WJEC **IT1, IT2**
CCEA **AS 2**

Since we communicate largely by speaking and listening it is important that we are able to include sound as part of our communication strategy in multimedia presentations. Both sound and video can be added to presentations in much the same way as adding images.

Essentially sound and video files can be set to:

- run automatically (sound files can play in the background)
- be embedded and play as an outcome of a hot-spot
- be loaded from an external source by following a hyperlink.

Key features of sound files

Computers convert **analogue** sound signals into **digital** ones by measuring the input signal at frequent intervals. The number of measurements taken each second is referred to as the **sampling rate**: a CD is sampled at 44.1 kHz – 44 100 times per second. Even at that rate there will be some gaps in the sound. If a lower sampling rate is used then longer sections of sound will be missed out. This means that the signal loses some of its definition. This may be noticeable when the sound is played back.

Sampled audio file sizes can be very large. Compression can be applied to some files. One of the most common file types is .mp3. This file type uses a compression algorithm to enable quicker downloads.

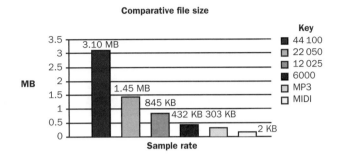

Comparative file size

As the sample rate decreases:

- sound quality reduces
- higher frequencies disappear
- bass notes are less distinct and lack clarity.

The .mp3 file is sampled at a high rate but is compressed so that the quality is not lost.

Feature	Attribute
Low sample rate	Acceptable for speech because the sound is concentrated in the mid range of frequencies.
Compression	In compression, items of high and low frequency sound data that are not likely to be heard are removed.
MIDI	Used with keyboards and synthesisers. Stores sound as a series of instructions (pitch, time, etc). Quality is dependent on playback equipment.
.WAV	Microsoft® multimedia extension. Can store mono and stereo sound up to CD quality.
.AIFF	Apple® multimedia extension.

Key features of podcasts

Podcasts are audio recordings that are posted on the Internet. They are known as podcasts as they can be easily downloaded to MP3 players.

To subscribe to a podcast users need access to the Internet and **feed aggregator software** such as iTunes® or Juice® . The details of the feed are stored in an XML file, which can automatically see if the material has been updated and will then download the new podcast ready for listening. This is useful when following a series or regular broadcast.

Searching for podcasts is supported by using **tagging software** to add information such as date and topic. Others can receive notification of podcasts through **RSS feeds**. This means that interested parties can subscribe to the feeds and hear the sound files that have been developed.

Key features of video files

There are many different file formats that apply to the use of digital video. Among the most common file types are:

Extension	Format	Company
.wmv	Windows media format	Microsoft
.qt	Quicktime	Apple
.mp4 .mpg .mpeg	Standardised series of formats usable cross platform	Moving Pictures Expert Group
.avi	Audio video interleave – windows	Microsoft
.ra .ram .rm	Developed for the Internet and allows streaming of video	RealVideo
.swf .fla .flv	Shockwave format: requires an extra component to play Files are typically viewed within a web browser	Adobe

Each format compresses and plays the video picture in different ways. To play back the video the data file needs to be decompressed in the correct way following the appropriate **codec** for the file (a codec is a program that can code and decode a digital signal).

The size of the video file is dependent upon the compression ratio and the intended screen size of the video when it is played. A 12 MB video clip saved as a .mpg file can be compressed down to 2 MB if saved in .mp4 format. As with bitmap graphics there is often an optimum screen size for videos saved in different formats: if the screen size is too large, the images will be blurred and indistinct.

Video terminology

When using video it is useful to be familiar with some of the terminology that describes how a video has been constructed. Aspects such as framing, pace and transition inform our understanding of fitness for purpose.

Framing is a technical term for the way a shot looks on screen:
- Telephoto lenses can bring the background forward to present a unified look to a moving image.
- Long shots are used to define locations to reduce the significance of people and objects.
- Mid-shots concentrate on actions and people. They are most common in interviews.
- Close-ups are used to draw attention to people and objects in detail.
- Focus can be used to draw attention to specific parts of the moving image.

Pace describes the length of time that a scene is shown. This is important when delivering key messages to the audience and to inject a sense of urgency or importance to the message. At other times the pace can be slow to reflect a relaxed and calm mood. **Transitions** are important too. They define how we move from scene to scene: swift and sudden cuts from one scene to another increase the sense of urgency; fades or dissolves contribute to a feeling that an overall message is being given carefully and with consideration.

Video broadcasts

Video broadcasts can be incorporated within multimedia presentations or can be uploaded to sites such as YouTube™. The increased specification of mobile telephones has given greater access to video technology, and the rise in the number of sites prepared to host video content for free has given everyone the opportunity to share their video files.

Manipulating audio and video to meet the needs of the audience

Audio and video files can be edited to ensure that they are fit for purpose.

> **KEY POINT**
>
> Audio and video files, like image files, may be subject to copyright. It is important to check that the rights attached to a file allow you to manipulate it.

Key features of manipulation may include:
- joining a number of files together for a background theme
- looping a file to play for a specified amount of time
- cutting unwanted elements from a file to better meet the needs of the audience
- cutting a file to play within a limited time frame
- adding fades so that the scene 'disappears' or 'appears' gradually
- adding special effects to change the nature of the file (e.g. adding base to a narration of a ghost story)
- moving clips about so they work better for the audience.

> **PROGRESS CHECK**
>
> **1** Give two advantages and two disadvantages of using clipart.
> **2** Describe the role of compression when incorporating bitmap images in a document.
>
> 1 Any suitable answer, e.g. Clipart is obtainable from a wide variety of sources and is often free at the point of use. It is also much quicker to use than beginning to design and then draw original graphics. On the downside, the images that you have to choose from may not be entirely appropriate to the presentation or document. They may also be from a widely used bank of resources. This could present a negative image to the audience as it may suggest that you were only using images to pad things out rather than to complement the message.
> 2 Choosing an alternative bitmap format that uses compression algorithms to store the image data could reduce overall document size when the document is saved. This could save valuable time, bandwidth and usage allowances when transmitting data and documents electronically.

7.4 Web authoring

LEARNING SUMMARY

After studying this section you should be able to:

● describe the features of web authoring including the use of:
  — HTML and CSS
  — web authoring software
  — frames
  — hyperlinks

Developing web pages

AQA **INFO 1**
OCR **G061**
WJEC **IT1, IT2**
CCEA **AS 1, AS 2**

HTML and CSS

Behind every web page is a set of coding that defines the shape and structure of the page. Colour, font size, image locations and sources, the direction of hyperlinks and other attributes are all controlled by this coding. Essentially web pages are written using **hypertext mark-up language** (**HTML**) and **cascading style sheets** (**CSS**).

HTML is a mark-up language designed for the creation of web pages that can be viewed in a browser. HTML is concerned with the way the information looks rather than what it is about.

There are three kinds of mark-up in common use:

Type of mark-up	Use	Example
Structural	Defines the purpose of the text	\<h1>Developing web pages\</h1> defines 'Developing web pages' as first level heading
Hypertext	Links parts of the document to other documents	\<a href=http://www.google.co.uk/>Google\</a> sets up the word 'Google' as a hyperlink to the specified URL
Widget	Small applications that can be installed and executed within a web page. They can create objects such as buttons or lists.	They often take the form of on-screen tools such as clocks, countdowns, local weather information, etc.

Cascading style sheets are used to define the presentational aspects of a web page such as formatting and animation. Like templates and master slides, they can define the presentation information for an entire website. This means that the look of a site can be updated quickly and easily when a new style sheet is imported.

For example, if a website required all level 1 headings to be large Times New Roman and centred in black italics, the style sheet coding would look like this:

```
h1 {
        text-align: center;
        color: black;
        font-size: large;
        font-family: "Times New Roman", serif;
        font-style; italic;
}
```

Web authoring software

Most websites are developed using **web authoring software**. These packages allow users to drag and drop objects into a page template to develop pages. What is seen during the development phase is what the page will look like when it is rendered as a live web page. This is controlled by the use of frames in very much the same way as they are used in desktop publishing.

Templates and wizards allow users to define text, line and background styles. They also enable users to position objects such as images, animations, audio and video clips.

> Being able to describe the differences between authoring software and generic software that can output web pages is important.

Although there are specialist packages available for web authoring, pages can be created using word processing, desktop publishing and presentation software by selecting the 'save as web page' option from the save menu. This makes the development of web pages pretty straightforward since the skill lies in developing the original document, rather than in developing a web page. While that can be seen as an advantage, it does have its drawbacks because objects can move around the page when it is converted. There is also a danger that some browsers may not present the page as intended because the HTML that is generated suffers from what is often described as **bloatware**: you get an awful lot of coding to do something that if scripted in HTML directly would only take a couple of lines. HTML leads to much more efficient coding of web pages. However, developers need to have specialist knowledge to develop web pages.

Frames

Some websites use HTML **frames**, where the pages are broken up into distinct areas. Each area consists of an independent web page. This means that frames allow multiple web pages to all show up in the same page.

Hyperlinks

Hyperlinks are a very common feature in websites. They can be internal links to other web pages or external links to other websites. Users are taken automatically to pages by clicking on the hyperlink.

Hyperlinks can be added to any web page and can even appear within publications and presentations. They can be attached to text or graphics. When attached to a graphic they would be defined as a hot-spot.

PROGRESS CHECK

1. Describe one advantage and one disadvantage of using HTML to produce web pages.
2. Explain how hyperlinks are used in web pages and presentations.

1. HTML allows for the precise coding, design and definition of a web page. Along with CSS it ensures that the web page is structured clearly and precisely according to defined and specific requirements. A key disadvantage is that you need to know the rules of the mark-up language to prepare a web page; you also need to be able to visualise what the page will look like.
2. Hyperlinks, when pressed, take users to other pages within the document, presentation or website; or to external websites. They can be inserted as URLs, attached to words or to images.

Sample questions and model answers

1. A village has a regular monthly newsletter that is printed as an A5 booklet. Describe three advantages of using a desktop publishing package to produce the newsletter. **(4)**

It is good to focus on a structural advantage for desktop publishing – it highlights your knowledge about the features.

It is good to give an advantage that focuses on the functionality.

A desktop publishing package has templates for producing A5 booklets and will ensure that each publication has the same look and feel. When the document is printed the correct amount of space for staples and folding will be in place. The production of the newsletter will be easier in desktop publishing because text and graphics are placed in frames. In word processing things move if you change other things - this can change the look of the whole document. Desktop publishing packages also have guides so that you can position frames accurately (clip to guide) and you can also layer frames so that text can be placed over a graphic easily to provide a caption.

2. The village shop has its own website. Describe three benefits of the village shop using a website. **(4)**

This is a key benefit that is extended upon by describing the customer base.

An Internet presence could provide opportunities for Internet shopping and therefore increase business.

This is about community relations – it is good for the community and for the business.

The Internet provides any retail outlet with an increased customer base that is potentially worldwide as anyone with access to the Internet is likely to be able to access it. It could mean that the shop is able to accept Internet orders and thus increase the hours of business and the turnover. Visitors looking to find out about the village can see the range of facilities available, and the shop site can provide access to other sites of interest locally - this could encourage the browser to become an actual visitor.

3. Describe how presentation software could be used to present details to the parish council about the distribution figures of the village newsletter. **(4)**

The use of graphics is good – it gets the message across.

Relevant graphs can be imported into the presentation to support the message that the parish council needs to hear about the newsletter. This could be supplemented by explanatory text. Animation effects can be added to provide emphasis as the presentation is being delivered, while speaker notes can be added to enable the presenter to make sure that all the key points are delivered. In order to help the parish council make decisions or to think more about the key messages, a handout of the slides could be produced.

4. What advantages are there in using HTML to develop web pages? **(4)**

The key focus here is on what HTML is.

The focus here is on the efficiency of using HTML.

HTML is a mark-up language specifically designed for the creation of web pages. It enables developers to focus on content and layout and when cascading style sheets are used, formatting conventions can be managed efficiently. Pages produced using HTML directly require less coding than pages developed using web authoring software, and much less than pages developed in word processing and desktop publishing software.

Practice examination questions

1 Word processing software can be used to perform a wide variety of tasks. Describe a task that you have completed using word processing software and explain how you used three elements of functionality to complete the task effectively. **(4)**

_____

_____

_____

_____

_____

_____

2 Many organisations have their own websites. Explain the following web authoring terms and give suitable examples in each case.

(a) hyperlinks **(2)**

_____

_____

_____

(b) frames **(2)**

_____

_____

_____

3 A master slide is used to ensure that a presentation has a consistent layout. Identify and explain two other benefits of using a master slide. **(6)**

_____

_____

_____

_____

_____

_____

_____

_____

8 Designing computer based systems for people

The following topics are covered in this chapter:

- **People and ICT systems**
- **Different types of user interface**
- **What ICT can provide**

8.1 People and ICT systems

LEARNING SUMMARY

After studying this section you should be able to:

- identify factors that need to be considered when designing a computer system
- describe the impact that making incorrect choices may have on people
- explain the advantages and disadvantages of choices of software and hardware

Human interaction with ICT systems

AQA **INFO 2**
OCR **G063**
WJEC **IT1**
CCEA **A2 1**

There are many different ways in which humans interact with computers.

> **KEY POINT**
>
> **Human–computer interaction** (HCI) is the study of interaction between people (users) and computers. This includes both software and hardware.

Components of an ICT system

In diagrammatical form every computer system consists of the following three main components:

INPUT → PROCESS → OUPUT

People are involved in each of these areas: they are involved in the overall design of the system, in setting up procedures, entering the data, and using the software and hardware to produce information for a purpose.

Design of the system

The following questions should be considered when designing a computer based system:

- What is the system required to do?
- Who will use the system (operator/user)?
- What output is expected? (i.e. What do you want from it?)
- Who will benefit from the output? (For example, management reports and/or sales predictions)
- What inputs need to be available in order for the output to be produced?
- How will this data be entered?
- What processes are required?

The above questions will help to identify what type of system is needed. This forms the basis of systems analysis.

End-user requirements

It is important to identify the requirements of the end-user. The design should result in a computer system that is easy, quick and productive for people to use.

Example

Mobile phones are used by most people, but individually we have certain preferences.

Jill wants to purchase a new mobile phone. She is in her late fifties, with good mobility but failing eyesight.

When matching a system with the end-user, thought must be given to:

- Characteristics/requirements of the end-user
- What can be incorporated into the design?
- Why should it be incorporated?
- Consideration of target group
- Consideration of options available
- Matching target group to options
- People and their fears and perceptions

In this instance, the end-user is a lady with failing eyesight so it may be helpful to incorporate design features such as large size of text on both the key pad and screen. It would also help to have a larger screen. A voice activated interface facility may also be included.

Consideration may need to be given to the potential decline in dexterity, such as arthritis. Big buttons could be a suitable option to enable the end-user to select and press more easily.

If Jill is a new user, then an interface that provides a limited number of options (i.e. only the ones that Jill might use and need) would be suitable as it is less confusing and easier to use.

Modern systems and their impact on people

As ICT systems develop, they become more dependent on other ICT systems, which may be integrated, web-based and/or networked. The knock-on effect is that the software and systems used are becoming more and more complex. It is important to:

- identify what skills are necessary to operate and use the ICT system
- carry out a skills audit to identify if the required skills already exist in the business
- consider buying in these 'skills' from outside the organisation
- consider how existing staff might benefit from training.

This may involve sizable investment for most organisations. However, if sufficient consideration and investment is not made at the design stage, it will likely result in costly systems being under utilised.

People have fears and preconceived ideas about what the solution might mean to them. In some cases where a new computer system is being installed, people may fear for their jobs as they may think that the computer can do more than it is actually programmed to do. People may fear that they will not be able to use the new system and feel frustrated and intimidated. It is important to address all these issues and make training available for all users so that they can gain confidence and trust in the impending system.

Designing ICT systems

AQA	INFO 2
OCR	G063
WJEC	IT1
CCEA	A2 1

Determining system requirements

The following factors should be considered when determining system requirements:

Consideration	Explanation
System makeup	In selecting a system to meet the user's needs, it is usual to consider the **off-the-shelf** business software applications that are available, such as databases or accounts that are used to keep records and produce management reports.
	The choice of Operating Software (Operating System (OS)) is likely to depend on the **budget** allowance, as well as its ability to run the chosen applications software.
	The choice of software will impact on the type and quality of processor as it will determine the minimum and recommended specification of hardware requirements.
Compatibility and need for integration	Thought must be given to existing systems, and how a new system may integrate with them.
	The need for integration will depend on whether the 'new' system is entirely new or an upgrade to an existing system.

Consideration	Explanation
Speed and processing capability	Optimum performance requires optimum processing power. The budget allowance will have an impact on the system used, and therefore the overall performance. The hardware should consist of a reliable and robust **motherboard**, good sized **RAM**, quality high-powered **processor** and **video card**.
Accessibility	Accessibility and ease of use issues must be given consideration. The importance of a friendly **Graphical User Interface** (GUI) is paramount in the design of modern computer systems for people.
Storage	The cost of **hard disks** and **flash memory** is reducing as the demand for higher capacity increases. The greater demand is due to the increase in use of digital libraries for photographs, video and music. Consideration must be given to the need for regular **backups** and the capacity to hold **generations** of files.
Maintenance	A good system should be reliable and easy to maintain. A maintenance contract and maintenance support may be included in the purchase of a hardware or software system. **In-house training** may also be conducted so that existing staff can feel comfortable in locating and treating the cause of a problem when one occurs.
Sustainability	Consideration for the environment should be part and parcel of any system design, for example using components with low emissions, safe disposal of toxic materials, refillable ink cartridges and, where possible, encouraging electronic dissemination of materials instead of printed.

Other factors to consider

A number of other factors must also be considered before a new computer system can be assembled. These include:

- Cost of hardware and software
- Time for implementation and delivery

Choosing appropriate software

AQA **INFO 2**
OCR **G063**
WJEC **IT1**
CCEA **A2 1**

In determining what software to purchase, consideration must be given to what is already available and the requirements of the end-user. The choices of software are:

- **off-the-shelf software**
- **tailored software**
- **bespoke software**

Software solution	Advantages	Disadvantages
An off-the-shelf solution is one that has been developed as a complete package to suit many organisations.	• Readily available. • Tried and tested. • Usually designed to link with other software systems.	• Will require software licence - which may be expensive. • May not do everything in the way that is required.
A tailored solution is developed using software that already exists, and modifying or customising it to meet the functional needs of an organisation.	• Can be easier to use to meet the specific needs of the business.	• May take time to develop. • Requires expertise in software development, therefore it may be expensive.
A bespoke solution is created to suit specific requirements for the business. It consists of designing and writing the program or suite of programs from scratch.	• Will produce outputs to match exactly what the business needs.	• Will take time to develop and test. • Expensive.

8.2 Different types of user interface

LEARNING SUMMARY

After studying this section you should be able to:

- identify different types of user interfaces
- describe where these types of user interfaces are best suited
- explain the advantages and disadvantages of various user interfaces

Types of user interfaces

AQA **INFO 2**
OCR **G063**
WJEC **IT1, IT3**
CCEA **A2 1**

What is a user interface?

> **KEY POINT**
>
> A user interface is the part of a system that allows the computer and a human operator to communicate with each other.

User interfaces exist for various systems, and provide a means of:
- **input** – to allow the user to access a system
- **output** – to allow the system to show the effects of the user's entry (it has reacted to what was entered).

For more information on user interfaces see pages 54–55.

Operating Systems connect with the user via either **commands** entered directly via a keyboard (**command line interface** – or **CLI**), by images (**graphical user interface** – **GUI**) or by menus.

CLI is the oldest form of user interface used in Operating Systems such as UNIX and MS-DOS® (Microsoft Disk Operating System).

A GUI creates a user friendly media rich environment for users to work in and uses a combination of moveable and resizable windows, icons and point and click mouse control.

GUI is based on **WIMP** (**W**indows, **I**cons, **M**enus and **P**ointers).

These are now the standard interface for modern Operating Systems. Some have voice recognition which allows the Operating System to respond to voice commands. In addition, **narrator** software can be used to relay messages and describe what is on screen.

'Menu driven' is a term used to describe software that is operated using a menu to select and activate the commands.

Advantages and disadvantages of user interfaces

Each of the main types of user interface has both advantages and disadvantages, and these need to be carefully considered when designing systems to meet a specific client's needs.

	Types of Interface		
	Command line	**Graphical user**	**Menu driven**
Advantages	• Uses little memory • Can be quick to operate when you know the commands • Uses little processing power	• Easy to use • Looks attractive • Easy to configure	• Easy to use
Disadvantages	• Difficult to use (a user needs to learn and remember lots of commands) • Different software will use different commands	• Uses a lot of RAM • Uses a lot of disk space • Can slow the computer down	• Slow and cumbersome (often having to find out what is behind the menu structure)

Examples of user interfaces

There are many ways in which users can interact with the interface of an IT system. These include:

- Graphical user interface (GUI) – such as Microsoft Windows®
- Graphics pads/Graphics tablets – these allow users to hand draw images and graphics as though they were using a pencil and paper
- POS systems (point of sales) – such as sales terminals at retail outlets
- Game playing devices – which use joysticks, games pads, buttons and levers for interactive gaming
- Touch sensitive screens – commonly used in mobile technology such as mobile phones, PDAs and iPads®; and also used for public information systems in locations such as train stations and libraries
- Biometric devices – such as iris recognition, fingerprints and hand prints
- Command line – such as MS-DOS® and other Operating Systems (although these have now largely been superseded by GUI).

> Note that graphic pads, POS systems, game playing devices, touch sensitive screens and biometric devices all use some form of graphical user interface.

Designing user interfaces

AQA **INFO 2**
OCR **G063**
WJEC **IT1, IT3**
CCEA **A2 1**

The design of a user interface should be as simple as possible. When a screen or piece of paper is overcrowded with information, has a mixture of font sizes and styles, uses garish colours, or complex language, it is difficult to read and understand.

When designing a user interface that is screen-based, consideration must be given to all types of users and how the information is to be accessed. Humans are attracted by colour and style so it is important to include some of these features in order to grab their attention. However, humans are more inclined to use an interface that they are comfortable with, without feeling blinded by the use of too much colour and flashing icons. The screen design should contain language that the user can easily understand, with controls such as **hot-spots** or **hyperlinks** that are easy to see so as to make using the interface straightforward.

Consideration should also be given to the methods of dialogue to include voice recognition, synthesisers, audio, visual, etc.

If another system is going to use the same software, it should have similar menu options and icons and these should be positioned on the screen in a similar way so that new users can identify them easily.

Human senses and perception

People use their senses to understand what they experience. These senses involve mostly the visual (colour, shape, movement, space) and the auditory (noise, beeps, music, voice) perception.

The design of the system should use colour and sound to help users navigate, but these should be chosen carefully. The sound should be user controlled to allow it to be turned down or off if needed.

The design should take into consideration that human memory is relatively short therefore options should be clearly visible in the form of icons or menus that are easy to find.

The system should include help in the form of a user manual with instructions on how it can be used and, where possible, have online help facilities (either on screen, as part of the software or available on the Internet). This will enable the user to fault find, as well as to obtain information on how to perform various tasks.

Model Human Processor

The **Model Human Processor** (**MHP**) was developed by Card, Moran and Newell as a way of comparing someone who uses a computer with the computer itself, and is used as an aid in the design of more effective user interfaces.

In essence, the MHP draws an analogy between the input, processing, storage and output of a computer system with the cognitive, perceptual, motor and memory activities of someone who uses the computer.

The MHP model is based on the fact that:
- human users interface with the world by receiving information through their eyes and ears; in a similar way to which data is input into a computer

- human users store different types of information in different parts of their brain (e.g. one area of the brain is used for visual images while another area is used for auditory images, at the same time different areas of the brain are used for short and long-term memory); in a similar way to which a computer uses internal RAM and external hard drives
- human users speak and/or take action after considering the information they have acquired; in a similar way to which a computer generates information and output based on data it has processed.

Examples of how the MHP can be used in the context of designing computer user interfaces include:

- the logical sequencing of inputs to help the user keep track of their actions
- the use of audible prompts (e.g. beeps) to inform the user that they have made an error and that they need to do something before progressing further
- the use of a flashing cursor to show exactly where data needs to be input.

PROGRESS CHECK

1 The user interface designer should take into consideration that humans can only cope with a certain amount of information at any one time. Give three examples of how this could influence the interface design.

1. Any three suitable answers, e.g. Use simple language; use menus that are easy to follow; have an uncluttered screen; gentle use of colour; clear format and style of design.

8.3 What ICT can provide

<table>
<tr><td>LEARNING SUMMARY</td><td>After studying this section you should be able to:

• understand how ICT systems can be used to help meet the needs of users
• describe the different types of processing and where they are best suited
• explain the advantages and disadvantages of using different processing systems</td></tr>
</table>

Meeting user needs

AQA **INFO 2**
OCR **G061**
WJEC **IT1**
CCEA **AS 1**

It is important when designing a computer system for people that consideration should be made to the many types of computer user that there are and their different needs and requirements. Thought should be given to the accessibility and ease of use of all computer systems.

Consideration	Explanation
Ergonomics	Ergonomics is the study of the design and arrangement of equipment so that people can interact with the equipment in a healthy, comfortable, and efficient manner. Ergonomics is concerned with such factors as the physical design of the keyboard, screen tilts, wrist and foot rests, chair and desk design, etc.
Design of web pages	Use of language, colour, complexity, size of text and graphics, quantity of information in one place. The intended end-user should determine what style and level of language and graphics are used. For example, a child will respond better to colours and objects; if there are too many words, they will not want to explore a learning environment.

Consideration	Explanation
Assistive technologies	Where users have disabilities, assistive technologies may be necessary in the design. The assistive technologies include speech recognition (input), speech synthesis, and sensors that cause a noise (output) to assist those with eyesight impairment. An example of this is on pelican crossings where the beeps are heard when it is safe to cross the road. Robotics can also be used as assistive technologies – such as vacuum cleaners and lawn mowers. Both can be programmed to move in a direction for a distance and then turn and repeat.
Mobile knowledge	Mobile knowledge connects knowledge workers to knowledge systems through portable handheld devices. Whether connecting through telephone networks or across the Internet, having instant connectivity to reference materials, decision systems, or colleagues brings new efficiencies to human performance. There are many palm top devices including mobile digital reading devices and other mobile devices such as graphics pads that use only a touch sensitive screen for input and output.

For more information on assistive technologies see pages 46–48.

Types of data processing software

AQA   **INFO 2**
CCEA   **AS 1**

> **KEY POINT**
>
> Data processing is controlled by the Operating System software within the Central Processing Unit (CPU). There are many different types of data processing software, which are all designed to do a specific job. When designing the data processing software, consideration must be made to speed and cost.

The common types of processing software are **batch**, **interactive/transaction** and **real-time**.

Batch processing is used for non-urgent jobs and usually for large volumes of data, for example employee wages. These are done at the same time every month, often at night and/or weekends so as not to interfere with busy daytime processing.

Interactive processing is where changes are made, usually following a system prompt. For example, a booking system for a cinema or Computer Aided Learning (CAL).

Transaction processing is where an update takes place within the processing – such as on the booking system. This is an example of interactive and transaction processing.

Real-time processing is for systems whose output changes immediately in response to the input. For example, computer controlled mechanisms for heat or other environmental maintenance, such as in-flight navigation systems, weather monitoring, or medical diagnosis.

The following table shows a comparison of each type of processing software.

Processing type	Access	Advantages	Disadvantages	User interface
Batch	Slow	Deals effectively with repetitive tasks. Can be carried out automatically at off-peak times. Less expensive than other types of processing.	A small error can cause major disruption (an error in input can ruin a whole batch or night's work).	Usually a pre-programmed macro requiring little user intervention.
Transaction/ interactive	Fast	Fairly fast (usually responds within a second or two – which is acceptable in the situation).	Must be properly monitored to ensure that more than one transaction does not occur at the same time, which may result in double booking.	Screen (GUI) key pad, joy stick to activate response.
Real-time	Instant	Fast (responds to an input and takes action to avoid collision).	Very expensive.	Screen (GUI) to show status, (e.g. temperature). Key pad or lever (joy stick) or voice activated response mechanism.

PROGRESS CHECK

1. Explain the type of processing that would be suitable for each of the following ICT systems:
   (a) Airline booking system
   (b) Web-based learning
   (c) Gas billing every three months
   (d) Wikipedia enquiry and update

1. **(a)** Interactive processing – there is a limited number of seats available, so immediate update and response is necessary.
   (b) Interactive processing – next question will be chosen based on response to previous question (i.e. responds to the user's needs).
   (c) Batch processing – the process can be carried out overnight, periodically and is non-urgent.
   (d) To find a definition using Wikipedia is an example of interactive processing. To change and update an entry in Wikipedia makes use of transaction processing.

Sample questions and model answers

A question like this is very open as it does not state how many advantages or disadvantages are required. There are six marks available and two different software solutions in the question so the minimum required is one advantage and one disadvantage for each software solution.

The clue indicating how much needs to be written is often given by the amount of space provided on the answer booklet. However, the clue here is also in the question, because when asked to 'describe the factors' it is clear that a more detailed response is required.

It is usual for a question like this to state a particular number of factors (normally two or three). This will give you an indication of the number of marks awarded for each factor. Where there is one mark awarded for each factor, it will be sufficient to just state the factor. However, where more marks are available, it is important to amplify the answer, by adding reasons relating to the context in the question.

1. Discuss the advantages and disadvantages of implementing an ICT solution using bespoke software rather than purchasing off-the-shelf software. **(6)**

Bespoke software is likely to be expensive and the solution will not be immediate - it will likely take time to be written but it will be written to suit the specific requirements of the user. Off-the-shelf software is ready to use straight away. It is tried and tested and is relatively cheap. The off-the-shelf software will hopefully do what is required - but may not be to the exact specification.

2. Human–computer interaction (HCI) can be affected by many factors.
   (a) Describe three physical (General, Computer, Health) factors which may affect HCI. **(6)**
   (b) Describe two psychological factors which may affect HCI. **(6)**

(a) Physical factors to affect HCI could include:
   General - lighting, heating, noise
   Computer - suitable ergonomics such as desk, chair, screen position
   Health - reason for ergonomics, i.e. to reduce the risk of repetitive strain injury (RSI) or skeletal disorder.

(b) Human perception may affect HCI. How users identify, interpret or attach meaning to what they experience through their senses, particularly visual perception, e.g. colours, shapes and movement and auditory perception, e.g. sounds and beeps.

Human memory may also affect HCI. Short-term memory should not be overloaded - humans can only store between 5 and 9 pieces of information in their short-term memory. Options should be clearly visible in the form of menus or icons that are easy to find. Standard interfaces should be used to make it straightforward to use.

3. When designing a user interface, what are the main factors to be considered? **(4)**

You will need to consider who the user is and how the system will be used, what information will be obtained (whether it is visual or audio - or a combination), the frequency of use, what is currently in use, whether it will need to match or complement existing systems and whether it will be in use while mobile or stationary.

Practice examination questions

1 Software packages can include a Graphical User Interface (GUI) or a Command Line Interface (CLI).

Explain how each of the following is used in a typical GUI.

(a) Icons   **(2)**

_____

_____

(b) Menus   **(2)**

_____

_____

(c) Windows   **(2)**

_____

_____

(d) Pointers   **(2)**

_____

_____

2 **(a)** Identify two advantages of using a GUI.   **(2)**

_____

_____

_____

(b) Identify two disadvantages of using a GUI.   **(2)**

_____

_____

_____

_____

9 Network systems and communications

The following topics are covered in this chapter:

- **Data communications**
- **Computer networks**
- **Internet communications**

9.1 Data communications

LEARNING SUMMARY

After studying this section you should be able to:

- understand composition of data
- understand what determines the rate of data transfer

Data composition

AQA **INFO 2**
OCR **G063**
WJEC **IT1**
CCEA **AS 1**

In Chapter 1, data types are covered in detail. As well as knowing about the data types, it is important to know about data files, their sizes and the speed of transfer.

All computers consist of a number of electric circuits. Each circuit can be in one of two states – On or Off. A circuit that is switched on represents the digit 1 and a circuit that is switched off represents the digit 0. This forms the basis of computing, which depends on the binary (base 2) system (0 or 1) for all forms of data storage and communication.

The capacity of a system to store data is referred to in bytes and is measured in multiples of approximately 1000.

> 1 single character (letter, number or symbol on a keyboard) can be stored as 1 byte – which is a very small unit.

Term	Approximate size/description	Exact size
Bit	A binary digit (*stored as either 0 or 1*)	1 bit
Byte	(*also referred to as a bit pattern*)	8 bits
Kilobyte	1 KB = 1000 bytes	1024 bytes
Megabyte	1 MB = 1 000 000 (1 million) bytes	1024 kilobytes
Gigabyte	1 GB = 1 000 000 000 (1 billion) bytes	1024 megabytes
Terabyte	1 TB = 1 000 000 000 000 (1 trillion) bytes	1024 gigabytes

Speed of data transfer

AQA	**INFO 2**
OCR	**G063**
WJEC	**IT1, IT3**
CCEA	**AS 1, A2 1**

Bandwidth is a word used to describe the rate of data transfer, throughput, or bit rate. It is usually measured in bits per second (bps).

The speed of data transfer depends on the following:

- **Volume** – the more people using the system, the slower the rate of transfer. For example, Internet access is slower in the UK in the afternoon, as that is when the USA is waking up and logging on at the start of their day.
- **Modem speed** – most modems work at speeds of 28 Kbps or 56 Kbps. (The higher the number, the faster the transfer speed.) The speed will be faster when both the sending and receiving modems work at the optimum speeds available.
- The **telephone line** – **digital lines** such as **ISDN** and **ADSL** speed up the data transfer between the **ISP** (Internet service provider) and the user. The data transfer through a normal phone network is normally about 56 Kbs (56 000 bps).

> For definitions of these terms see pages 199 and 202.

At the start of the Internet revolution in the mid 1990s, everyone used 'dial-up Internet' – as that was all that was available. The acceptable data transfer rate was 9.6 Kbps, and later 14.4 Kbps. When downloading any sizable file, often there was time to have a cup of tea (in the local tea rooms a bus ride away) and still be back in time to watch the download bar slowly moving from left to right. Because of this 'slow' experience, people referred to their Internet usage by how long it took to download files. Internet lines were therefore being measured in terms of speed.

This is, technically, not quite accurate. A dial-up line of 9.6 Kbps would be described as being 'slow' while a 100 Mbps broadband line would be described as being 'fast'. This comparison is actually referring to the maximum amount of data (Kilobytes or Megabytes) that can move through the line in one second. So it is really referring to the capacity or 'bandwidth' of the line. However, since having a higher capacity means you are able to get more data through in the same time period, the end result is that it takes less time to download files. From the human perspective, it is a faster experience; therefore the words 'speed' and 'bandwidth' are used interchangeably in the Internet world.

The importance of bandwidth depends on the intended use. It is particularly important to have a high bandwidth when accessing content that is being delivered in real time. Otherwise, image and sound become out of sync and freeze. For example, if the user is taking part in a video conference a high bandwidth is required, so as to avoid breaks in transmission. Whereas if the user is downloading a pre-recorded radio programme, it may take a long time for the download to take place but when they are listening to that programme at a later time, the listening experience will not be affected.

PROGRESS CHECK

1. Why is bandwidth so important to the effective transfer of large quantities of data?

1 Any suitable answer, e.g. The importance depends on the application the user is running, how much data needs to be downloaded and how quickly it needs to be downloaded. Video conferencing will require high bandwidth whereas a user who sends an occasional email will require smaller bandwidth.

9.2 Computer networks

After studying this section you should be able to:

- describe the different types of computer networks
- identify the key features of the hardware for each type of network
- explain the advantages and disadvantages of each type of network
- identify the components of a network system

Types of networks

AQA **INFO 2**
OCR **G061, G063**
WJEC **IT1, IT3**
CCEA **AS 1, A2 1**

A **network** is two or more computers connected together. All computers on a network can communicate with each other. The Internet can also be classed as a network (see pages 200–204).

Local Area Networks

Local Area Networks (**LANs**) are networks seen in most small organisations and schools. A LAN is always in one physical location (office, building or even campus). They consist of:

- Individual workstations (terminals) that allow access to networks, software, hardware and information files.
- A **network file server** – this is a dedicated computer that runs the network software and is responsible for the central storage and management of data files, so that other computers on the same network can access these files. A file server allows users to share information over a network without having to physically transfer files by some external device. A file server may be any Personal Computer (PC) that handles requests for files and sends them over the network. Any computer can be configured to be a file server. In a larger network, a file server might also contain a dedicated **Network-attached Storage Device** (**NASD**) that also serves as a remote storage device. Anyone on the network can store files on the NASD as they would to their own hard disk drive. A file server can be any software program or any mechanism that enables the required processes for file sharing.
- A **print server** – this manages the print requests and makes printer information available to users and network managers. In a large organisation, a print server might be a dedicated computer, managing hundreds of printers. In a small organisation, a print server can often be a specialised plug-in board or small network device that performs the same function as a dedicated print server, but frees up valuable disk space for use on the network.
- **Links** in the form of wire cables, fibre optic cables or radio signals.

Intranets are usually LANs within the same organisation.

> Understanding and explaining the differences between different types of networks are key areas of knowledge that examiners will be looking for.

Wide Area Networks

Wide Area Networks (**WANs**) are used when computers need to be connected together across different sites and even different countries. A WAN is different to a LAN in that it connects different physical locations.

- Like LANs, WANs need servers to operate the network. Users have to connect to the network using either **modems** or **wireless links**. The wireless links such as **microwaves** and **satellites** can be expensive, but are much faster and much more reliable.

You will find more about teleworkers and distance learning in Chapter 13.

- WANs are normally used by large multinational companies, companies that have **teleworkers** and often colleges and universities that support **distance learning**.

The Internet is the largest example of a WAN.

Peer-to-peer and client server networks

Networks can be described as **peer-to-peer** (**P2P**) when each computer has the same status and has permission to communicate with each other and with all peripherals and all recourses connected to the network. Peer-to-peer networks are usually used for home networks. If the users want to share all files and printer use, then peer-to-peer is suitable.

More peer-to-peer is being used across the Internet to allow users to share files between them. This has caused problems about legality. Issues regarding the sharing of copyrighted images, video and music through this unmanaged route have been raised.

Advantages of using peer-to-peer networks include:
- Low operating costs – no server required, reduced set up and maintenance
- Easy to set up – simple network link
- Easy to access.

Disadvantages include:
- Poor security – users are sharing what they have on their computer, so they need to make sure that they are only sharing the files that they want to share and not other confidential information
- Some computers may be slow – depending on amount of access.

Larger networks tend to use **client server networks**. Usually within a client server network there is one more 'powerful' computer that is used as the central computer, which holds all the programs and files. This computer is called the **server** and the other computers connected to it are called **clients**.

Advantages of using client server networks include:
- Security is better
- Data is centralised
- Better control over the quality of data and the frequency and reliability of backups
- Access is faster and more reliable.

Disadvantages include:
- Expensive – both in hardware (with having a server) and software with network Operating Systems (for larger networks it may be necessary to purchase network management software)
- Needs specialist knowledge of networks, to ensure continual connection
- All clients are dependent on the server, so if problems exist with the server, it will affect all clients
- Permission to access certain files and peripherals may be different for users.

Network topologies

AQA **INFO 2**
OCR **G061, G063**
WJEC **IT1, IT3**
CCEA **AS 1, A2 1**

In describing network **topologies**, there is sometimes confusion between the physical and the logical. Whereas the physical topology defines the arrangement of servers, workstations, cabling, scanners, printers, etc. the logical topology defines the way in which data is transmitted around the network. The two main logical networks are **Ethernet** and **token ring**.

Ethernet

In the main, networks transmit data using a packet-switching system. This is where a block of data (a spreadsheet file for example) is split into manageable chunks (packets). These packets are then assigned a destination address, a sender's address, a checking method (to check if errors have occurred – e.g. a check sum), and coding to include instructions on how to reconstruct the original file (as the order may be mixed up). Ethernet is based on a token called **Carrier Sense Multiple Access/Collision Detection** (**CSMA/CD**). It basically allows computers in the network to send the packets across the same channels. If more than one computer sends a packet of data at the same time, a collision will occur. This is monitored and acknowledged by the computers in the network. A random time period will then elapse before these computers resend their data packets. This time period is not noticeable as it is usually nanoseconds (although if there is a lot of traffic using the network at the same time, this will result in the network running slowly).

Token ring

The token ring system also uses packet switching.

Here is a brief overview of how it works:
- Empty information packets are continuously circulated on the ring.
- When a computer has a message to send, it inserts a token into an empty packet and inserts some information and a destination identifier in the packet.
- The packet is then examined by each workstation in turn. If the workstation sees that it is the destination for the message, it copies the message from the packet and changes the token back to the received signal.
- When the packet returns back to the sender, the original workstation can detect that the token has been changed to 'received' status and therefore their message has been copied and received. It then removes the message from the packet.
- The packet then continues to circulate as an 'empty' packet, ready for a workstation to take it when they need to send a message.

A token ring system is a robust system that works well with both twisted pair and fibre optic cabling (see page 203). It is more costly than the Ethernet, more complex in the running and therefore more difficult to locate errors when they occur. The biggest disadvantage of a token ring system (now almost obsolete) is that if the wire breaks it takes down the entire network.

Star network

A **star network** is used when a large number of workstations need to be connected to a central hub. The hub takes a signal that comes from any **node** (services and workstations) and passes it along to all the other nodes in the network. A hub does not perform any type of filtering or routing of the data. It is simply a junction that joins all the different nodes together.

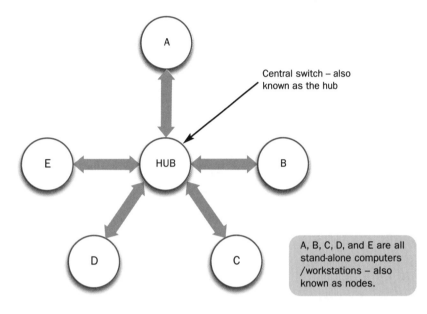

Central switch – also known as the hub

A, B, C, D, and E are all stand-alone computers /workstations – also known as nodes.

Advantages of using a star network	Disadvantages of using a star network
• Each workstation has direct contact with the central computer • Fast response time • Can withstand heavy use and give consistent performance • Reliable • No problems with data collision as each station has its own cable • If one workstation (or cable) has a problem – it is unlikely to affect the rest of the network • Security can be centrally placed in the hub	• When the central computer (hub) has a problem – it affects the whole of the network • More cabling therefore more expense • Restricted by the length of cabling unless extra equipment is used • The speed of the data transfer is dependent on the quality of the central hub/switch

KEY POINT

A star network consists of one central node and several outlying nodes.

Line or bus network

In a **line** or **bus network** a common backbone connects different devices in a single run of cable (similar to Christmas lights). The data is sent to and from the file server along a single line of cable. All the nodes are connected to this single line. If there is a fault in the line it will affect all devices after that point. Each end of a bus network must be terminated with a resistor to keep the signal sent from the node from bouncing back when it reaches the end of the cable.

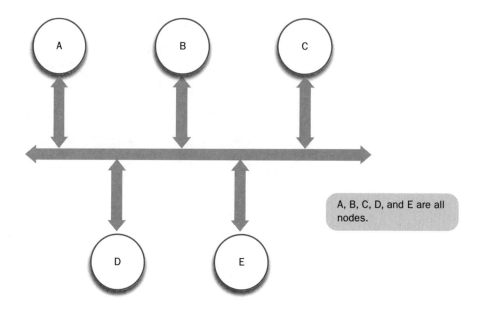

A, B, C, D, and E are all nodes.

Advantages of using a line/bus network	Disadvantages of using a line/bus network
• Each workstation is connected to the central line • Less cabling therefore cheaper • If one workstation (or cable) has a problem – it is unlikely to affect the rest of the network • More devices can be easily added	• When the central cable has a problem – it affects the whole of the network • Very slow as data travels along a central line • Cable failure may be difficult to isolate without specialised equipment • Data travels in either direction therefore there is a risk of data collision

KEY POINT

In a line or bus network data travels along a single line to reach the outlying nodes.

Ring network

A **ring network** is a series of nodes that are connected like a daisy chain. Each node takes a turn sending and receiving information. Ring topologies typically use a **token passing scheme**. In this type of scheme, only one machine can transmit on the network at a time. The machines or computers connected to the ring act as signal boosters or repeaters, which strengthen the signals that travel the network.

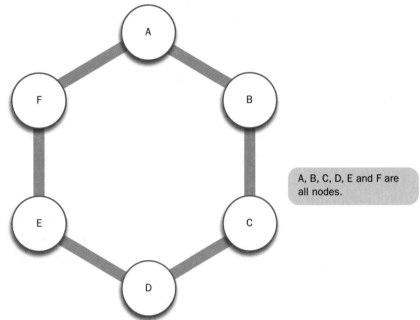

A, B, C, D, E and F are all nodes.

Advantages of using a ring network	Disadvantages of using a ring network
• For a small network – can be cheap • Not dependent on a central computer or server • Easy access • Fast • Data flows in one direction only – so no risk of data collision • Problems can be easy to locate	• Not as reliable as a line or star network • Each node is dependent on each other to make the ring. If there is a problem in one node the whole network is disrupted • Expensive if over long distances as extra amounts of cable are needed • Signal degrades over long distances

KEY POINT

A ring network is connected like a daisy chain.

Hybrid networks

Hybrid networks use a combination of any two or more topologies in such a way that the resulting network does not exhibit one of the standard topologies (e.g. bus, star, ring, etc.). Two common examples of hybrid networks are:
- star bus network
- star ring network

The **star bus network** is probably the most common network topology in use today. Star bus combines elements of the star and bus topologies to create a versatile network environment. Nodes are connected to hubs (creating stars), and the hubs are connected together along a network backbone (like a bus/line network). Stars are sometimes nested within stars.

The **star ring network** consists of two or more star topologies connected using a **Media Access Unit** (MAU) as a centralised hub.

> **KEY POINT**
>
> A Media Access Unit is a device that attaches multiple network stations in a star topology in a token ring network.

Network components

AQA **INFO 2**
OCR **G061, G063**
WJEC **IT1, IT3**
CCEA **AS 1, A2 1**

A basic network consists of a number of computers and the hardware devices such as scanners and printers connected in such a way to allow communication between them. Within any network solution a number of other components are also required to ensure that communication is possible.

Component	Definition
Bridges	A connection between two LANs (must have same protocols). Can create a virtual network which appears as one network though is likely to be several different networks. Bridges use a different OSI layer for addressing to a router.
Data packet	A data packet is the basic unit of data to be communicated across a digital network. A packet is often also called a segment, a block or a frame, depending on the protocol in use. When transmitting data, it is broken down into smaller chunks, which are then reassembled into the original data chunk once they reach their destination.
Ethernet	A network standard of communication using coaxial or twisted pair, widely used in LANs. Most new computers will have Ethernet already inbuilt. For computers that do not, Ethernet adapters can be added via USB, or by plugging in an Ethernet card.
Gateways	A combination of hardware and software that links two computer systems. By using a gateway with computer systems that are different in terms of make, Operating Systems, etc., the data is converted and passed through into the format required by the other system. It allows two different network types to be connected securely. For example, a gateway on an email system allows different email systems to exchange data.
Hubs	A hub can receive data and broadcast it to all the output ports. A hub does not screen the network traffic unlike a switch.

Component	Definition
IP	Internet Protocol (IP) uses a set of rules to send and receive messages at the Internet address level.
OSI	Open Systems Interconnections – the standard of how data can be transmitted between two end points in a telecommunications network.
Modem	**Mo**dulator **Dem**odulator – a device to modulate a wire line, dial-up, DSL or cable. The original modems worked with dial-up and can be described as a device or program that allows a computer to transmit data across telephone lines. A modem converts the digital to analogue signals in order to send the data and then converts back from analogue to digital at the receiving computer. With DSL and cable, the modulation technique is different. Dial-up uses sound to modulate the line in a single channel whilst DSL and cable use electromagnetic signals over many channels.
Protocols	A set of rules/standards that are used to make sure that transfer of data between devices is possible. Protocols are often described in an industry or international standard. On the Internet, there are the TCP and IP protocols. Other protocols exist such as File Transfer Protocol (FTP) and Hypertext Control Protocol (HTTP); each has their own set of rules. The protocol determines the format of the data packets, in terms of content to include a header and the type of error checking to be used, the data compression method (if needed), how the receiving device signals when the packet has been received and how the sending device signals the end of the information packet sent.
Repeaters	A device used to link two cable segments. With a loss of signal over distance, a repeater amplifies the signal before passing it on. This allows you to extend the distance of a cable run and the overall length of the network.
Routers	A communications device (either hardware or software) which receives data and forwards it to the correct location via the most appropriate route. Can be a modem as it allows an internal network to connect to the Internet.
Switches	Can be used to connect two LANs together even if they use different protocols. A switch can be referred to as a multi-port bridge. It channels incoming data from multiple ports to a specific output port that will forward it to the intended destination. Switches can be used to manage the flow of data in the network.

For more information on protocols see pages 38–39.

Component	Definition
TCP	Transmission Control Protocol (TCP) uses a set of rules to exchange messages with other Internet points at the packet level.
TCP/IP	Like other network protocols, TCP/IP is based on layers. Each layer builds upon the layer below it, adding new functionality. The lowest level protocol looks after the sending and receiving of raw data using specific network hardware. At the top are protocols designed specifically for tasks like transferring files and delivering emails. In the middle, the levels deal with things like routing and reliability. The advantage of the layered protocol stack is that if you invest in a new network application or a new hardware, you only need to create a protocol for that application or that hardware.

PROGRESS CHECK

1 Suggest **two** reasons why protocols are important within a network.

1. Any two suitable answers, e.g. to ensure the same language is being spoken and understood by all involved; to allow communication to take place between different devices; to allow signals to be sent across the Internet and enable Internet users to communicate with each other; to allow computers to connect with an ISP; to allow users to send and receive emails.

9.3 Internet communications

LEARNING SUMMARY

After studying this section you should be able to:

- describe how data packets are used in data communications
- identify the key features that determine the speed and quality of transmission
- explain the advantages and disadvantages of different communication technologies

The Internet

AQA **INFO 2**
OCR **G063**
WJEC **IT1, IT3**
CCEA **AS 1**

The Internet is a very large network of computers; it is often described as a network of networks. It works by allowing individuals to connect to each other on a world wide basis. The Internet revolution has had a major impact on human interaction.

The Internet has:

- made communication between people who live long distances apart relatively cheap
- allowed for a richer level of communication over long distances – like the exchange of video images and sound
- enabled large organisations to have effective and timely communication
- given people who live in remote locations and/or those that are house bound through illness or disability the opportunity to connect with the rest of the world and feel part of the wider community

- provided the opportunity for distance learning, as students can have access to a wealth of information from their own home
- allowed a new type of business where sales and business transactions can take place over long distances
- along with mobile technology allowed individuals to be connected while they travel.

Data packets

AQA   **INFO 2**
OCR   **G063**
WJEC **IT3**
CCEA **AS 1**

When surfing the **World Wide Web**, data packets travel from your computer through the vast jungle of interconnected networks (the Internet) to the web server that is hosting the requested content and back through the Internet to your computer. Throughout this vast journey there are many different routes for the data to take to reach its destination and return. This can be compared to a long road journey, where part of the journey may be on narrow country lanes where other cars are travelling in the same lane and traffic is moving slowly, and part of the journey may be on motorways where the traffic is moving more quickly. In the same way, data will travel on congested pathways where it will take a longer time to get through, but once through the congested part, it may well reach a part of its journey when a faster speed is attainable.

The number that is on the broadband plan (i.e. 512 Kbps, 100 Mbps, etc.) cannot refer to the whole network, as it will not be able to show what the bandwidth is on other parts of the journey. That number will refer only to the part connected to the receiving end. It is important to know the end-to-end rate of data transmission, i.e. the amount of data that actually gets transmitted from the computer, through the Internet to the web server, and back in a single unit of time. This is known as **throughput**. When files are downloaded it is possible to see a bar that shows the progress of the download and a number that shows the rate of that download. Throughput is never a constant – it fluctuates within the same download session.

Communication technologies

AQA   **INFO 2**
CCEA **AS 1**

There are many different ways in which IT devices can communicate with each other. Most users currently connect to the Internet via use of **broadband** technology. However, broadband is simply any telecommunications signal that has a greater bandwidth than standard telephone lines (see page 191). Although broadband tends to be measured in terms of the maximum bandwidth available, the speed of data transfer varies considerably depending upon the number of users trying to access the system at the same time.

Technology	Explanation
Dial-up	This method uses the standard telephone line with a modem. The modem converts the analogue signals into digital signals to be processed by the computer. The main disadvantage is the slow transmission and the inability to use the telephone for voice calls while the Internet is in use.
Integrated Services Digital Network (ISDN)	ISDN digital telephone lines facilitate: <ul><li>video phones</li><li>use of a keypad to select options and enter data</li><li>conference calls</li><li>use of computers as automated answering machines. This allows an increase in the number of messages. Can use tones to deliver messages to different numbers (recipients), allow choice of menu options and personalised messages, etc. Can be used to receive and send faxes, allow multiple Internet connections and email by phone</li><li>greater bandwidth and faster transmission of data</li><li>use of ring tones to identify individual callers</li><li>screen display to show caller identification</li></ul>
Digital Subscriber Line (DSL)	Common standard for broadband. This system uses existing telephone lines but sends and receives all data in digital format. It is much faster than dial-up, and can be used simultaneously with telephone communications. The dedicated line means that data transmission is more secure. A disadvantage is that if the distance between the user and the telecom provider is great, the connection quality will not be very good (the further away the weaker the connection). This means that this type of connection will not work very well in remote locations.
Asymmetric Digital Subscriber Line (ADSL)	Works by splitting the functions of a phone line into separate channels to cope with both voice transmission and data transmission. ADSLs come in different speed specifications and are a much faster option to the original dial-up facility that was available at the start of the Internet revolution. The majority of ASDL connections are used for downloading data from the Internet. The downstream bandwidth is much greater than the upstream bandwidth. This explains why it takes much longer to upload files than it does to download them. Designed for users who tend to download more data than they upload – bandwidth is allocated on this basis, so as to maximise the download speed. Other lines are available – mainly VDSL – (Very High Speed DSL) and SDSL – (Symmetric DSL).
Cable	Coaxial cable is used to connect telecommunication devices which use high frequency broadband connections. Types of coaxial cable include thin Ethernet (used for shorter distances) and thick Ethernet (used for longer distances). These are difficult and expensive to install.

Technology	Explanation
UTP and STP	Unshielded Twisted Pair (USP) has superseded the coaxial cable in the development of networks. Both UTP and Shielded Twisted Pair (STP) use copper wire, which is an excellent conductor and easy to work with. Crosstalk can occur between two wires, which run in parallel. Both UTP and STP cables have twisted cables in order to cancel out this interference. STP is more expensive as it has a metallic-coated plastic foil to remove the chance of electromagnetic interference. UTP is prone to interference from stray signals. STP is expensive.
Optical fibre	Uses light transmission, generating light pulses which travel down the fibre (thin threads of glass). Photodiodes detect the light pulses at the other end. Optical fibres are capable of high transmission rates and broadband applications such as video, music and voice. They are expensive to install and signal deformation occurs over long distances.
Radio	Digital signals can be converted into radio waves, which can be reflected, absorbed or refracted as they travel through different materials. An antenna is needed to amplify the signal when it reaches the destination. Radio signals become weaker over distance and may be intercepted making security an issue.
Microwave	Modern microwave-based networks are becoming more popular. They can offer high bandwidth at a relatively low cost.
Satellite	Satellites orbit the earth and provide high bandwidth solutions for data transmission across countries. They are suitable for high volumes. Satellite links are cheaper today and are being used more and more by businesses due to their higher bandwidth and their ability to cope with the growth of data traffic. New developments are looking at in-flight broadband connections for travellers.
Bluetooth®	Bluetooth® is not a full scale wireless Ethernet networking standard. Instead it was developed as a specialised wireless technology for short distances. Its ideal use is with printers, palmtops, mobile phones, PDAs and other external devices. Bluetooth® requires little power and no base station so it is used in portable, battery operated devices.
GPRS	General Packet Radio Services (GPRS) is a packet-based wireless communications service that provides continuous connection for mobile phone and computer users. It allows portable (handheld) devices to use multimedia websites, video-conferencing and similar applications as well as notebook and notepad computers. GPRS is based on **Global System for Mobile** (**GSM**) communication and works alongside existing circuit switched services such as **Short Message Service** (**SMS**) (see page 204) and cellular phone connections. GPRS complements Bluetooth® technologies.

Technology	Explanation
SMS	Short Message Service (SMS) uses standardised communications protocols to allow short text messages between fixed line or mobile phone devices. It was seen as a non-intrusive method of phone call/messaging, to allow the receiver to respond at a time to suit. It is now the most widely used application in the world. Most SMS are mobile to mobile text messages. SMS gateway providers facilitate SMS traffic between businesses and mobile phone users, including all different uses of SMS and its content delivery. Entertainment services also use SMS, such as TV voting.
WiFi	WiFi is a trademark for the WiFi Alliance that identify certified products that belong to a class of wireless local area network (WLAN) devices based on the IEEE standards.
WPAN	Wireless Personal Area Network (WPAN) is a network for connecting an individual's personal devices.
ZigBee®	ZigBee® is ideal for home, business, and industrial automation where control devices and sensors are commonly used. Such devices operate at low power levels, thus helping to give a long battery life. Applications well suited to ZigBee® include heating, ventilation, and air conditioning (HVAC), lighting systems, security, fire sensing, and the detection and notification of unusual occurrences. ZigBee® is compatible with most network topologies including peer-to-peer and star and can handle up to 255 devices in a single WPAN.

PROGRESS CHECK

1. What does ADSL stand for?
2. Why is DSL not viable in remote locations?
3. What is throughput?

1. Asymmetric Digital Subscriber Line
2. The further away the user is from the telecom provider, the poorer the quality of the connection.
3. The amount of data that gets transmitted from the computer, through the Internet to the web server and back in a single unit of time.

Sample questions and model answers

When answering this question it is important to be clear what are the advantages for each method and what are the disadvantages for each method. This may be best shown in columns. The examiner must be certain that you know the differences for each method otherwise no marks will be awarded.

1. There are many ways in which ICT is used in communication. Give at least one advantage and one disadvantage of each of the following methods of electronic communication: Email, Web pages, Word processing, Collaborative software. **(8)**

Email	Advantage: Quick, efficient, quietly invasive (they can be opened and read at a time to suit)
	Disadvantage: Can be seen as obtrusive as unsolicited Spam often appears in the inbox
Web pages	Advantage: Interesting, Interactive
	Disadvantage: Needs to be updated regularly
Word processing	Advantage: Permanent record, easy editing
	Disadvantage: Word processing skills required by the user
Collaborative software	Advantage: Saves travel as meetings can be carried out effectively over long distances
	Disadvantage: Lacking in physical contact

2. **(a)** STP and UTP are susceptible to interference.

    (i) State what is meant by STP and UTP. **(2)**

    (ii) Explain how each is affected by interference. **(2)**

    (ii) Explain how STP is designed to minimise interference. **(2)**

    (b) Describe the main features of fibre optic cable. **(3)**

    (a) (i) STP (Shielded Twisted Pair), UTP (Unshielded Twisted Pair)

       (ii) Interference can occur between two wires, which run in parallel, electromagnetic interference from electric circuits.

       (iii) Both UTP and STP cables have twisted cables in order to cancel out this interference. STP is more expensive as it has a metallic-coated plastic foil to remove the chance of electromagnetic interference.

    (b) Fibre optic cable consists of a bundle of glass filaments / threads, each of which can transmit a message in digital form. The glass threads are covered in an outer jacket / cladding / buffer material / sheath.

When asked to describe differences between items it is clearer if you write about each difference in sequence (as shown here) rather than grouping them together for each item.

3. Describe the main differences between a WAN and a LAN. **(3)**

    A LAN generally uses physical connections whereas a WAN uses a variety of connection types such as cable, satellite or modem to suit the transmission required.

    A LAN is usually limited to a single site whereas a WAN often consists of several networks over many sites.

    A LAN is normally private to that company whereas a WAN (e.g. the Internet) is open.

Practice examination questions

1 The four computers in a small office are linked as a network.

(a) Describe two disadvantages of networking these computers. **(2)**

_____

_____

_____

(b) Describe two advantages of networking these computers. **(2)**

_____

_____

_____

2 A company is planning to implement a new network system. They are looking at topologies including star, ring and bus network.

Describe each of the following network topologies.

(a) Ring **(3)**

_____

_____

_____

_____

(b) Star **(3)**

_____

_____

_____

_____

(c) Bus **(3)**

_____

_____

_____

_____

10 Implementing ICT systems

The following topics are covered in this chapter:

- **The importance of ICT policies**
- **Organisational systems and information**
- **Development and implementation of an ICT solution**

10.1 The importance of ICT policies

LEARNING SUMMARY

After studying this section you should be able to:

- understand company legislation and policies
- know what laws are in place to protect the individual and the organisation
- understand the measures taken to keep information secure

Legislation

AQA **INFO 2, INFO 3**
OCR **G061**
WJEC **IT3**
CCEA **AS 1, A2 1**

For more information on legislation see pages 268–269.

The growth of computing technologies over the past few decades means that computers are increasingly being used to store and process important data. It has become increasingly easy to transfer data electronically so a number of Acts of Law have been passed to control computer use. Many of these Acts are specific to information and how it is used by organisations. They protect individuals and organisations by setting out guidelines that must be adhered to. Failure to follow these guidelines can lead to prosecution and even imprisonment, as it will be a criminal offence.

Data Protection Act (1998)

Both individuals and organisations that obtain and hold personal information about other individuals must register with the Information Commissioner's Office and let them know that they are holding such details and pay an annual fee. The holder of the information must make sure that the information follows the eight principles set out for personal data.

The eight principles (as set out by the British Computer Society) require personal data to be:
- processed fairly and lawfully
- obtained for and used only for specific and lawful purposes
- relevant, adequate and not excessive
- accurate and up-to-date (if necessary)
- only kept as long as needed
- held in accordance with the rights of the person to whom the data refers
- kept securely
- only transferred to countries that offer adequate data protection.

Freedom of Information Act (2000)

The Freedom of Information Act allows an individual to approach the organisation that is holding their personal details and request information about what exactly is being held, why it is being held and for how long. There is a set of guidelines available when requesting such information. These include:

- Requests should be written.
- The request should be processed within 20 days.
- The holder should respond in full and inform the requester if the information cannot be made available and why.
- The requester can appeal the decision.

The guidelines cover most occasions where a request is made. However, the Freedom of Information Act cannot authorise any release of information which is:

- in breach of National security
- commercially secret
- used in court
- over 50 years old.

Copyright, Design and Patent Act (1989)

The Copyright, Design and Patent Act makes it illegal to copy a file without permission from the owner or copyright holder. The Act covers:

- using software without a licence
- downloading images, text or sound from the Internet and not acknowledging their origin when you use them, or using them without the owner's permission
- copying business software and/or games from one computer and using it on another, without permission or licence.

There are some exceptions to the Copyright, Design and Patent Act. These include:

Open Source – software, which is freely available and does not require a licence. Users can make changes to the source code and adapt it to suit their needs. An example of an Open Source Operating System is Linux; an example of Open Source applications software is OpenOffice.

Freeware – copyrighted software, which is often offered free to non-commercial users (for example, students). This is usually a cut-down version, in the hope that the user will eventually buy the full product.

Shareware – usually offered for a period of time to allow an evaluation of the product on a 'try before you buy' basis.

Computer Misuse Act (1990)

The Computer Misuse Act was brought about to cope with the problems of **computer hacking** and viruses.

> **KEY POINT**
>
> Computer hacking is gaining access to computer systems illegally, with the intention to steal or do some malicious damage to the content.

This legislation serves to protect against attacks such as **Denial of Service**. This attack involves disabling ports or intervening in the transport of data across a network to dramatically increase the bulk of traffic and slow down speed of access or, indeed, prevent access completely.

The Computer Misuse Act makes the following three things illegal:

- Unauthorised access to computer material (e.g. hacking). This includes accessing parts of a network that you are not permitted to and also illegal copying of software programs.
- Unauthorised modification or changing of computer files – including deleting files and planting viruses.
- Unauthorised access to information with intent to commit offences like fraud and blackmail.

Terrorism Act (2000)

The Terrorism Act guards against using a computer to intimidate individuals and groups, or hacking into a website for political gain.

Organisational policies

AQA **INFO 2, INFO 3**
WJEC **IT1, IT3**
CCEA **AS 1, A2 1**

As well as these externally set conditions, many organisations set their own internal codes of conduct or organisational policies which they impose on their staff. If an employee is in breach of the terms in the **code of conduct**, their employer may justifiably terminate their contract.

The organisational policies determine what is expected by that organisation and therefore will be different from those of another organisation. They usually relate to **ethical issues** such as the general behaviour that is expected from employees.

Organisational policies will specify the action required to deal with problems that occur. **Security issues** are vital and must be considered as a priority.

Security policies

As ICT technologies continually evolve, security procedures must also be updated regularly. This is usually done at senior management level to safeguard the whole organisation at a responsible level. It may also be done using outside agencies such as ICT security consultants and the police security services. As this is a crucial aspect in any organisation, it is important that security audits are carried out on procedures, equipment, and logical operations to identify any irritations, loopholes and potential threats.

Employees are considered a high risk as far as security of information is concerned. In the **conditions of employment**, it would be expected to have guidelines on the following:

- Rights and privileges as user/supervisor dependent on role and responsibilities.
- Advice on password use – to include strength, privacy, recommended time in which it should be changed.
- Storage space within own working area.
- Who can have access to other storage areas.
- What software to use for each process.
- Where and how to obtain/request upgrades and new software.
- Illegal and unauthorised software.

Organisational expectations of employees

An employee's contract of employment will contain or have reference to:

1. Communications policy

A communications policy is often included as part of the contract of employment. It will detail the rights and permissions granted as part of the employee's responsibility within their job role when interacting with the organisation's ICT systems.

The purpose of this policy is to improve the security of all ICT systems within the organisation. It may contain advice and guidance on the individual's responsibility for:

- Internet use
- Email use
- Software installation
- Reporting of security breaches
- Reporting of system and software errors
- Hardware purchases

As part of this policy, management may set up monitoring and surveillance policies, which may observe activities and keep electronic logs of usage.

2. Internet and email usage

There is an expectation within most organisations that employees will use the Internet and email for only business purposes. These will include external messages to suppliers and customers, as well as internal messages to work colleagues concerning business-related affairs. However, some organisations will allow some personal use during working hours. This is usually monitored carefully to ensure that the employees are also doing their allocated work.

The following table shows what organisational email and Internet usage policies will advise on.

Email usage policies	Internet usage policies
<ul><li>Use acceptable language</li><li>Observe the restrictions to print emails</li><li>Turnaround time for reading and replying to email</li><li>Use of attachments</li><li>Expression of personal views</li><li>Authority to email external clients</li><li>Use of spam, jokes and chain mail</li><li>Opening and checking attachments for viruses</li></ul>	<ul><li>Authorisation of appropriate websites</li><li>Observe the restrictions to printing content</li><li>Personal use in own time (e.g. before 9am or at lunch time)</li><li>Posting of personal views on message boards or organisation's newsgroup</li><li>Use of appropriate and sizable downloads.</li></ul>

3. Procurement

Guidelines for the acquisition of hardware and software must be clear and unambiguous. Employees must be aware of where and who they approach with such requests and if there are favoured suppliers.

4. Allocation of employee duties

As part of overall project development and the security of the project, an important consideration is that of roles and responsibility for each stage. The management must ensure that no one person has one hundred percent control of the project from start to finish. Separation of duties between different employees will facilitate the opportunity to catch malicious, fraudulent and genuine mistakes.

By making sure that employees complete activity logs, this process becomes more transparent.

5. Responsibility of ownership and privacy

Often employees have access to privileged information in their day-to-day tasks, such as medical or financial records of an individual. In order to protect that individual's privacy and ensure repeat custom, it would be common practice for such organisations to ask employees to sign a **non-disclosure agreement**. These agreements ensure that their employees promise not to pass on any information belonging to the organisation (business or individual).

Within the organisation's policies, the onus is placed on the employee to protect the organisation's interests as far as misuse of time and/or resources by any employee. If an employee is witness to inappropriate behaviour, such as a colleague's misuse of the Internet while at work, they have a duty to report this to the organisation. Another example of misuse may be that of hacking into the organisation's computer systems and stealing information (such as customer details), excessive use of personal email and/or inappropriate use of the Internet.

In addition some organisations may dictate that computer screens are positioned so that unauthorised users will not be able to read what is displayed. This will help keep information confidential.

Many **professional bodies** exist to offer businesses advice and guidance on security issues. These bodies include the Association for Computing Machinery (ACM), British Computer Society (BCS), Business Software Alliance (BSA) and Federation Against Software Theft (FAST).

> **PROGRESS CHECK**
>
> 1 What are the two main reasons why data should be kept confidential?
>
> 1. To comply with the Data Protection Act in terms of privacy of information; if the data relates to commercial sensitivity – such as plans for a new product.

10.2 Organisational systems and information

	After studying this section you should be able to:
LEARNING SUMMARY	• understand different information needs within an organisation and how information is required for all internal operations as well as external operations • understand management of information at different levels

Information needs within an organisation

AQA **INFO 3**
OCR **G063**

Within every organisation the need for business information is crucial to its survival. Information is of no use or value unless it is fit for purpose. In Chapter 1, the characteristics of effective information has been explained. These characteristics include: validity; reliability; timeliness; fitness for purpose; accessibility; accuracy; relevance; cost effectiveness.

Information flow

Information flow is the communication between all parties involved in an organisation, both internal (departments) and external (suppliers, banks, the outside world, etc). Effective information flow is essential to enable efficiency in maintaining a stable and current presence. It includes:

- An awareness of what is happening in the world that will impact on current business – to include new developments, competitors, as well as disputes, volcanoes and adverse weather – all of which will impact on the internal operations of the organisation.
- Sending and receiving crucial information between customers and suppliers.
- Information flow between departments, e.g. knowing when goods are ready to be dispatched, where they should be sent, when invoices need to be sent out, etc.
- Informing employees about changes, events, etc.

Most of the information flow through an organisation is formal. The formal flow of information normally involves planning, requires a particular format and is usually documented. However, the informal flow of information, such as email and conversations, also plays an important part in getting the work done.

Internal information

Normal day-to-day business activities generate internal information. The size and nature of the business will determine exactly what form this information takes. The information tends to be generated from specific departments (or functional areas) within the organisation but is often used by more than one other business function. The main functional areas of any business include **finance**, **purchasing**, and **sales**. Other functions do exist and many organisations have different titles for these.

The sales area is often combined with **customer support**. In general, the internal information necessary within a sales area will include: sales targets, product lists, price lists, marketing brochures, customer questionnaires. Their task is to produce sales orders for the sales they have made. These will include customer details, and costs and delivery details, where appropriate. The customer questionnaire will help feed back on which internal areas could be improved. The size of the organisation will determine the information needed and generated. For example, the National Health Service (NHS) does not have a sales department as such. The patients (customers) come to the NHS. Within the NHS the type of information required by this area will include patients' details, appointment times, specialist/doctor details. Whereas, the sales function in a mobile phone retail company will require slightly different information.

The purchasing area is responsible for the ordering of goods and services, such as stationery and office equipment as well as raw materials needed for production purposes. The purchasing department will need to liaise both externally and internally. The internal information will be exchanged between all other functions as they will buy in on behalf of the whole organisation. They will need to get the detail of requirements for purchase, as well as feed back on expected delivery and let finance know what is being purchased and from whom.

The finance area of an organisation deals with the monetary activities, both internal and external. Within the finance area, there are many sub functions or activities. These will include **payroll** and **accountancy**. The payroll will look after the employees' salaries and make sure that the correct pay is allocated to the correct bank accounts at the same time each month as well as pay the National Insurance contributions to the Inland Revenue when required. The accountancy area is responsible for recording the business' activities such as purchase orders, sales invoices, details of creditors and debtors, and pay VAT for the whole organisation.

Both these areas use information that is generated by other departments and will provide information to those departments in return.

Some of the internal flow of information is likely to be in the form of email with attachments and in some cases in the form of an internal organisational messaging system. Most organisations will use integrated software systems, which facilitates the data entry from different departments and uses the information to inform other departments of progress. Many organisations will have an **Intranet**, which is like a website that is managed internally for the use and benefit of all employees. This will contain information and links to organisational policies, company news and important events.

External information

Most organisations interact with external agencies, providing and receiving information as and when required. These external agencies include:

- Government – All businesses are legally required to pass certain information to government departments. This information includes: tax and National Insurance paid by employees, VAT details, business turnover (to account for company tax payable).
- Suppliers – Information such as marketing leaflets, purchase orders, price lists and delivery notes, invoices, statements.
- Banks – Information about loans, overdrafts, banking facilities, statements and advice.
- Customers – Information about delivery notification, promotional materials, details on special offers, magazines, price lists, invoices and letters of invite to launch events. Information from the customer will include order requests, payments, completed customer satisfaction questionnaires, complaints and grievances.

Management systems

AQA	**INFO 3**
OCR	**G063**
WJEC	**IT3**
CCEA	**A2 1**

From an operational perspective, the organisation will need to ensure that all data and information is secure and can be recovered in the event of any mishap. It is also important to realise that it is costly to ensure that data is used for the intended purpose and kept secure at all times. Systems are becoming more complex and staff working with these systems should be suitably trained.

Operational decisions

Operational decisions are based on what needs to be done today and in the immediate future of the organisation. It can be referred to as fire fighting – but these fires should be anticipated and regulations should be put in place for their eventuality. For example, major disruption was caused to the supply of raw materials by the volcanic ash cloud in April 2010. This disruption in the main could not have been foreseen but good planning would mean that sufficient raw materials were already in stock to prevent any such disaster from having a major effect on the production line. This is a man made decision, aided by computer systems that give information about stock in hand and delivery time.

Strategic decisions

Strategic decisions have a longer time frame and require a management team to be planning into the future. These include decisions about expansion, restructuring, relocating, etc. Information is needed for these types of decisions to be made, including estimates, premises costs, e.g. projected heating, lighting, taxes. Budget setting for the purchase of replacement equipment should be part of the organisation's overall strategic plan.

Many organisations use a four-year cycle for updating hardware and applying upgrades to the Operating Systems, and carrying out reviews and upgrades to current application systems. The process that enables this to happen successfully should be drawn up many months before it actually happens. It will involve research being carried out to establish what the latest updates are and will review what is currently in use. Decisions on what updates are to be purchased are made and a suitable schedule drawn up to identify a suitable period for the updates and upgrades to take place. These plans are then communicated to the management and implementation team.

PROGRESS CHECK

1. A heavy and prolonged period of winter snowfall often renders many roads impassable. This means that transport is severely disrupted and many supplies do not get delivered when expected.
   (a) What plans should a production company make to predict any such disruption and keep their production line in work as long as possible?
   (b) What level of decision making will this decision be made at?

1. **(a)** Any suitable answer, e.g. Where finances permit, the company should stock well in advance and hold a supply of raw materials sufficient to carry over in such an event. **(b)** Any suitable answer, e.g. Operational level (with consultation at strategic level where long term finance planning might be involved).

10.3 Development and implementation of an ICT solution

LEARNING SUMMARY

After studying this section you should be able to:

- understand the different types of implementation
- understand the importance of implementation and maintenance
- understand that the user must be involved in decision making and offered training to use the new system

Factors that contribute to a successful implementation process

AQA **INFO 3**
OCR **G063**
WJEC **IT3**
CCEA **A2 2**

Training and communication

Organisations that are committed to **Continued Professional Development** (CPD) will provide regular training for their employees. This ensures that employees are capable and confident in performing their tasks and are aware of any updates to regulations that may affect their working environment and responsibilities.

A good channel for internal communications is vital for improved security. It is important that employees understand their personal and professional duties within the organisation and understand the overall strategic aims of the company.

Large scale organisations v small scale organisations

Policies, such as the Data Protection Act, apply equally to a small newsagent as they would to a multi-national organisation. For example, a newsagent can justify that they require holding an individual's personal details such as name and address and subscription records on a database so that they can ensure that the customer receives the correct magazine or paper on the correct day at the correct address.

The growth of e-commerce has been of particular benefit to customers throughout the world. Apart from being able to purchase a wider range of products at competitive prices, improved business efficiency and distribution logistics ensure that products bought online usually arrive between 24 and 72 hours from time of order. Mail order facilities, only a few years ago, prided themselves on a 28 day delivery service.

Traditionally larger multi-national organisations were operated from large headquarters. With e-commerce much of the work can be outsourced, with call centres and functional areas such as finance, being set up in different countries where labour and facilities are less expensive. Multi-national companies such as Tesco, Sainsbury's and Marks and Spencer have also set up online trading facilities as well as having a high street presence. The main advantage to these organisations is that they can offer 24/7 trading hours and the customer can make their purchases at a time that suits them without leaving home and can have heavy items delivered directly to their door, at their convenience. At the point of ordering, no human intervention is necessary. When a customer has a query, they will send an email or make a telephone call. This means that customer services can operate between normal business hours, even though the company is effectively open for business around the clock.

Many of the larger organisations use **transaction processing**. For example, supermarkets use this when they offer a loyalty card scheme. To encourage customers to join this scheme they offer incentives such as money off vouchers and a points collection reward. However, their main reason for having such a scheme is to allow them to collect valuable information about each and every customer and item that is purchased. Software exists to collect the information about each purchase made and link it to the customer details (made available when the card is produced at point of sale) held on a database. The **Customer Relationship Management systems** (CRM) can then use this information to get a view of customers' spending habits, which include the frequency, the type and quantity of products purchased. This information can be used to market products to susceptible customers. The same information can be fed into the supermarket's **management information system** (MIS) at a tactical level to determine reorder quantities, and at a strategic level to understand buying behaviour by sites and/or geographical areas.

For more information on management information systems see page 146.

KEY POINT

A management information system (MIS) is a system that is designed to help executives to manage an organisation. It is set up to provide sufficient and effective information to allow them to control the day-to-day activities and the overall direction of the business.

Implementation

AQA	**INFO 3**
OCR	**G063**
WJEC	**IT3**
CCEA	**AS 1, A2 2**

Implementation of a new system may involve replacing everything in the old system or implementing an upgrade to an existing system. Depending on the circumstances, there are different ways in which a changeover can occur.

Direct changeover

Direct changeover is where the old system will cease to operate after a given date and will be replaced outright by the new system. The main advantage to this is that it is fast and efficient. For example, the old system could close down on a Friday at the end of business and the new system come into operation at the start of business on the Monday morning. To make sure that this happens smoothly, every effort must be made to have all the data transferred completely and accurately to the new system – this is likely to take place over the weekend. The main weakness of this method is that the old system can no longer be used, if any problems or errors are found in the new system.

Parallel running

Parallel running is a more cautious approach as it allows new and old systems to run alongside each other for a trial period. The advantage of doing it this way, is that it allows any problems to be ironed out, as the old system will be there as a backup. It also allows users time to familiarise themselves with the new systems and gain confidence by comparing the old with the new. The business can run as normal with no disruption if a problem with the new system occurs. This period is likely to be very short – usually only a few days. When the new system is running correctly, the old system will cease. The main disadvantage of doing it this way is the expense. It is clearly a duplication of effort, with staff time and resources.

Phased implementation

Phased implementation is where one part (functional area) of an organisation will implement the new system. This will be observed and monitored by the whole organisation and then phased across other areas when initial problems have been ironed out. The main advantage of this method is that it will cause minimum disruption to the organisation as a whole at any one time. Parallel or direct methods can be used within phased implementations.

Pilot implementation

Pilot implementation is common in larger, multi-sited companies, such as chains of restaurants or outlet stores. One site might implement a change and run for a while, feeding back information to management, who can then take their time to compare value and decide whether to implement the system in other branches in the same way. As with phased implementation, pilot implementation can be carried out using parallel or direct methods.

Maintenance

AQA	INFO 3
OCR	G063
WJEC	IT3
CCEA	AS 1

Once the implementation is complete maintenance of the system will begin. There are different types of maintenance, which will occur at different stages:

- **Corrective maintenance** is necessary for minor oversights such as column totals missing, or other mainly aesthetic problems, which users have a preference to change. These are referred to as reactive modifications of the software product. They are carried out to correct discovered problems, usually within the first few days.
- **Perfective maintenance** is usually changes identified by the user. The system will perform as it was designed but the end-user will be able to identify where and how it may be better utilised. Perfective maintenance is about making the system work more efficiently and effectively. There is normally no urgency on this and it may happen over a period of time. This is modification of the software product to improve its performance or sustainability.
- **Adaptive maintenance** is carried out over a longer period of time. This is where modification of the software product is performed to keep it usable in a changing environment.
- **Preventative maintenance** is where modification of the software product is carried out to detect and correct latent faults in the software product before they become effective faults. This will take place by carrying out several tests of robustness, which will test the system in extreme situations.

The cost of software maintenance rises considerably if the system is accompanied by poor quality system design documentation and/or insufficient staff training.

PROGRESS CHECK

1. What is the main difference between corrective maintenance and perfective maintenance?
2. What is the main advantage of phased implementation?
3. What is the main disadvantage of direct changeover?

1. Corrective maintenance (if necessary at all) is for minor oversights in the development and programming of the system. Perfective maintenance is carried out on a system which was developed according to the design specification but when operational, some 'alterations' are seen to be beneficial.
2. It will cause minimum disruption to the organisation as a whole at any one time.
3. The old system can no longer be used if any problems or errors are found in the new system.

Sample questions and model answers

1. Which piece of legislation governs the illegal copying of software? **(2)**

The Copyright, Design and Patent Act states that it is illegal to copy a file or software program without permission from the owner or the copyright holder.

2. What are the main principles of the Data Protection Act? Who is it set out to protect? **(5)**

The eight principles (as set out by the British Computer Society) require personal data to be:
- Processed fairly and lawfully
- Obtained for and used only for specific and lawful purposes
- Relevant, adequate and not excessive
- Accurate, up-to-date (if necessary)
- Only kept as long as needed
- Held in accordance with the rights of the person to whom the data refers
- Kept securely
- Only transferred to countries that offer adequate data protection

The main aim is to protect the individual.

3. A communications policy is often included as part of an employee's contract. List four issues that this type of policy would be likely to cover. **(4)**

A communications policy is likely to contain advice and guidance on an employee's responsibility for:

- using the Internet in a responsible manner
- sending and receiving emails appropriately (including procedures for opening attachments)
- reporting of actual or suspected breaches of security
- reporting systems and software errors to the appropriate person/department

4. What is meant by the term 'parallel running' when implementing a new system? **(4)**

Parallel running is the term used to describe a period of time where a new system is run alongside the original system. During this trial period problems can be ironed out, and if there are any problems with the new system the old system can be used as a backup. Parallel running also allows users time to familiarise themselves with (and gain confidence in using) the new system, thus resulting in minimum disruption to the organisation.

Marks are awarded here for each correct principle stated. In this case it will be to a maximum of four marks with an additional one mark being awarded for the second part of the answer.

As this question is asking about a 'communications' policy, you have to think about how communication occurs within business. As only four marks are awarded here, think carefully about the communication that a general employee would be involved with and keep the responses general.

In this question, the examiner will be looking for an answer that shows that you understand what is meant by the term 'parallel running'. In your answer, you need to identify that the new system will run at the same time as the old system. It is also important to identify what advantages this may have and show the benefits to the organisation.

Practice examination questions

1. Many supermarkets use transaction processing systems and loyalty cards to gather information about their customers. Describe how the Data Protection Act helps to control what information is collected by the supermarkets, and how that information is used. **(4)**

_____

_____

_____

2. Explain what is meant by:

(a) Corrective maintenance **(2)**

_____

_____

_____

(b) Perfective maintenance **(2)**

_____

_____

_____

(c) Adaptive maintenance **(2)**

_____

_____

_____

(d) Preventative maintenance **(2)**

_____

_____

_____

11 Implementing and managing change

The following topics are covered in this chapter:

- **Managing ICT and its impact on business**
- **Implications of ICT**
- **Training and support for users**

11.1 Managing ICT and its impact on business

LEARNING SUMMARY

After studying this section you should be able to:

- recognise the importance of staying up-to-date with changes in ICT
- understand what Management Information Systems and ICT strategies are
- understand how changes in ICT are managed
- understand the impact ICT has had on businesses

Changing with ICT

AQA **INFO 3**
OCR **G063**
WJEC **IT3**

In the world of ICT, changes are happening all the time. In order to respond to change, organisations will need to constantly update their systems. This means that systems will need to be modified to ensure that they still meet the needs of the organisation.

Organisations must be aware of the latest technologies and what their organisation will benefit from. They must also be aware of the lifespan of their current systems and make sure that continual review takes place so that they keep as up-to-date as possible.

Many organisations have staff at senior management level with relevant knowledge and technical expertise and good understanding of the current developments in ICT. At a strategic level this senior management can then inform and support the process of change ensuring that any changes that are being implemented are appropriate and will meet the overall organisational needs.

There is a general assumption that all managers have a good understanding of ICT and the new technologies and their uses. However, this is not the case. Many managers are incapable of sending emails effectively and some are not even IT literate. This being the case, it is often the responsibility of an IT department manager to be involved in the decision making in order to identify the technical information needs of the functional areas within the organisation.

Making use of management information systems

AQA **INFO 3**
OCR **G063**
WJEC **IT3**
CCEA **A2 1**

As discussed in Chapter 6, an effective **management information system** (**MIS**) is key to the successful operation of any organisation. An MIS should give all the information about the day-to-day operations of the organisation by having a well documented information flow from customer (and all other external sources) to and from the organisation and all the processes within. The purpose of an automated MIS is to give the senior management sufficient information to enable them to control the overall direction and all day-to day activities. In the design and development of an MIS, consultation and constant communication with managers (users) is extremely important.

For more information on management information systems see page 146.

The key elements of any information system involve **data**, **people**, **software systems** and **hardware systems**. The data will originate from a variety of sources – from the internal functional areas as well as from outside the organisation. The people (staff/management) must know what data is relevant and how to interpret the information obtained. The software and hardware must be of a standard to operate and handle the volumes of data and produce the required output. In addition, many organisations will need to have some **telecommunications system** in place to allow the organisation to communicate over multiple sites.

In the design of an effective MIS, there should be open communication channels with the management team at all times. The systems designers will need to ask relevant questions to find out how the organisation works and what they what from a new system, and ensure that:

- relevant data is collected from the correct source(s)
- management receive information that they require
- information is accessible by a wide range of users
- information is timely
- information is in a format that is meaningful and usable
- the system is sufficiently flexible to allow analysis, and/or add on where necessary.

KEY POINT

It is important not to make the implementation of new ICT systems too complex as people will shy away from something they do not understand.

Legacy systems

Legacy systems have come about as a result of the individual functional areas using computer systems to suit their own needs and replacing existing manual systems. This was justified by organisations as it meant there was relatively small financial outlay and the costs could be spread over a period of time as each area became computerised in turn. However, in many cases it was soon realised that this led to incompatibility of equipment and communications and duplication of effort. Ideally organisations should be looking at creating integrated systems so that sharing of information between functional areas can occur easily. This reduces any duplication of effort where individual systems are reproducing the same information. It will also feed into a more efficient management information system.

ICT strategies

AQA **INFO 3**
OCR **G063**
WJEC **IT3**
CCEA **AS 1**

> Note the business case for the development of ICT within an organisation. Look for examples in the media so that you can expand on this area.

Within any successful organisation, ICT implementation should be managed at a strategic level. It makes sense that any ICT development should provide tangible benefits to users, the organisation and customers. ICT is only as good as its application to people and organisations. Lots of money can be thrown at a fantastically well-specified, very powerful system. However a system such as this is useless if it does not meet the needs (human, financial, organisational, customer) of the organisation.

Strategic ICT is about leadership and positive attitude. New systems take time to develop and implement, cost money, cause disruption and if not properly managed, can cause disillusionment. However bad the current system is the new one will change the way people work and it could mean that files end up in different places.

In the planning, design and implementation of any ICT system, working together with management and employees is crucial.

Identifying why the organisation needs ICT, taking ownership of the plan and making sure that it is backed and supported by senior management will tend to lead to a more positive outcome.

The ICT strategy should do the following:
- Consider financial implications – how much it will cost and what impact this cost will have on the organisation.
- Consider the impact on people and what, if any, training will be needed.
- Consider the technology as far as hardware, software and infrastructure. What is needed to make it all work?
- Consider what success will look like – how will you know if your ICT system is working?
- Be short and simple to understand – everyone in the organisation must be able to follow it.
- Be able to clearly articulate benefits (for employees, customers, profit, effectiveness) – it needs to be clear who gets what out of it.
- Not be too technical.
- Be able to support and accommodate change – a three year plan looks great today but might be very different in a year's time.
- Build in time for constant review.

Many companies see emerging technologies as too expensive and decide not to invest in ICT for that reason. However, the growth of computing technologies over the past few decades means that computers are increasingly being used to store, process and transfer important data, and businesses are benefiting from the fast responsive world that it supports. Any company that does not invest in ICT may soon find that they are unable to compete and survive in the market. As part of their feasibility study, a company should be able to assess what level of return they should get from any investment in ICT. It is pointless investing more than the return is likely to be.

Managing change

AQA **INFO 3**
OCR **G063**
WJEC **IT3**

Managing change is fundamental to the success of ICT implementation in any organisation. Every ICT strategy will have to establish the effect on people (employers and customers) and advise on how to cope with change.

Implementation of new technology can often lead to organisations needing to restructure. Some organisations can do this with little or no disruption and little resistance from employees. However, depending on size and structure, some organisations will find restructuring very difficult. In general, people are not positive receptors to any kind of change, especially older people. Many traditional organisations tend to be autocratic and unwilling to respond positively to change. In such archaic organisations implementation of new technology may lead to a total restructuring of the organisation and give way to a totally new operation. Organisations must be very careful with impending changes to make sure to guard against:

- employees leaving if they fear that the implementation of new technologies may push them out
- employees feeling devalued and a feeling that they are being replaced by machines
- employees feeling resistant to change, especially when they think that their own jobs and livelihood may be at risk
- division between organisational areas.

This type of reaction is often referred to as being 'closed'.

Organisations that are 'open' to change are likely to accept any change as a natural and progressive part of the overall organisational behaviour. This open response:

- makes people feel part of a team and more valued and therefore motivated
- can encourage new employees to join the organisation
- has the potential of creating new opportunities (promotion)
- encourages forward thinking, which leads to company prosperity.

External sources of support

Often an organisation will consider **outsourcing** projects or tasks. This might involve buying in skills and expertise from self employed contractors, or the complete project being carried out by a different company. In the main, it is likely that an organisation will maintain a number of key (core) staff, primarily to ensure that adequate security measures are in place.

Advantages of outsourcing	Disadvantages of outsourcing
- Inexpensive – only paid for what they are contracted to deliver. - Already experts – so no training implications. - Contract agencies will normally supply staff with little notice – so always available.	- Security – there is greater chance of a breach to security. - External staff will deliver only what they are paid to do – so no motivation or interest in the organisation as a whole. - The organisation has given the control of the project over to the outside agency – so has to trust that the job will be done correctly.

The impact of ICT on business organisations

AQA **INFO 3**
OCR **G063**
WJEC **IT3**
CCEA **AS 1**

ICT has had a great impact on the way in which data is gathered and handled:

- Data is gathered must faster than before.
- Much more data is being gathered than before. For example, surveys ask for information about whole households e.g. age, hobbies, car insurance, etc. The resulting information is passed to third parties, which will feed marketing campaigns so that, for example, older people will automatically receive information about stair lifts and orthopaedic chairs.
- There is greater opportunity to collect data. For example, data is gathered through loyalty cards, credit and debit cards at EPOS.
- Demographic statistics are available through Government websites.
- Websites record data about the purchases made and by using hit counters can calculate which websites have received most hits (numbers of visits).
- Identifying trends is easier with the use of new graphical software.
- Information is available much more quickly.

With the use of up-to-date ICT systems, organisations can have a competitive edge within their sales and marketing if they:

- gather data faster
- have the capabilities to analyse data faster
- have the ability to respond much faster
- can manage sales teams more effectively
- can provide accurate and timely information more successfully.

It is widely accepted that the introduction of ICT systems within an organisation has had a positive effect on the business as far as productivity and profit.

In summary the general benefits of ICT to an organisation include:

Benefit	Explanation
Greater efficiency	<ul><li>Response time increases.</li><li>Direct order status, leading to orders being placed as and when needed (not a capital outlay and tied up in a warehouse).</li></ul>
Increase in profitability and reduction in costs	<ul><li>Less wastage of materials due to precision measuring and cutting.</li><li>Fewer staff, as processes become more automated and therefore less costs in wages.</li><li>Use of electronic transmission of data (email, Internet) means less cost in postage and down time.</li></ul>
Gains in productivity	<ul><li>Longer periods of production (machines can be operated over 24 hours if necessary).</li><li>Consistently accurate therefore a greater quality of production.</li><li>Faster production line.</li></ul>

Benefit	Explanation
Improved MIS	• Greater quantities of data leads to more available information. • Information and data is easily accessible. • Data can be analysed and viewed from different perspectives. • Great quantities of data can be held and used as comparative data for future sales. • Sales projections can easily be made and progress charted.
Improved customer service	• Use of emails and automated directed telephone calls can make it easier for customers to address a query to the correct port. • Customers can be contacted quickly and easily using mass email to alert them to a special offer or change in a specification. • Calls/emails can be analysed and trends identified.
Improved communications and integration of systems	• Well designed systems will communicate easily internally leading to greater quality. • Well thought out designs will allow an organisation's systems to communicate easily with external sources.

PROGRESS CHECK

1 List three main benefits of ICT to an organisation.
2 Why might some companies decide not to invest in the latest technologies?
3 What can an organisation do to ensure that they have the cooperation of their staff when planning to implement a new system?

1 Any three suitable answers, e.g. Greater efficiency; increase in profitability and reduction in costs; gains in productivity; improved MIS; improved customer service; improved communication and integration of systems.
2 Any suitable answer, e.g. It may be too expensive; The benefits may not justify the initial outlay of costs; The timing may not be suitable due to relocation or other reasons.
3 Any suitable answer, e.g. Involve staff at all stages; Ask for opinions, ideas and support from employees from the initial planning; Offer training and up-skilling where necessary.

11.2 Implications of ICT

<table>
<tr><td>LEARNING SUMMARY</td><td>After studying this section you should be able to:
• identify emerging technologies and their impact
• identify the health and safety issues of ICT systems
• understand the impact of ICT on the workforce</td></tr>
</table>

Emerging technologies

AQA **INFO 3**
OCR **G063**
WJEC **IT3**
CCEA **AS 1**

> **KEY POINT**
>
> Emerging technologies are making a big impact on the way we live today. There has been major development of technology in areas of medicine, crime, leisure and education.

Within medicine, people are living longer due to techniques such as those used in key hole surgery. There have also been advances in scanning systems like MRI, which allows diseases to be detected and treated earlier. The advancement in genetic research has seen the cloning of embryos such as Dolly the sheep.

There is an increasing use of **embedded computers**. Embedded computers are contained inside the machine that they control. For example, in microwave ovens, digital recording devices, televisions and other sensor devices.

Tracking devices are worn by people who have been convicted of a crime in order to track their movements so that curfew conditions can be imposed. They can be used on people as part of a sentence, as an alternative to a prison sentence or whilst a person is on temporary leave from prison.

The use of simulation and games technology is being used in leisure and education. Many are interactive and intuitive, with responses dictating the next action. **Chatbots** (or talkbots, or chatterboxes) are also used in education. A chatbot is a computer program, which is designed to simulate an intelligent conversation with one or more human users via auditory and/or textual methods. Characters interact and help teach problem solving in a way that engages the learner. Such computer programs can also be referred to as 'Artificial Conversational Entities'. Although many chatbots appear to intelligently interpret human input before providing a response, many simply scan for keywords within the input and pull a reply with the most matching keywords or the most similar wording pattern from a verbose textual database. A well known chatbot is ALICE (the Artificial Linguistic Internet Computer Entity).

Geographical Information systems (**GIS**) combine information in a database with mapping software to produce an output in map format. These can be used within a portable satellite navigation system where the driver can enter the destination and the map and directions will be generated to assist the journey. This system works with the guidance of a satellite, by detecting where the receiver (satnav system) is located. An addition to this system is a service that updates travel information in real time, warning of traffic delays and advising on alternative routes.

Sensor systems are used widely in many walks of life. For example, a journey by car or public transport will encounter the use of sensors in a variety of places. One example may be at traffic lights where the flow of traffic may determine when the lights change. The sensor detects the volume of traffic and the system responds using the data from the sensor. This means that the lights may stay green for longer during peak times when the traffic is heavier. Speed cameras use light sensors to measure the speed of a moving vehicle. If the vehicle is going at a higher speed than is recommended for that area, a signal is sent to the camera, which photographs the vehicle's registration number. The owner's details can then be obtained from the national database of registered car owners – who will then be sent a speeding fine. Sensors are also used by some car parks to detect how many cars enter and leave. In this way it is possible to determine how many spaces are available and flash a sign when there are no spaces left.

For more information on emerging technologies within the automotive industry see Chapter 12.

Developments are being made to home security systems to allow owners to install sensor equipment with close circuit television (CCTV) surveillance. This enables owners to view what is happening to their property from a distance. People can have peace of mind while on holiday abroad knowing that they can view what is happening at their home at any time. The implications here are that burglaries can be detected at an early stage.

Health and safety

AQA	**INFO 1**
OCR	**G061**
WJEC	**IT1**
CCEA	**AS 1**

Many people consider IT working environments to be extremely safe. And indeed, in comparison with many other working environments, they are. However, even in the IT workplace there are many health and safety issues that relate directly to the use of computers and the environment in which computers are used.

Organisations (both commercial and educational) are obliged by law to ensure that all employees, or people for whom the organisation is responsible, who work with computers do so safely.

Health hazards

Most health hazards within IT environments arise from either posture or prolonged and/or repetitive use of equipment. These include:

Issue, cause and symptoms	Precautions
Ulnar Neuritis can result in tingling sensations in the fingers and pain in the elbow joint. It is caused by compression on the elbows, which (in IT) can arise when people rest heavily on their elbows when working at a desk.	For people who tend to lean heavily on their elbows on a regular basis, the use of elbow pads can help distribute their weight more evenly, thus avoiding unnecessary pressure on the arm and nerve as it runs behind the elbow joint.
Deep vein thrombosis (DVT) is the formation of a blood clot in a deep vein (most commonly in the legs) and is often associated with long haul airline flights. However, recent research suggests that an increasing number of people who sit working at a computer for long periods each day are also getting DVT.	The best way to avoid DVT is to take regular breaks and to ensure that your legs get regular exercise during the day.

Issue, cause and symptoms	Precautions
Repetitive strain injury (RSI) occurs when muscles and tendons (especially in the arms and hands) are damaged as a result of continuous repetitive use of particular muscle groups. When using a computer, RSI is usually caused by over use of a keyboard or mouse. The symptoms include aches in fingers, wrists and muscles in arms.	RSI can be prevented by setting up desk equipment in a way that encourages good posture. RSI can also be avoided by taking regular breaks to ensure that your muscles get time to relax, and varying your work pattern to avoid long periods of repetitive actions. Using wrist pads or ergonomically designed equipment (e.g. keyboard and mouse) also help considerably.
Eye strain is often caused by long periods of looking continually at a computer screen. The level of screen glare and screen resolution (e.g. looking at bright and poor quality images) can significantly add to the strain placed upon your eyes.	If possible, the best way to avoid this is to reduce the brightness level of the screen; and where it is not possible to adjust the level, to use an anti-glare filter. Good lighting can help alleviate this problem, particularly by reducing the contrast between the screen and the surrounding workplace; and in workplaces where direct sunlight shines on screens, window blinds or tinted windows should be installed. It is also important to take regular breaks in order to allow your eyes to rest, and when working to change the focal length of your eyes by regularly looking at objects that are both nearer and further away than the screen.
Back and neck problems can be caused by sitting in the same position for long periods of time without adequate support or posture.	The best way to avoid this is to have a well designed workstation, to use a chair with adequate back support and to adjust the height of the chair to encourage good posture. As with many other health hazards it is also advisable to take regular breaks in order to relax and vary the position of your limbs and muscles.
Carpal tunnel syndrome (CTS) is caused by compression (squashing) of a nerve in the wrist and results in pins and needles and pain in the fingers and palm of the hand. As with RSI it often occurs as a result of significant repetitive wrist movement.	As with RSI, the best way to avoid CTS is to set up your workstation in a way that encourages good posture, to use wrist pads and ergonomically designed equipment, to take regular breaks to ensure that your muscles get time to relax, and to vary your work pattern to avoid long periods of repetitive wrist action.
Electromagnetic fields (EMFs) such as electric fields, magnetic fields and radiated fields (e.g. TV, radio and microwaves) are emitted by most types of electrical equipment. Overexposure to EMFs can result in a number of serious medical conditions. Whilst the level of EMFs emitted within the workplace is relatively low, it is still worth taking precautions to avoid overexposure.	The best way to reduce exposure to EMFs is to ensure that electrical equipment (such as your computer) is turned off (or automatically switches to standby) when not in use.

Physical hazards

In addition to being aware of the health hazards associated with the use of computers and computer technology, it is also important to be aware of the physical hazards that can cause potential problems in the IT workplace.

Issue	Precautions
Risk of fire	Wherever there is electrical equipment there is also a risk of fire. It is important to check the location of fire extinguishers, to ensure that the correct type of fire extinguishers are available and to make sure that only carbon dioxide (CO_2) extinguishers are used to put out electrical fires.
Risk of electrocution	The risk of electrocution rises considerably when equipment is poorly maintained (e.g. loose wires, frayed cables, disconnected earth connections). The best way to avoid electrocution is to ensure that all equipment is well maintained, and that liquids are kept well away from electrical equipment. It is important to know the location of circuit breakers in order to be able to turn off equipment quickly if a problem occurs.
Unsecured equipment	It is important to ensure that all equipment (especially heavy equipment such as PCs and screens/monitors) are positioned securely so that the equipment is not easily knocked off the working surface.
Trailing wires	Trailing wires are a common hazard within most offices and usually result from poor installation and/or maintenance of equipment. Wires should normally be gathered together in a 'loom' (or bound together by cable ties) and positioned in a way that does not allow them to be tripped over by the computer user or by other employees who might be passing the workstation.
Food and drink	Not only does the consumption of food and drink at an IT workstation pose a risk of electrocution, it also results in an increased build-up of germs and bacteria on and around the keyboard. It is recommended that food and drink always be consumed in an appropriate environment (e.g. not at the workstation).

Health and Safety Regulations

In accordance with the **Health and Safety Regulations** (1992) all employers must:

- analyse workstations, assess and reduce risks
- ensure workstations meet the minimum requirements (proper chairs and lighting)
- plan work so that there are breaks and change of activities (opportunity for non-computer work must be provided)
- provide free eye tests
- provide health and safety training and information.

Perhaps the most important thing to remember is that the safest type of IT working environment is one that is well maintained, neat and tidy, and that is used by well trained employees.

The impact of ICT on the workforce

AQA **INFO 3**
OCR **G063**
WJEC **IT3**
CCEA **AS 1**

With the increased use of ICT in the workplace, some employee skills may become unnecessary or redundant. For example, the manufacturing of automobiles once required highly skilled lathe operators to cut the metal with precision. Pre-programmed CAD/CAM machines now produce these components. The disadvantage for those employees is their loss of work and income. The advantage to the industry is that there are fewer rejected components because the machines can work with greater accuracy and consistency and are not subjected to human error. The turnaround time is also much faster. There are many other examples of this in the service industry. One example is in supermarket checkouts. Many of these now offer self-service where the customer can purchase items by self-scanning the bar code and paying without any intervention from the checkout staff.

People who find that their skills are no longer required within the organisation are often offered a position elsewhere in the company, with some being retrained to suit a new position. Sometimes this repositioning and retraining is not possible and the employee is made redundant.

With the improvement in technologies comes the opportunity for many people to work from home. The benefits of this include potential savings to the environment, saving of fuel and travel time to and from work each day, while the downsides are that some workers can feel isolated and miss the interaction with people that they would normally have in the office environment.

See advantages and disadvantages of working from home in Chapter 13.

In order to work from home, most workers will require a network connection (modem), a computer and the appropriate software to enable them to do the required job. Many organisations will provide this equipment to enable their staff to work from home.

PROGRESS CHECK

1. How could you avoid eye strain when using a computer?
2. How could you avoid back problems when using a computer?
3. What is the best way to avoid DVT?

1. Good lighting; adjustable screen; anti-glare filters; window blinds; taking adequate eye rests.
2. Well-designed workstation; adjustable computer chair with back support; get up for leg stretches and short walks.
3. Ensure that your legs get regular exercise during the day.

11.3 Training and support for users

LEARNING SUMMARY

After studying this section you should be able to:

- understand the different ways in which users of ICT systems can obtain training
- understand the importance of customer support

Training users of ICT systems

AQA **INFO 2, INFO 3**
CCEA **A2 1**

> **KEY POINT**
>
> A user in this context is anyone who uses the computer system – either from the organisation perspective (i.e. the employee) or the end-user perspective (i.e. the customer).

One of the most important considerations within any organisation is the workforce and their competencies. With the increased use of ICT in the workplace, there is a persistent need for organisations to make sure that their workforce is continually and appropriately kept up-to-date and skilled through appropriate training. This is usually quite expensive and will be a large portion of the implementation costs of an ICT system. Failure to train employees to use the systems properly will result in inefficient working, which will be to the detriment of the organisation and to the benefit of its competitors.

Identifying the training that is most appropriate to the individual's needs can be problematic as there is such a wide range available. Training one-to-one often works better than group training courses. The system's installers can provide the in-house training to suit the system and its users. The organisation could decide to train a few of their staff with a view to **cascading** this training throughout the organisation (e.g. paying for two people to be trained and then getting the trained people to train the rest of the team). Other courses may be available in local colleges (often with accreditation) and for the technical users it may be appropriate to consider qualifications in network building and maintenance or specialist courses in software engineering. Within the internal functional areas, courses in word processing, accountancy software, spreadsheets and databases may be required. If the implemented system includes bespoke software, it would be usual for the developers to provide customised training as part of the overall delivery package.

Consideration to the choice of training will include a number of questions. The following table compares the type of training and its benefits:

Type of training	How much?	Where?	Is it worth it?
Preset generic courses, such as word processing, DTP, spreadsheets, databases	Relatively inexpensive	Local college Books Web-based	Good for beginners, in particular individuals. Will cover all the basics. Generic training may not get to the breadth and depth required by the organisation.
Bought-in tailored training	Expensive	In-house (delivered by consultants)	Tailored to suit the requirements of the organisation. Designated tutor, so all questions should be addressed.
Cascade training	The initial cost is expensive for the first few staff, but much cheaper for the other staff they train.	Initially either external or internal	Can put a few staff through greater training. The more staff to benefit from the cascaded training, the less expensive it will be overall.

Often organisations operate a **Continued Professional Development** (CPD) scheme where each employee is offered a number of hours training and development per year.

It is good practice to encourage employees to identify their own training needs. However, it is more likely that management will recommend specific training after the employee's annual appraisal meeting. This yearly meeting gives employees and management the opportunity to discuss and evaluate performance over that period and identify any training needs.

Customer support

AQA **INFO 2, INFO 3**
OCR **G063**
WJEC **IT3**
CCEA **A2 1**

Some people perceive new technologies to have had a detrimental effect on **customer support**. For example, the debate continues as to whether call centres have been a success. Many customers have complained about the fact that they end up speaking to someone at the end of a phone miles away from the business itself. The main advantage to any organisation is that by using Internet technologies, they have the ability to apparently offer their service 24 hours a day, 7 days a week.

Good customer support is key for repeat business so it is important for an organisation to find out what kind of support their customers are likely to respond to best. Offering good customer support includes being able to respond quickly in answer to a customer complaint. When using email across a number of time zones, this often is not the case. Customers expect a complaint to be dealt with straight away in a courteous and favourable manner. If this does not happen, it may result in bad publicity and no repeat business.

Many organisations offer online support via electronic user manuals, procedures and policies, health and safety, specifications of products and FAQs. The advantage to customers is that they can access this information in their own time and at their own pace.

PROGRESS CHECK

1 Give one advantage of bought-in tailored training.
2 Give one disadvantage of generic training courses.
3 What is cascade training?

1 Tailored training suits the needs and requirements of the organisation so all questions should be addressed.
2 Generic training courses may not get to the breadth and depth required by the organisation.
3 Where a few members of staff are trained and then the trained staff train the rest of the team.

Sample questions and model answers

1. In an information system, sources of external information are generated from various departments. Identify two sources of external information. **(2)**

Appropriate sources that could be identified include:

Government, Commerce (other businesses), Databases, Market research companies

2. An organisation is expanding and looking to implement a new ICT system. What factors should be considered to ensure successful implementation of the new ICT system? **(6)**

With any expansion and/or implementation of ICT systems some change is inevitable. It is important that this change is managed correctly. One of the most important factors to ensure successful implementation and changeover is that a proper consultation with managers and employees takes place. It is important to involve the people that will be using the new system, so that a proper understanding of the system needs will be met. Other factors to ensure successful implementation include:

- End-user involvement
- Thorough analysis
- Consideration of financial implications
- Build in review time

3. Many companies see emerging technologies as too expensive and decide not to purchase ICT systems for that reason. What other options might be available? **(4)**

In order to spread the cost of investing in emerging technologies over a longer period of time companies could opt to lease equipment from a service provider rather than buy it. They can also reduce their costs by outsourcing some of their IT services such as network management, security and user support.

4. With the advancement in modern technologies many people have objections to the use of such devices as body scanners being used at airports. What are the main advantages of such a device and why might its introduction be an issue for some people? **(4)**

The main advantage is that it provides additional security as it can show if items are being smuggled on a person. Some people may object to it on religious and moral grounds, and feel that it is an invasion of privacy, as the outline of body parts will be visible.

An exam question may be set in context, e.g. a clothes shop, so that you can identify with who the workers are and respond using the example given.

Exam questions may be on topical issues that are in today's news, and have not been covered specifically in the classroom. It is important to identify the knowledge that you have and transfer that to an alternative context.

Practice examination questions

1 A local spa is having a simple network installed to assist with stock control and appointment booking. As a small business dealing directly with the public, certain health and safety procedures must be adhered to. What health and safety issues will the employer need to take into consideration when planning the layout of the computers and what advice can be given to employees who will be using the computers?

(6)

_____

_____

_____

_____

_____

_____

_____

_____

_____

_____

2 How can an employer train staff to use a new computer system? What types of training are available and what factors need to be considered?

(8)

_____

_____

_____

_____

_____

_____

_____

_____

_____

_____

_____

12 ICT and society

The following topics are covered in this chapter:

- The impact of ICT on society
- The impact of ICT on services to the consumer
- The impact of ICT on individuals

12.1 The impact of ICT on society

LEARNING SUMMARY

After studying this section you should be able to:

- describe the moral and ethical issues that ICT developments raise
- discuss the legal, social, cultural, economic and technical issues associated with the implementation of ICT solutions
- present a balanced argument outlining the benefits and problems associated with ICT and society

ICT and the way we live

AQA **INFO 2, INFO 3**
OCR **G063**
WJEC **IT1, IT3**
CCEA **AS 1, A2 1**

There are lots of claims made about ICT and its impact on the way we live and function. As always there are positive and negative effects. You should consider the impact on our culture as well as moral, legal, social, economic and technical issues.

Moral and ethical concerns

For each benefit of the use of ICT there are concerns about the impact on the way we live, and the way society conducts itself. ICT is often seen as the solution to problems, but could in some circumstances lead to other problems (see table below). With all moral and ethical concerns there are aspects that differ depending upon our circumstances or our beliefs.

You could also consider the benefits and concerns surrounding:
· car number plate recognition
· monitoring employees to measure their work-rate
· identity cards
· the use of cookies to record information about web-searches.

Benefits of ICT	Moral and ethical concerns
Increased productivity leading to an all round sense of wellbeing as economic growth increases spending in the economy.	A greater use of technology in the work place can mean that some entry-level (low skilled) jobs are no longer required.
Monitoring by close circuit television (CCTV) can lead to reductions in crime; it can deter criminals simply by being there; it can also enable face recognition in large crowds.	Over-use of CCTV can lead to the so called 'Hawthorne effect' – we are so used to seeing it about that we begin to ignore it – this minimises its impact on crime or unruly behaviour. Because CCTV has a ubiquitous presence (it is everywhere) it reduces our privacy. Combined with electronic ticketing, passes, mobile telephony, debit and credit cards, our movements could be tracked at any time.

Give examples to show that you understand this benefit, e.g. online banking and shopping.

Benefits of ICT	Moral and ethical concerns
More flexible approaches to working and an increased sense that business can be conducted 24/7.	Greater access can lead to other problems: • illegal **file sharing** and downloading of **copyright** materials like films and music have raised questions about the viability of the music industry • the availability of gambling, pornography, chat-rooms, gaming and social networking sites has led to reviews about Internet addiction • **auction sites** enable sellers to sell counterfeit or stolen goods more easily since the buyer cannot necessarily see what is being bought • more of our personal details are 'online' and there is an increased risk of **identity theft**
As we experience more and more online or telephone voting systems, ICT may bring about changes to the way we conduct our democracy. Or at the very least it makes us feel that we can question what our politicians are doing.	We may be more susceptible to voting with our emotions rather than thinking things through fully. We may also become susceptible to **pressure groups**: very much in the way that recently people got together to prevent a talent-show winner from getting to number one in the charts.
ICT offers a clear range of health benefits and could improve life expectancy through things like the DNA genome, better medical scanners, and **nanotechnology** that can be used to undertake small internal medical procedures.	Increased knowledge about hereditary disease could lead to increases in insurance costs for those 'potentially' affected, or could lead to questions about state sponsored euthanasia or vivisection.

Legal issues

As the use of ICT expands and changes the way that we do things, national and international laws are being amended or introduced to minimise unwanted consequences.

We have already mentioned the illegal file sharing and downloading of copyright materials. For some, this is merely an issue of differing ethics. For others, it is more about the impact on their livelihoods. Law has developed to protect the rights of individuals and there have been calls to amend laws further so that Internet service providers are required to allow the authorities access to the identities of all those making illegal downloads.

Advances in technology, therefore, have implications about how our privacy is protected. We can be monitored in everything that we do, and while this can make our lives easier and more efficient – it can give rise to unwanted invasions of privacy.

Take, for instance, the increased use of **biometric data** for security purposes in airports. Regular travellers through some airports can make use of iris recognition to speed their way through customs and border controls. Some people might be concerned about the amount of personal intrusion that access to such data could give.

There are other, emerging concerns that may require new or altered legal responses. In 2010 there was a series of advertisements on television that reworked fairytales, with one looking at the story of Little Red Riding Hood. Here the wolf is challenged for 'stealing grandma's bandwidth'. This might seem insignificant – but where the wireless network is insecure the person paying for the service may find that their bandwidth is being used freely by others. This has cost and efficiency implications – but could also have implications for identity theft.

It is good to find up-to-date examples to support your work.

Also in 2010 there was a problem for second home purchasers in Bulgaria. Foreigners were entitled to buy a house in Bulgaria but first had to set up a company and provide personal and passport details. These details were recorded and stored in a database that could be accessed online. This led to questions about the security of those details and the potential impact of any identity theft that could occur.

Social issues

The increased use of ICT has led to changes in the way that people access entertainment. In the 1970s, many families sat together to watch TV and some shows had regular audiences of over 20 million (a third of the UK population). Today very popular TV shows attract something between 9 and 11 million viewers. This is in part due to the availability of satellite television. In the 1970s there were three main terrestrial channels; today there are hundreds. But our viewing habits have changed even further. We now have online access to TV shows, greater access to recording technologies and an increased use of portable devices for accessing a wider variety of transmissions.

This means that advertisers have to respond differently, and TV companies have had to reconsider their advertising reach; especially when there is an increased use of recording technologies that can filter out the advertisements.

These views might well conflict with the way that you feel about social networking. Do you have a view on this? If you can explain and justify alternative responses it will add a useful and important dimension to your work.

Increased access to televisual and other online and onscreen entertainment is believed to be playing a part in the increased levels of obesity and type 2 diabetes in young people. Too much time playing computer games, or engaging in 'social networking' are often cited as the contributory factors.

Social networking is also cited as giving rise to changes in the way that people interact with each other: people are increasingly confident and more open in their online dealings with people but are unable to recognise the social implications of their behaviour when in public situations.

Employment patterns have changed as ICT has grown as a tool. More and more jobs have been outsourced to developing countries where costs are seen to be lower. Other jobs have disappeared altogether, or have been de-skilled as technology makes some aspects of work more straightforward. This has led to increased levels of unemployment in some sectors, and the need to re-skill the workforce. This results in social problems for those who find themselves looking for work.

Cultural issues

Increased access to ICT has led, in part, to a smaller world view. There is greater access to an international perspective on things. This could mean that smaller countries lose their cultural identity as they access the language, culture, entertainment and eating habits from larger nations.

The way in which we listen to music and watch television has changed over time. This began with the advent of the Sony Walkman in the late 1970s. Now with MP3 and MP4 players, and with mobile computing and Internet access, the opportunity to download music and video allows people to watch what they want, when they want, and where they want. The development of Internet-based television players has also contributed to greater flexibility. This could mean that people have more time to engage in other cultural activities – it could also mean that they are just watching more television.

Social networking and Internet telephony (**voice over Internet protocol** or **VOIP**) is enabling contact between people all over the world. This is important for families and friends that are widely distributed. It is also important for people who find themselves restricted in their movements: social networking for the elderly or the disabled may be their only contact with the outside world.

Economic issues

Like the industrial revolution before it, the ICT revolution has the potential to provide great economic benefits for nations that are prepared to embrace the changes technology can bring.

> **KEY POINT**
>
> There is a balance between the economic and the social issues: advances in technology may bring economic benefits – but there may be some short term social upheaval as the economy adjusts.

Any industrial or technological revolution can only be ultimately successful if the political environment fosters:

- open and sustained access to ICT resources – some countries limit access to the Internet for example; others (like Finland) believe that everyone has a right to Internet access
- a clear policy on education and workforce development – people need to be confident in using new systems as they emerge, and need training to develop their knowledge and skills
- support for active research and development in new methodologies
- investment in the developing sectors; this can be risky as with the dot com 'bubble' of the 1990s.

Technical issues

The speed at which technology develops can enable or hamper the way that we use ICT. The developments that we have seen in entertainment technologies have increased demands for **bandwidth**, faster processing speeds, greater battery life, greater portability (size and weight) and increased storage capacity. ICT development is limited by local, national and international capacity to deal with these emerging technological requirements.

Bandwidth is a hotly contested area: you only have to see the advertisements claiming speeds of up to 20 Mbps. The highest speed could very well be dependent on how far you are away from a telephone exchange, whether you have access to optical fibre cabling, the strength of your mobile phone signal, or even whether your access is provided with your mains electricity. So where you live could have a major impact on how you access and use the technology that is available to you. In India approximately 50% of all Internet connections are slow and expensive because they rely on dial-up. Therefore in India Internet usage is likely to be for short periods of time and for very focused reasons. In England the availability of broadband connections is much higher and as a consequence users could be online all day.

PROGRESS CHECK

1 What examples of moral, social or ethical issues might be linked with Internet usage?

1. Any suitable examples, e.g.
   - Pornography is seen as exploitative, and may have a number of consequences in changing our views of acceptable body images, or even our approach to members of the opposite or same sex.
   - Spam mail offering dubious products is also an outcome of increased Internet usage. The automatic generation of email addresses and the sending of 'important' emails about financial transactions have been of some concern.
   - There are also concerns about increased social isolation of people who spend increasing amounts of time engaged in Internet gaming or social networking.

12.2 The impact of ICT on services to the consumer

LEARNING SUMMARY

After studying this section you should be able to:

- describe the present and potential future impact of ICT on:
  - transport   – commerce
  - medicine   – marketing
  - education   – communications
  - entertainment   – manufacturing

ICT and transport

AQA   **INFO 2, INFO 3**
OCR   **G063**
WJEC   **IT1, IT3**
CCEA   **AS 1, A2 1**

Fifty years ago, people could use very much the same range of transport that is available to us today. If we had asked someone in 1960 about the transport of the future they would no doubt have spoken about rocket cars, supersonic air travel, and personal air travel. Actually all of these things have been developed, but were too expensive to be practical for everyday use. What has happened is that ICT has made the internal combustion engine much more efficient, and has enhanced our travel experience.

Air travel

Travelling by air has changed massively as a consequence of the application of ICT.

Application	Outcome
Airline simulation	Enhanced training opportunities enable pilots to experience take-off and landing in new aircraft and on tricky landing strips.
Flying by wire	Many aircraft have auto-pilot and computer systems that enable the pilot to pass control to an automated system. A fly-by-wire system replaces manual flight control of an aircraft with an electronic interface. The movements of flight controls are converted to electronic signals and flight control computers determine how to provide the expected response. Commands from the computers are also input automatically to stabilise the aircraft and perform other tasks.
Security	ICT is being used to increase levels of security. Airports have introduced a wide range of ICT mediated security measures: • luggage scanning that identifies metallic, electronic and liquid items • biometric data – taken from passports, iris scanning, photographs taken at entry to security and before boarding • whole body scanning – currently only used for selected passengers though it has raised some concerns about the level of detail it shows • hand-held scanners to detect metal and other objects
Design	ICT-based design of aircraft, engines and fuel storage and delivery systems has enabled aircraft to increase in size and range. The DC7 developed in 1953 had a maximum passenger capacity of 104 passengers. The Airbus A340-600 in current service has a maximum passenger capacity of 500 passengers, and the Boeing 747-400 a capacity of 568 passengers. Flights to Australia often had to make fuelling stops in the Middle East and the Far East before arriving at the final destination. Today it is possible to make the trip without fuel stops. This was made possible, for example, by using ICT systems to monitor engine performance, and by using ICT design to make wings more aero-dynamic and efficient and so increase fuel economy.
Global Positioning Systems (GPS)	GPS enables pilots to know exactly where they are. It is also possible to transmit this data to passengers using in-flight video, and also to keep air traffic control informed of the flight's progress.

Intelligent motors

Motor cars have benefitted greatly from the application of ICT. Safety legislation and demands for better fuel economy have led to the development of higher technical specifications, even in the very cheapest of cars. Modern cars may have something in the region of 50 **microprocessors** that manage a whole range of functions.

Application	Outcome
Anti-lock braking system (ABS)	The anti-lock braking system microprocessor controls the braking system to ensure that the car stops safely and securely in a range of weather conditions. The system may also handle such functions as traction and stability control.
Engine Management Systems (EMS)	• Engine Management Systems (EMS) enable the smooth operation of the engine and will include microprocessors such as the Engine Control Unit (ECU). • The ECU controls engine functions such as the spark timing and the ratio of fuel to air. Data held by the EMS make servicing and repairs easier – although this means that servicing at home is much more difficult without the 'readers' that can decode the data held by the EMS. • Fuel management – delivers fuel in the most efficient way to decrease consumption.
Driving controls	• Cruise control, which locks the speed at which a car can travel, has become increasingly sophisticated. Some cars have distance control sensors that warn drivers when they are driving too close to the car in front. • Parking control – most often seen as parking sensors and/or cameras that help the driver to park in tight spaces. Recent innovations have seen the development of automatic parking systems which use the data from sensors to park the car without the need for driver intervention. • Wobble control – this is a development that warns the driver that they have waivered from their lane and crossed the white line. It is seen as a useful development for drivers who may be tired.
Safety controls	• Airbag monitoring – sensors that set the airbags off should impact occur. • Seat belt pretensioners – these tighten seatbelts automatically in the event of a crash. They are triggered by sensors.

GPS and navigation

There has been an increase in the range of cars that include satellite navigation (supported by **Global Positioning Systems – GPS**). Where it is not included as a standard piece of kit, portable navigation systems are available. The range of portable navigation systems has increased at the same time as the price has decreased. There are also mobile phones that offer satellite navigation as an application.

In-car navigation enables travellers to find their destinations quickly and easily: though the accuracy of the data set used by the navigation system can lead to people getting lost. Like most aspects of computer usage we have to remember the old adage, 'Garbage in, garbage out'. If the data that went into the system is wrong, or if it has not been updated to include the post codes for a new housing estate, then the data out of the system will be wrong. There are stories about people following instructions and ending up at the edges of cliffs or on impassable roads. Under these circumstances it is probably useful to remember that we have other processing capabilities when we are driving – our brains!

Some manufacturers include access to real time data, which presents the driver with information about traffic jams and other delays and provides options for detours.

> **KEY POINT**
>
> There are some disadvantages with satellite navigation aside from incorrect or outdated data. Some would argue that an over-reliance on GPS-based navigation has reduced our capacity to read paper-based maps. This is especially important for the rescue services who may be working in locations where signals for portable devices are not available.

Servicing and repairs

The number of microprocessors in modern cars enables service engineers to 'plug into' the engine management systems and diagnose problems accurately and quickly. This takes away the requirement for trial and testing – and so makes the servicing and repair of cars much more efficient. For some problems it may be about the replacement of the microprocessor rather than the replacement of mechanical parts. This means that the servicing of modern cars has been professionalised. It can no longer be carried out by knowledgeable amateurs.

ICT and medicine

AQA **INFO 2, INFO 3** OCR **G063** WJEC **IT1, IT3** CCEA **AS 1, A2 1**	Medicine and health services have benefitted from the increased application of ICT-based solutions. It has led to greater life expectancy and a reduction in disease. Patient treatment has been enhanced by the use of technology, as has the accuracy of diagnosis and care of patients.

Expert systems, virtual reality and medicine

Doctors can now use **expert systems** to support the diagnosis of medical conditions and to prescribe drugs to relieve symptoms. The expert systems (developed using data from medical practitioners) take the doctor through the symptoms that the patient is presenting and enables them to hone in on the disease or illness and to prescribe appropriate medication.

Virtual reality (**VR**) is emerging as a valuable tool for the medical profession. **Imaging technology** is already being used by plastic surgeons to show the 'after effects' of the surgery once the bruising and swelling have reduced. In ground-breaking whole face transplants the use of imaging technology was vital: providing the patient with the assurance of what they would look like after the operation.

> **KEY POINT**
>
> VR is a useful tool in medical training. It allows doctors to experience rare and life threatening conditions before they engage in practical training on live patients. If we believe what we see in televised forensic dramas the use of VR is (or will be) a vital tool in supporting post-mortem diagnoses.

Medical services make extensive use of both analogue and digital sensors to track and monitor the progress that patients are making. These sensors could check things like breathing rates and carbon dioxide for babies at risk of cot death, or check for heart function abnormalities for people with heart disease. Data taken from sensors can be used to make judgments or to inform future practice as the medical profession find out more about things like sleep patterns, for example.

Scanning devices can be used to diagnose illness. **MRI** (magnetic resonance imaging) scanners are often used to diagnose health problems that affect organs, tissue and bone. They use magnetic fields and radio waves to produce a detailed image of the inside of the body.

Advantages of MRI scans	Disadvantages of MRI scans
• Does not expose the body to radiation • Patients can often wear their own clothes	• MRI scanners are very expensive and this may limit their use

CT or **CAT** scans (Computerised Axial Tomography scan) also produce images of the inside of the body. The scanner is ring shaped and contains an X-ray scanner within the ring that makes small rotations around the body as the patient lies on a bed that moves backwards and forwards through the ring. This means that the body is exposed to a series of X-rays which build up a detailed picture of the body. These images are called tomograms, and are much more detailed than traditional single-beam X-rays. They are used to provide detailed images of structures inside the body such as: internal organs; blood vessels; tumours and bones.

Advantages of CT scans	Disadvantages of CT scans
• Provides detailed images that enable medical professions to diagnose such conditions as cancer or bone disease • The benefits of having a CT scan will often outweigh any potential risks	• CT scans use X-rays so some groups of people may well be advised to avoid them

ICT and support for the differently abled

Devices are increasingly available to support people who have sight, hearing, mobility or medical impairments.

Application	Outcome
Remote assistance	For the elderly or infirm, systems can be installed and linked to the telephone system, which will call for aid if they cannot get to the telephone or see someone in person.
Transcription aids	Braille printers, or voice enabled dictation systems can transfer the written or spoken word into a format that is readable by the intended audience.
Hearing aids	Hearing aids with microprocessors are much smaller and less obtrusive than they were in the past. Linked with induction loops, the quality of sound available to those with hearing difficulties has improved.
Bio-mechanical prosthetics	Complex limb movements, such as those requiring high levels of manual dexterity, are becoming increasingly available to those who need artificial limbs.
Organ management systems	When the heart cannot operate on its own, units can be inserted and attached to regulate the heart functions. When organs like the kidneys fail, patients are often attached to a dialysis machine. This uses a combination of mechanical functions (pumping and filtering fluids) and electronic functions (monitoring the quality of fluids and patient wellbeing) to replicate the normal functions of the kidneys.

For more information on adaptive ICT devices see pages 46–49.

Administrative and support systems

Patient records are held in databases that, with each visit, build a profile of the patient and ensure that the doctor is able to follow the history of the patient accurately.

Increasingly, patients are able to book appointments with their GP online (especially in busy urban practices). There have been developments in surgeries where the doctor has been able to liaise with the patient and make decisions about the time and place of follow-up consultations in hospital.

There are also systems that enable the patient to self-diagnose, using the principles of expert systems. NHS Online supports patients in making healthy lifestyle choices as well as providing information about illnesses, their diagnosis and their treatment. NHS Direct is a practitioner mediated system, which can be used to support the diagnosis and treatment of common and minor ailments; or to direct people to visit their local doctor or hospital should the symptoms indicate a more serious problem.

Review the range of choices available to the patient. Your own examples are always useful.

Surgeries use integrated systems which:

- provide access to patient records
- support prescription of medication
- enable forward booking of appointments
- provide links to external services such as blood testing and hospital appointments
- provide budgetary information.

ICT and education

AQA **INFO 2, INFO 3**
OCR **G063**
WJEC **IT1, IT3**
CCEA **AS 1, A2 1**

More than anywhere, the impact of ICT on education is keenly felt. The nature of the modern classroom is very different from that of the classroom of 20 years ago.

ICT in the classroom

The introduction of the **interactive whiteboard** into the school classroom has enabled teachers to develop and use interactive presentations and demonstrations to support learning. Students are able to engage with the presentations and demonstrations by taking an active role by, for example, moving objects on the whiteboard to their correct location.

This aspect can be applied on the screen: students can move objects or control work areas using a touch screen. This is especially beneficial for kinaesthetic learners.

Find some practical examples from your own school experience.

Internet, online and on-screen resources often come with internal assessment and tracking systems that enable the students and teachers to see how learning is progressing. This internal assessment allows for built-in flexibility where the pace of learning is managed by the learner. These systems are often referred to as Computer-Based Training (CBT) or Computer Assisted Learning (CAL).

Such ICT learning systems can enable the personalisation of learning. Students can be directed along, or can follow their own choice of, learning pathways suited either to their own learning needs, or to their personal learning interests.

Distance education and home schooling

Classroom-based teaching and learning is not necessarily an option for all students. For students who choose not to engage in classroom-based learning, distance education, supported by ICT, is a real option. Providers of distance education have learning sites where students can download course materials and upload assessment activities. This provides support for both individual students and for parents and carers who have made the decision to educate their child at home. Distance education providers offer education at all levels – from primary school, through to doctorate level.

Learning technologies

The use of **virtual learning environments** (**VLEs**) allows teachers to establish their own online presence and to provide access to their classes, and to associated e-learning and teaching resources. VLEs tend to be restricted to validated and registered students who can log in, access the teaching and learning materials, engage in activities and complete assessments. VLEs can be a useful complement to traditional teaching, or provide the basis for distance education. VLEs often have chat room functions so that students can engage in dialogue with other students or subject experts.

Administration and assessment

An increasing number of schools is making use of **swipe card** systems to register attendance at school, and at lessons. The readers, at the entrance to classrooms, log students and transmit the data to the main office. This data can be used for daily, weekly, termly and annual reports on attendance. Links from the database to parent and carer contact details means that letters, emails and texts can be automatically generated.

Swipe cards are also being used to support cashless transactions in schools as well.

Assessment is an interesting area for ICT. **Optical mark readers** have long been used to mark and calculate the results of multiple-choice tests. The way in which answer papers are distributed has also developed: from the sending of parcels to the scanning in of papers and the transmission of the output online, or via email. A recent development is the emergence of **intelligent marking systems** which scan for words and phrases in answers in order to award marks. This is an area of much debate – it could lead to answers being made up of key words and phrases rather than intelligible sentences.

ICT and entertainment

AQA	**INFO 2, INFO 3**
OCR	**G063**
WJEC	**IT1, IT3**
CCEA	**AS 1, A2 1**

Our view of entertainment has changed dramatically as a consequence of ICT. Internet and independent handheld gaming is now a regular feature of our lives, and current advertising is pushing the age and gender boundaries of ICT-based gaming and entertainment products. Handheld and Internet gaming and entertainment used to be seen as the domain of young men and boys but with the advent of Brain Gym®, Wii Fit® and family-based entertainment that profile is being challenged.

Digitising television and radio

Major changes in access to television and radio have been emerging since the 1980s. The access to both terrestrial and satellite television stations has seen a wider choice of television channels available, but has also seen a move from analogue to digital signalling.

This move has been formalised in Great Britain with the switching off of the analogue television signal planned for 2012. This has a social and economic impact: every television will either need to be replaced or enhanced with the attachment of a digital signal receiver and decoder.

The move from analogue to digital radio is not quite as straightforward as television, although the timetable for the transition was originally the same. New digital radios (**digital audio broadcasting – DAB**) are not as expensive as digital televisions – but a significant proportion of radio listeners listen to radio as they travel in their cars and these radios only receive analogue signals. This makes the transition from analogue to digital an expensive option, since to change the radio you need to change the car. The termination of the analogue radio signal has been postponed – for future consideration.

Entertainment on demand

Access to entertainment is very much available **on demand**. Audio and video players have become increasingly portable, and as mobile broadband speeds have increased, **video streaming** has been made more accessible to people as they travel.

Internet video applications and video download (and upload) sites are widely available.

Entertainment modules, applications and downloads are available for all kinds of mobile systems: computers, MP3 and MP4 players, portable video players, games consoles, mobile telephones. Indeed the range of applications for the latest mobile phones is growing massively every day.

Television stations have responded to the demand to have television programmes available out of slot. The demand began as radio stations began to develop podcasts of popular programmes. Television responded initially with **vodcasts** (video on demand), but extended it to a much more sophisticated offer. Each of the terrestrial stations in Great Britain now has their own system for television on demand.

ICT and commerce

AQA	**INFO 2, INFO 3**
OCR	**G063**
WJEC	**IT1, IT3**
CCEA	**AS 1, A2 1**

The service industries are heavy users of ICT. The importance of ICT in commercial activity such as shopping, banking and insurance has grown with the advent of the Internet. The Internet allows suppliers to offer their services twenty-four hours a day, seven days a week, and three hundred and sixty-five days a year (24/7/365).

Shopping

Many stores have an online presence, which allows them to trade their wares far beyond the physical boundaries of their stores and warehousing, and outside normal trading hours. The range of goods and services to purchase includes: housing; insurance; food; furniture; clothing; cars; holidays; flights; books; audio and video.

This list is not exhaustive, but it does highlight the diversity of goods on offer online. Indeed, many commercial activities take place only online, and for each of the categories above you will be able to find traders whose only avenue for generating sales is through their website.

Advantages for the consumer	Advantages for the trader
• Can compare prices quickly without physically going from store to store. • Online payments are secure and, if made using a credit card, are backed by guarantee. • Shopping can be cheaper: no charges for travelling; no parking charges; no temptation to spend money on snacking. This has to be balanced against the cost of delivery. • Shoppers can avoid queues. • Because the suppliers have lower overhead costs prices can be cheaper.	• There is access to a much wider customer base. • There is no need for expensive shop fronts or fancy warehousing. • Fewer staff are needed in order to sell the products: the focus will be on warehousing and despatch rather than on staffing the shop floor. • The business can be based anywhere. • Overheads are much lower – while prices can be lower, profitability can be much higher.

Disadvantages for the consumer	Disadvantages for the trader
• Are dependent on the reliability of the delivery service. • It is difficult to choose the correct size and colour – trying on is not really an option. • As the goods have to be delivered you have to plan in advance. • Concern about the security of payment.	• Need to let customers know that the outlet is online and available. • Difficulties in getting to the top of search-engine listings. • Reliable on delivery services – if they are unreliable they give the company a bad name.

As ever it is important to be aware of a range of advantages and disadvantages.

There is an increasing number of auction sites online. These sites enable everyone, including regular businesses, to present their goods and services and to allow potential customers to browse through what is on offer. Buyers can make instant comparisons and the opportunity to bid low and 'bag a bargain' is attractive to many prospective purchasers.

Many stores, both physical and online, make use of **Electronic Point of Sale** (EPOS) systems. These track purchases that have been made and enable stores to manage their stock control and payment functions directly from the till (or point of sale). This would mean that each time a tin of baked beans passes the scanner, information is passed on to stock control – as well as to the billing system that the customer sees. If stocks of baked beans pass a 're-order level' at the moment of that sale – an order for new stocks would be placed automatically.

Banking

Online banking has developed an increasingly visible presence since the beginning of the twenty-first century. Almost all services that are available in branch are now available online, and with the reduction in the number of physical branches, online banking is providing vital services to customers who find getting to a branch difficult. It is possible to open accounts, transfer money between accounts or to other account holders, pay bills, organise loans and mortgages, plan investments and book virtual appointments with an account manager.

Insurance

Many insurance companies have an online presence, which allows customers to provide the required information and get a quotation instantly.

The insurance industry has been affected by the emergence of comparison websites. These allow customers to enter their details once and get a wide variety of offers and prices from which to make a choice.

Making reservations

It is possible to make reservations for hotels, rail and air travel, restaurants, and theatre, cinema and concert seats. Many of the reservation agents provide consumers with access to discounted tickets, and some provide access to critiques of the venues so that comparisons and judgments about suitability can be made. Using reservation agent websites enables customers to make many bookings or enquiries at a time, without having to make one telephone call to enquire, and then another to make the booking.

Secure payments

Technology enables us to make secure payments online and in store without using cash. The development of 'chip and pin' has allowed faster processing of transactions, which means that funds can be debited from a customer account quickly and securely. Recent improvements in the process has seen some banks introduce contactless purchasing where the card is simply pressed against a reader rather than inserting the card and validating with a personal identification number (PIN).

The security of online payments is often presented as a barrier to transactions. The vast majority of online transactions go through secure servers – recognised by the symbol of a padlock and the use of https to signify the security of the system.

ICT and marketing

AQA **INFO 2, INFO 3**
OCR **G063**
WJEC **IT1, IT3**
CCEA **AS 1, A2 1**

Advertisements are a regular feature of our Internet and web-browsing experience. Advertisers and marketers have recognised that as consumers move away from printed and televisual material there are other avenues for bringing their goods and services to the attention of potential customers.

Reaching consumers

Many websites have advertisements attached to them. Attracting an advertiser is one way of ensuring that a website generates income. The key to successful advertising using ICT is careful targeting of the advertisement to the browsing preferences of the consumer.

You might, for example, be looking for a popular club in Newcastle to plan for a night out. You may find the club that you are looking for, but may well be presented with advertisements for related services like restaurants, hotels and taxis.

You will often find 'complementary marketing' is a feature on many websites that you visit. For example, looking at a car trading website may present you with advertisements for insurance, loans, tyres and exhausts.

Loyalty cards are used by many stores. Data about customer preferences are recorded with each transaction made. This can lead to targeted discounts or 'rewards' being offered to the customer, or can be used to support complementary marketing (e.g. because you bought cat food you might be interested in cat litter and flea powder).

Viral marketing

Viral marketing is a relatively new area of marketing and is heavily reliant on Internet and email services to 'spread the message'. The focus of the message is to encourage people to pass on the message to existing social networks such as colleagues, family or friends; and as such viral marketing always has something to hook you in, for example:
- the latest must have product
- a fantastic special offer
- an amusing video or joke
- a game that others may want to play.

The most effective viral marketing campaigns are those in which the marketer identifies the hook and gets it out there! Video sharing sites have often been the source of successful campaigns that get hold of the public imagination, for example:
- Susan Boyle
- Mint sweets and Cola
- Million Dollar Web-Page (a page made up of a million pixels, which are each sponsored by an advertiser)

There are even TV programmes that focus on showing viral videos.

Legal implications

All marketing and advertisements are subject to the rules and regulations administered by the **Advertising Standards Authority** (**ASA**) and by local trading and standards officers. Advertising has to be seen as being 'legal, decent, honest and truthful'; something which is sometimes difficult to 'police' on the Internet.

ICT and communications

AQA	**INFO 2, INFO 3**
OCR	**G063**
WJEC	**IT1, IT3**
CCEA	**AS 1, A2 1**

ICT has really changed the way that we communicate. The development of email, social networking, chat, text and Internet telephony have each, in their own way, been as radical as the introduction of the Penny Post in 1840.

Email

Emails are electronic messages that can be sent from one electronic device to another. Email can be accessed either through web browser software, or through company-based servers who will use specialist email software like Microsoft Outlook® or Lotus Notes®.

All emails follow a consistent structure and contain details of the:
- sender
- recipient

- subject of the message
- message content (including the facility to attach files as text documents or images).

Communication by email is much faster, easier and cheaper than paper-based communication systems. Distance is no object with minimal delays between the sending and the receipt of the communication.

Email technology is largely based on **SMTP** protocols and besides being easier and faster, email allows for many possibilities such as:

- copying (Cc) the message to a range of recipients at the same time
- using blind copy (Bcc) to keep identities of multiple recipients hidden from each other
- filtering certain types of messages or recipients.

One of the biggest problems with some email systems is the amount of spam or junk mail that is sent and received every day.

Telephony

The nature of social interactions has changed immeasurably as ownership of simple mobile telephones has grown; and continues to develop as phones become increasingly sophisticated. The ability to receive email, browse the web, and use the telephone as a watch, camera and video camera has changed the way that some people live their lives, but has also seen reductions in the sales of wrist watches and cameras.

> Smart phones are a rapidly developing area of mobile telephony. Have some up-to-date examples ready: any that might be included here would certainly be superseded by a new and improved model very quickly.

In some peoples' views, the rise in the use of mobile telephones is both a cause and symptom of social and moral decline. It is not uncommon to see two people sitting together at a table communicating by text or by tweets to anyone but the person they are sitting with. For some people this is seen as normal behaviour; for others it seems rude and anti-social.

Internet-based telephony has made it cheaper to talk to people all over the world. Bundled within the price you pay anyway to access the Internet, voice over Internet protocol (VOIP) technology reduces the cost of international phone calls significantly.

ICT and manufacturing

AQA	**INFO 2, INFO 3**
OCR	**G063**
WJEC	**IT1, IT3**
CCEA	**AS 1, A2 1**

ICT enables manufacturers to take advantage of developed ICT systems to mass produce goods that retain high quality and high levels of precision and accuracy. The use of robots and computer controlled design and manufacturing has led, in part, to a decrease in demand for skilled crafts people and an increase in demand for computer literate operatives.

Design

Specifications for products can now be developed using industry specialist software. Both minor and major amendments can be made without having to redraw the entire design. Customers are able to request and see 3D renderings of designs so that the process from design to manufacture is much quicker and more likely to fulfil client expectations.

Manufacture

More and more elements of production and manufacture have been automated as technology has become more sophisticated. Automation in the manufacturing process became prominent in Europe in the 1980s with the widely advertised use of robots in the production of the Fiat Strada. Automation and the use of robots is now commonplace in car manufacturing (Citroen and BMW have used specific advertising campaigns that include robots) and in food production. This has meant that a number of jobs have been made obsolete.

For manufacturers the cost of installing the production machinery and ICT systems has meant heavy capital investment. This has been offset by increased capacity (automated machinery can operate 24/7) and a reduction in the overall manufacturing cost per unit. It also means that changes in design and in the manufacturing process can be managed by changing the production software.

Simulation modelling

Simulation modelling is a process that takes various scenarios and applies them to the design and manufacture of all types of product.

Example	Impact
Seat belts	Over years tests on lap-only belts determined that injury to passengers was much greater than if they wore three-point belts (those that cross the lap and go over the shoulder and across the chest). Modern cars no longer have lap-only belts for rear seat passengers.
NCAP safety tests (New Car Assessment Programme)	All motor vehicles go through a range of safety tests, including crash testing and the use of crash test dummies, that determine how well the vehicle conforms to safety requirements. Such conformity testing has an impact on design processes – with safety being designed in rather than added on.
Aircraft configuration	Simulation modelling enables designers to calculate the impact of seat configuration on passenger safety in the event of an air accident.

PROGRESS CHECK

1 How might stores benefit from an online presence?
2 Give two advantages of online shopping for the consumer.
3 What is viral marketing?

3 Viral marketing is a relatively new area of marketing that relies on Internet and email services to 'spread the message' to colleagues, family and friends.
2 Any two suitable examples, e.g. They can compare prices quickly; Shopping can be cheaper; Shoppers can avoid queues
1 It extends the physical boundaries of trade and the hours of trading.

12.3 The impact of ICT on individuals

LEARNING SUMMARY

After studying this section you should be able to:

- identify how ICT has had an impact on individuals
- evaluate the changes that have taken place in the workplace
- review how present and future systems affect our home lives

ICT and the workplace

AQA **INFO 2, INFO 3**
OCR **G063**
WJEC **IT1, IT3**
CCEA **AS 1, A2 1**

There are very few areas of working life that have remained unchanged as a consequence of ICT and as job requirements change, so do the skills needed to carry out those jobs.

Workplace skills

As the need for manual and clerical skills has declined, new ICT skills have come to the fore. Many roles in organisations today are what can be defined as portfolio roles, i.e. ones that have a variety of aspects and skills: financial management; report writing; developing presentations, etc. In the past, financial calculations were often carried out by teams of people using manual calculators. New skills are rapidly replacing old skills as the pace of technological change quickens. This means that the need for ongoing training and skills development needs to be available within the modern workplace.

A wide range of new technologies has given businesses access to faster communication, increased efficiencies, and the ability to work away from the office (see Chapter 13). The growth of new technologies to be used in the workplace is showing no sign of slowing down. Some examples of technology currently in development for commercial use are wearable computing, free urban and region-wide access to WiFi, and nanotechnology. Teams are also able to facilitate virtual meetings where participants will be able to teleconference on their computer screens, while creating or changing documents and product designs using a 'virtual whiteboard'. These technologies and many more, including all the unforeseen advances, will continue to contribute to an increasingly mobile workforce. There will be challenges for businesses and organisations, not only in implementing new technology as it emerges, but in preparing their workforce effectively for these changes.

ICT in the home

AQA **INFO 2, INFO 3**
OCR **G063**
WJEC **IT1, IT3**
CCEA **AS 1, A2 1**

ICT has not only had an impact on our workplaces. Our homes too have changed, and will continue to change. Only 30 years ago the impact of ICT and technology on our homes was negligible. According to the Office for National Statistics the proportion of households in the UK owning a home computer rose from 70 per cent to 72 per cent between 2007 and 2008; up from 67 per cent in 2006. The percentage of households in the UK with an Internet connection rose from 61 per cent in 2007 to 66 per cent in 2008. It is not just about computers and access to an Internet connection: many of our small household devices have a microprocessor, and the development of 'smart household goods' is becoming a reality.

Security

As concerns about home safety and security are often in the headlines there have been developments in home security systems. Rather than relying on contact breakers (such as when a door is opened) many home security systems can be linked to movement sensors, web-cams and telephone services to contact the police without 'alarm bells ringing'.

Domestic services

Many of our services can be controlled by ICT. There are systems and devices available for homeowners to review their energy usage and to make changes so that their bills can be reduced, e.g. monitoring gas, electricity and water usage.

As more and more people are generating electricity at home using solar panels and wind power, microprocessing systems have been developed to identify how much home generated power is being used by the householder, how much is being taken from the National Grid, and so calculate the bill for electricity.

There are also early developments of home robots that can provide services in the home. The Japanese are at the forefront of developments in this area. Perhaps the most commonly available home robot currently available is the automated vacuum cleaner, which uses sensors to negotiate its way around the room.

Entertainment

Although we are very used to digital and satellite television in the home, newer applications require the television to be connected to the telephone line. This enables regular updates to be made, provides cheaper access to broadband services, and allows **video streaming** on demand to the television screen rather than just to a computer screen.

ICT in the kitchen

It may seem odd to think of ICT in the kitchen, but there are developments being made in this area. For example, developments to enable householders to get recipes based on what is in their refrigerator and cupboards. This works by scanning barcodes on products as they go into and out of storage. There is even talk of intelligent waste bins that can scan what has been used and so come up with next week's shopping list.

The range of functions on microwave ovens has become much wider allowing users to programme the weight, size and type of food being cooked: the oven calculates the cooking time based on the data entry.

PROGRESS CHECK

1. How has the spread of ICT in the home changed in the last 30 years?
2. How has ICT affected skills in the workplace?
3. What developments have there been in home safety and security in the last few years?

1. Computer ownership has risen – 72% in 2008; Internet access has risen – 66% in 2008
2. There has been a decline in the need for manual and clerical skills and an increase in the need for new ICT skills.
3. Many home security systems can now be linked to movement sensors, web-cams and telephone services to contact police without 'alarm bells ringing'.

Sample questions and model answers

1. What are the implications of a growth in e-commerce for society? **(8)**

The growth of e-commerce can result in a change in employment pattern because businesses that trade entirely on the web need fewer traditional shop-floor staff. Employers such as Amazon® and Ocado® have no retail premises and therefore no shop-floor staff.

What they do have is central warehousing and distribution depots that benefit from computer controlled storekeeping. They do of course need ICT trained staff to support the e-commerce.

For society as a whole, since customers may travel less to visit shops and retail centres then there could be less pollution and smaller carbon footprint. However, since e-commerce can be global, the distribution of goods bought abroad and shipped by air could counterbalance the reduction in personal carbon footprint.

There are concerns that increased reliance on e-commerce could change the nature of our town centres and also lead to a decrease in social interaction (although as e-commerce has grown so has the number of coffee shops and cafes). There are other issues that have emerged as e-commerce has increased: gambling sites operate 24/7/365. These range from the National Lottery, to bingo, poker and betting sites. There are concerns that these leave people vulnerable to gambling addiction, which is a problem for the individual but also for society as a whole.

2. Explain how ICT can cause problems for society at large and for individuals. **(10)**

The misuse of ICT can raise a number of issues for individuals and for society as a whole. Of widespread concern currently is the issue of identity theft. This occurs when someone else gets hold of your bank or credit card details and uses these details to buy goods and services. At a higher level there have been instances of people gaining access to passport and other official documentation to develop a whole new identity. Some access to personal data can be gained as an outcome of hacking: getting through password protection and sign-ins to then be able to change or access stored data. Malicious interference comes from virus attacks which can cause software functions to fail, or to alter the content of data files. For both individuals and for organisations this type of attack can be extremely damaging. Other problems arise when people feel that they are living and working in a surveillance society: everything we do seems to be monitored by CCTV, our use of mobile phones, or our use of debit, credit and customer loyalty cards.

Our general use of ICT can highlight inequalities - those who can afford access to ICT services can get savings and services not available to those without access. At a national and international level this means that the rich nations of the world are able to benefit greatly from ICT. Countries where electricity and telecommunications are unreliable or insufficiently developed are unable to benefit from ICT. Some third world countries are, however, benefiting from globalisation as cultural and economic barriers break down.

Because ICT allows us to work anywhere jobs, such as software support, can be carried out where labour costs are cheaper. This could be seen a symptom of de-skilling of the workforce. This is problematic for the individual, but also for society as a whole as a disaffected workforce could give rise to social and political unrest such as the `poll tax riots' or the miners' strike of the 1980s.

The answer is extended here by giving a couple of examples.

This is a strong opening to the paragraph. The argument is balanced – as one element of work changes another emerges.

Again, a balanced argument is given here. This shows the examiner that you have a broad understanding of the impact of ICT on society.

Identity theft is a key area of concern and one that is good to explore in detail.

Hacking and viruses are also 'popular' issues to explore.

Note the examples that are given to expand upon the symptoms of de-skilling the workforce.

Practice examination questions

1 Social networking sites have grown in popularity. Discuss the possible effects of using these sites on individuals and society.

Your discussion should include reference to:

- Use of the Internet for socialising

- The protection of personal data

- Moral and ethical factors

- Cultural factors **(20)**

13 Working in and with ICT

The following topics are covered in this chapter:

- **Telecommuting**
- **Codes of conduct**
- **Careers in ICT**

13.1 Telecommuting

LEARNING SUMMARY

After studying this section you should be able to:

- describe how remote workers access office networks from home
- identify the key features of the hardware available to remote workers
- explain the advantages and disadvantages of teleworking for organisations and individuals

Teleworking

AQA **INFO 3**
OCR **G061, G063**
WJEC **IT3**
CCEA **AS 1, A2 1**

Teleworking is when an employee works away from the main centre of work, usually at home. Teleworkers are defined as people who work from their own home using computers, telephones and other communication devices for their work. The UK Labour Force Survey (2002) defined three categories of remote or teleworker:

- **Teleworker home-workers** – those who work mainly from home as an outcome of their main occupation.
- **Home-based teleworkers** – those who work in a number of locations but who use their home as a base.
- **Occasional teleworkers** – those who have the option to work from home for at least one day per week.

The UK Labour Force Survey (2002) is the most recent available to us. At that time there were 2.2 million teleworkers; around 7.4% of the working population. This number has been growing steadily, increasing at around 13% per year since 1997. The growth in other forms of employment is around 1.6%.

Organisations that allow their employees to work as teleworkers need to be engaged in the type of work that can be done remotely. Examples include: directory enquiries; secretarial work; data entry work; advice and consultancy. There has to be a significant amount of trust – as an employer you need to know that the work is going to be done. There are also set-up arrangements to be considered: the employer would need to provide the relevant equipment – computer, telephone line, network connection (Internet and company intranet); and the employee would need to ensure that they have space available to set aside for work.

> Reduced costs and increased flexibility for both employer and employee are often cited as benefits of teleworking.

	Advantages of teleworking	Disadvantages of teleworking
Employee	Saves time and money on commuting to work.	It costs more at home because you spend more on lighting and heating.
	You can choose where you want to live – you are not restricted by the time it takes to travel to work.	Some teleworkers feel isolated.
	It is easier to work flexible hours – you might be able to start work early and work later in the evening to fit around family commitments.	Some employers may decide that the pay rate for teleworkers can be lower.
	It can be less stressful since you are not dealing with transport problems.	There are fewer opportunities to meet other colleagues, to 'get the gossip', or to go out after work.
	Many employees can set up their working space to suit themselves.	Some employees lose the distinction between work-time and home-time, or become distracted easily during the working day.
Employer	Employers need smaller offices if their staff is based elsewhere. This reduces office overheads (gas, electricity, insurance, furniture, cleaning staff) and could contribute to greater profitability.	Set up costs can be high as all the computer equipment has to be provided. Dedicated telephone lines and remote working support services can also be expensive to run. Heavy use of mobile telephones and other mobile communication devices can prove costly. With so much computer equipment based outside the office, and potentially on the move, there are greater data security risks.
	Without office distractions teleworkers are often more productive.	It can be difficult to ensure that staff are working hard enough, and it can be hard for managers to monitor the flow of work. It can be more difficult to hold meetings – if staff are working in many locations you can't quickly get people together for an ad-hoc meeting to discuss how things are progressing.
	Since workers are not restricted to working at specified centres, organisations can recruit them from anywhere, without having to pay relocation costs.	The organisation may have to restructure itself – what sort of workers are working remotely, are they all 'lower-tier workers' or are there managers working away from the office as well? Do other sections of the organisation need to grow – such as support and technical services?

	Advantages of teleworking	Disadvantages of teleworking
Society	As fewer people commute to work traffic congestion is reduced. This leads to lower CO_2 emissions and less air pollution.	As people become increasingly isolated in their work there could be increased incidences of depressive illnesses.
	Rural communities benefit because people can still work at organisations based in the cities and remain at home.	A significant reduction in the number of commuters could lead to cut backs in public transport services – this could affect rural communities disproportionately.
	Workers have more time at home and have more time to spend with their families.	

High-quality video-conferencing

AQA **INFO 3**
OCR **G061, G063**
WJEC **IT3**
CCEA **AS 1, A2 1**

Video-conferencing is becoming an increasingly important tool for split site organisations, for remote workers and for education. It enables colleagues (and learners) from anywhere in the world to communicate with each other and to discuss key issues that are important to the organisation in which they work and/or to discuss topics which they are studying. Whilst the use of web cams is an inexpensive way of video-conferencing, the quality can vary considerably according to how busy the Internet is at the time communication is made. For business purposes it is important to have a high quality and reliable service, and this requires the use of specialist equipment.

Advantages of high-quality video-conferencing	Disadvantages of high-quality video-conferencing
Allows for regular meetings between differently-located individuals.	Video-conferencing is very dependent on expensive hardware: it is expensive to set up, and ongoing running and maintenance costs can be high.
Allows everyone to see faces and to be able to pick up important messages through body language.	Subtle nuances in body language can be missed – the face may tell one story, the tapping feet that you can't see may tell another.
Can be used along with the Internet to facilitate the sharing of presentations.	Costs could be offset by the use of cheaper Internet or telephone-based systems – but the quality is often low.
If an organisation has many centres, or if staff are distributed widely because the organisation supports teleworking, video-conferencing can help to maintain and enhance the company ethos.	Organisations need to establish a clear etiquette for video-conferencing since it is often difficult for more than one person to interact at a time, and it is more difficult to signal that you want to make a point than it is in a traditional face-to-face meeting.

Essentially there are five stages in setting up a high-quality video-conferencing system:

1. Get the room
A room needs to be available and set up like a normal meeting room. It also needs to have a camera to capture the visual images, a large screen (so you can see the participants in the other location) and at least one microphone to capture the voices.

2. Convert the signal
The camera and microphone will pick up analogue signals, which need to be converted to digital (binary) signals. This can be done using a codec which can convert analogue to digital and digital to analogue. It is also possible to combine the video and audio signals into one file – such as a .AVI file.

3. Compress the signal ready for transmission
Compressing the signal means that transmission is more efficient: it will be both cheaper and faster. The trick is to make sure that compression can be done without a loss of quality (both in image and sound). A popular compression methodology is one that removes pixels from images with lots of high contrast. This is known as lossy compression.

4. Transmit the data
Data is usually transmitted using an ISDN line. This ensures that audio and data arrive together, which is very important for video-conferencing. There is nothing worse than watching lips move and hearing the sound a few seconds later.

5. Reverse the process at the receiving point
The process is reversed at the destination – decompressing and converting back from digital to analogue. This happens in real time, in both locations, so that the transmission is live and two-way.

PROGRESS CHECK

1. **(a)** Define the term 'teleworking'.
   (b) Describe three advantages of teleworking for an employer.
2. What are the three main categories of remote worker?
3. Why is it important to digitise analogue video signals and to compress the signal before transmission?

1. **(a)** Teleworking happens when an employee works away from the main centre of work, usually at home. **(b)** Any three suitable answers, e.g. Company overheads can be reduced as the employer should need to spend less on office overheads such as gas, electricity, insurance, furniture and other office-based staff. Most teleworkers are more productive. Since staff can work anywhere there is no need for an employer to pay relocation costs when taking on additional members of staff.
2. Teleworker home-workers; home-based teleworkers; occasional teleworkers.
3. As the signal is usually transmitted using an ISDN line the signal needs to be sent in binary format. Compressing the signal means that the transmission will be cheaper and faster, and so more efficient.

13.2 Codes of conduct

LEARNING SUMMARY

After studying this section you should be able to:

● identify the key features of codes of conduct
● explain the difference between an ICT code of conduct and a professional code of conduct
● describe the key legislation that governs working and professional practice in ICT

Types of code of conduct

AQA **INFO 3**
OCR **G063**
WJEC **IT3**
CCEA **A2 1**

> **KEY POINT**
>
> A code of conduct is an agreement made by an employee to follow the rules and guidelines set by their employing organisation. Sometimes this is referred to as a code of practice.

There are two types of **code of conduct**:

● **ICT codes of conduct** relate specifically to the use of ICT and the use of Internet, email and telephone systems.
● **Professional codes of conduct** are set by professional organisations at a more strategic level than a code of practice. These, like Asimov's Laws of Robotics, outline the general principles that govern the way a professional behaves in relation to society, employers and individuals.

The agreements made by an employee to follow specific rules and guidelines are designed to protect the employer and employee from a range of potential ICT-related problems and issues. Some of these issues are covered by legislation; others relate to conduct in the workplace.

The following table outlines the issues relating to the use of ICT facilities:

Issue covered	Specific direction within the code of conduct	Rationale
Virus protection	Employees may be forbidden from using portable storage media.	They may introduce viruses to the organisation's facilities.
Misuse of ICT facilities	There could be specific reference to the use of printers for personal work. Use of Internet, email and telephones (landlines and mobile).	The employee should bear the cost of such activity. Employers could consider the use of consumables such as paper and ink for purposes other than work as theft. Codes of conduct will specify what is allowed and disallowed. A key focus will be on the amount of time an employee gives to their work – personal use of these facilities can be seen as time expensive, and of course will incur costs (e.g. use of telephones).

Issue covered	Specific direction within the code of conduct	Rationale
Distribution of and access to material that is offensive to others	Generally the focus of this area is on material that is racially, sexually or morally offensive.	Employers will view access to and distribution of such materials for personal gratification as a severe misuse of facilities. Since ICT facilities at work are potentially available to everyone within the organisation, the risk of causing offence is high. There could be legal consequences for such actions.
Misuse of data for illicit purposes	Data owned by, or generated by the employer should not be shared with others outside the organisation.	Some data may be seen as commercially sensitive. It may damage the company if sensitive information is leaked to a competitor. For some employees this may have an impact on national security as they may have access to security data that should not be shared outside the organisation. Others may have access to personal data, e.g. credit card or bank details.
Inappropriate use of mobile phones	Employees may be reminded, or indeed required, to think about the nature of their call and to be sensitive about their location.	How often do you sit in a public area and hear details of company or personal transactions taking place over a mobile telephone? Sensitive information can be overheard and others may make use of that information. Other aspects of misuse may involve: sending offensive texts; engaging in workplace bullying by text; inappropriate use of video and Internet facilities where they exist.
Inappropriate communication	Employees may be specifically directed about their use of email or company letter headed stationery and logos.	There is a danger for organisations that individual personal views could be seen as representative of the organisation if they are made on company stationery or by company email.
Copyright or software agreements	Many organisations have policies about software that is available to employees and about their access to, and use of, text and images from outside sources.	The majority of software has licensing agreements that must be followed. Images, text, sound and video from other organisations may have copyright; use of such media may constitute as a breach of copyright. Failure to comply with these agreements could result in litigation.

Content of an ICT code of conduct

Codes of conduct generally have at least nine specific elements:
- An outline of the responsibilities of the organisation and of the employee
- A statement about the need to respect the right of others
- Reference to current legislation
- The need to protect hardware and software from malicious or accidental damage
- The need to comply with licensing agreements
- The levels of authorisation needed to perform certain actions (such as installing new software or installing a new printer driver)
- Permissions on data access
- A definition of rules about:
    - password disclosure
    - personal use of emails and the Internet
    - the transfer of data
- A section on the penalties for misuse or a transgression of the rules, including:
    - informal warnings
    - written warnings
    - dismissal
    - prosecution

Example

This is an example code of conduct. You might want to have a look at other examples. Your school or college is likely to have an ICT code of conduct. You might even have signed one. It's always good to have a practical example you can refer to.

The purpose of this code of conduct is to provide guidance on our systems with a particular focus on the use of email, the Internet and instant messaging. It outlines our policy regarding personal use and offers guidelines on what is not acceptable. Used properly ICT systems can assist the organisation in improving business performance. However, it is important that we all accept responsibility for our actions when using these facilities.

The code has been approved by the Management Team and applies to all users, including full time, part-time, secondees, contractors and agency staff.

It is the responsibility of all users to comply with this code of conduct. You must ensure that you are familiar with its contents. Ignorance is no excuse.

The ICT facilities are provided to fulfil our business objectives. As such they are owned by the organisation – which in turn is liable for all equipment, material, and any emails and cached Internet pages generated or stored on company equipment. Staff are permitted to make limited personal use of the ICT facilities in their own time, or when working outside normal working hours.

You may use company systems to prepare personal documents. These documents must not, however, be stored on the C: drive of your working computer, nor on the F: drive. Our registration under the Data Protection Act only covers work-related data.

Use of company systems in connection with running a private business, or in preparing materials which could be held to be of direct financial benefit to you, is not allowed.

You may send brief personal emails with small attachments to internal and external contacts, providing they are flagged as 'personal'.

You must not use official templates for personal documents. Private use of chat-rooms, newsgroups and instant messaging is forbidden.

Disciplinary action will be taken against any user who makes improper or excessive use of the email facility.

Accessing the Internet for personal purposes is permitted provided that this is done outside normal working hours. All Internet usage is monitored. Line managers and the HR unit will be alerted and take disciplinary action if there is a concern about attempted access to inappropriate sites or if excessive personal time is spent on the Internet.

If you misuse the system you could be committing a criminal offence. Email can be spontaneous: think before you send it and aim to reflect the high professional standards expected of all employees. If you make defamatory, libellous or untrue statements about internal or external contacts you may be seen as committing a serious disciplinary offence and may be deemed to have undertaken an action which falls under the laws of libel.

Examples of misuse of ICT facilities are listed below. This list is not exhaustive. Discretion can be applied, but misuse may lead to disciplinary action. Those items in the list marked * are more likely to be treated as serious misconduct and could lead to dismissal:

- Attempting to gain access to an inappropriate Internet site that would offend others on the basis of race, religion, colour, sex, disability, national origin or sexual orientation; or which contains material relating to illegal or prohibited activities. *
- Disclosing your password for someone else to use. *
- Loading software for personal use onto your PC, laptop or network drives.
- Subscribing to mailing lists through the Internet for purposes other than those that are work-related.
- Generating messages in a way that makes them appear to have come from someone else. *
- Sending messages which are abusive, offensive, libellous or which cause a nuisance. *
- Generating and/or distributing chain email. *
- Using the ICT facilities for personal gain. *
- Disseminating or printing copyright materials in contravention of the copyright laws. *
- Using the ICT facilities for activities that are politically sensitive, or potentially controversial. *
- Running/hosting a personal website or making private use of chat rooms or instant messaging.
- Improper use of official templates or logos.

We recognise that there may be times when Internet users connect accidentally to websites that may be deemed to contain illegal or offensive material. If this happens, or if you receive an email which you believe may contain pornographic or offensive material, you must disconnect from the site or close the email and then contact ICT Services and inform your line manager.

ICT Services and the HR Unit are responsible for monitoring the use of ICT systems to ensure that we comply with security standards and that all users comply with the code. All email activity is logged. Similarly all Internet activity is logged whether the attempt to access the site was successful or not.

Any possible cases of misuse or misconduct will be drawn by the ICT Director to the attention of the HR Unit who will decide, in consultation with line management, what action should be taken. Cases of serious or gross misconduct could lead to dismissal. In extreme cases it may be necessary to involve the police.

You are required to familiarise yourself and comply with this code of conduct. You will be deemed to agree to its terms and conditions, including the monitoring arrangements. You should inform your line manager in the case of accidental or questionable access. You should also inform your line manager if you believe that a colleague is misusing the system.

Professional codes of conduct

AQA **INFO 3**
OCR **G063**
WJEC **IT3**
CCEA **A2 1**

Professional codes of conduct often begin with a statement relating to **ethics** and define details of a code of ethics and a set of related standards of conduct. Ethics relate to our understanding of what is right and what is wrong. Businesses make these decisions all the time. So do we all, both in our personal and in our professional lives. Some decisions that we make may have a very small impact on those around us; other decisions that are made may have an impact far beyond our initial understanding. A misjudged decision can give rise to a number of unintended outcomes: it may cause offence or hurt; it may present a negative image of the company or product and reduce demand; it may lead to a company going bankrupt.

> It is always useful to have a range of current examples of how ethical or unethical decisions or actions have an impact on individuals or on society.

Most professions have a set of guidelines that govern the way that their members should behave. For example, there are guidelines for the way that teachers, lawyers and doctors should conduct themselves in their professional dealings. People who work in ICT are no different. The British Computer Society (BCS), the Association of Information Technology Professionals and other ICT and Computing professional associations have their own codes of professional conduct. As with the general codes of conduct there are specific elements that make up a code of professional conduct. These include:

- The contribution that engagement in professional activity makes to society.
- The need to keep professional knowledge current and to support others in the development of knowledge and understanding.
- The need to be honest and open in all professional undertakings and to expect the same from others.
- To respect privacy and confidentiality.
- To respect and value the work that others have done and not to claim it as your own.

Legislation that influences ICT and professional codes of conduct

AQA **INFO 2, INFO 3**
OCR **G061**
WJEC **IT3**
CCEA **AS 1, A2 1**

You have seen that in the general ICT and professional codes of conduct there is reference to associated legal rights and responsibilities. There is also specific reference to the ethical or moral decisions that we are required to make in our day-to-day personal and professional interactions.

There are a number of laws that have informed the development of professional and legal codes of conduct.

For more information on legislation see pages 207–209.

Telecommunications Act (1984)

The transmission of an obscene or indecent image from one computer to another through a public telecommunications system is an offence under section 43 of the Telecommunications Act. For traditional mail the same sort of offence is covered by the Post Office Act of 1953.

Protection of Children Act (1978) and Criminal Justice Act (1988)

The Protection of Children Act and Criminal Justice Act make it a criminal offence to distribute or possess scanned, digital or computer generated facsimile photographs, deemed to be indecent, of a child under 16.

Protection from Harassment Act (1997), Sex Discrimination Act (1975) and Race Relations Act (1976)

It is unlawful to engage in activities that lead to another person, or other persons, feeling that they are being harassed or that they are suffering discrimination. This applies whether or not work-based communication systems have played a part. Comments sent by email, text, or through instant messaging are capable of contributing to harassment and give rise to complaints of harassment and discrimination.

Data Protection Act (1998)

Personal data as defined under the Data Protection Act should not be included in any proposed Internet web page, or other Internet entry. Care should be taken not to disclose personal information when replying to email enquiries.

Defamation Laws

Information stored on web servers is subject to laws relating to defamation. For example, in 1997 a large insurance company was required to make a payment of £450,000 in damages to a rival insurance company because untrue emails had been circulated that implied that the rival company was facing financial difficulties and was likely to go out of business.

It is important to remember that emails and records of web access can be stored for many years, and that items deleted on hard and network drives are recoverable. Defamatory material can be restored and used as evidence in legal cases.

Copyright laws

The use of material from the Internet is subject to similar copyright conditions that apply to other media. Sources should always be acknowledged and permission should be sought if large scale or systematic use of material is to be made. You will probably have seen messages relating to software or video piracy.

Computer Misuse Act (1990)

There are several criminal offences linked to the Computer Misuse Act. It is an offence for a person to knowingly attempt to gain unauthorised access to a secure computer system. It is also an offence to gain such access with the intention to modify data or programs. The deliberate introduction of a virus to a computer system is forbidden.

Companies Act (2006)

Company Directors must act not just in the best interests of the company but also in the interests of employees, the community and the environment. As with other aspects of law, ignorance is not considered a reasonable defence.

Bribery Act (2010)

Under the Bribery Act legislation companies can be held liable for the actions of any employee or agent who offers bribes or inducements in order to gain commercial advantage, even when the company is unaware that such actions are taking place.

Ethical and moral issues in ICT

AQA	INFO 3
OCR	G063
WJEC	IT3
CCEA	A2 1

Disinformation

ICT can provide us with a wider access to data about the range of products and services that is available to us. An online store may find themselves with an overstock of items that need to be sold on quickly before an upgraded model is introduced. An advertising campaign that focuses on the price and features of the model with a strap line about the 'latest model' would not be informing potential customers of all the available facts concerning that product.

Privacy

The distinction between an individual's right to **privacy** and the needs for an organisation to comply, for example, with the Companies Act (2006) or the Bribery Act (2010) is one that needs careful consideration. It is important that organisations make it very clear which aspects of privacy are subject to review by the organisation, and which aspects remain private to the individual. For some organisations this will be an ethical decision, for others it will simply be a matter of complying with the law – how people feel about scrutiny will not play a part in this.

The development of ICT systems has enabled all kinds of organisations to hold a great deal of private and personal data. Individuals are protected under the terms of the Data Protection Act (1988), but not all 'data subjects' know that this is the case. Not all organisations behave ethically with the data that they have, and we need to recognise that some organisations do not store personal data securely and it may become more widely available than expected. We have seen in the example ICT code of conduct that the monitoring of emails can happen on a regular basis – this company has informed its employees of this, and has provided some justification for doing so, but this is not always the case.

Employment patterns

ICT has changed the workplace in ways that workers in the 1980s would not have been able to predict accurately. The ability to calculate complex sets of figures, produce reports, design the layout of kitchens, plan the building of technically advanced engineering projects, etc has changed dramatically – and this change has had a dramatic impact on the way people work. For some, working life is richer and more varied; for others, perhaps working in call centres, the working day can be full of drudgery. The fluctuation in employment patterns (the rate at which people move jobs) is much higher in call centres than in many other areas.

Equity

ICT, since it relies on the ownership of, or access to, relatively expensive equipment has led to what has been called 'information poor' and 'information rich' societies. For many individuals the relationship between knowledge and power is important: access to ICT systems that provide ongoing access to knowledge systems can mean the difference between economic success and failure. This means that those less well off could find themselves constantly at the wrong side of the divide between information rich and poor. Many western countries have developed plans and schemes to enable the poorest members of society to have access to ICT systems. For example, Finland has made it a legal right to have access to 1 MB broadband. We have also seen the development of the sub-$100 laptop for use in the developing world.

Intellectual property rights

The development of highly effective ICT tools and products, and the expansion of the Internet have led to questions about **intellectual property rights**. Who owns what we as individuals produce using ICT? Access to the written word, music, images and film is much easier over the Internet than it was before. The tension between the creator and the user is obvious when, for example, a musician wants to be paid royalties for their music, but that music has been made available on a free-file sharing basis. Some accept the principle of free downloads – others do not.

There are issues too about when or how work is done. The development and publishing of an idea or thought that has taken place on 'company time' will be claimed as the intellectual property rights of the organisation rather than the individual. This does not only apply to inventors or researchers – staff working on the compilation of large databases, complex financial analyses or the production of sales and marketing materials could be generating intellectual property that belongs to the employer.

Many employment contracts will make intellectual property rights very clear. Intellectual property may also have moral rights attached to it. For example, a musician may have produced a jingle for a product. The intellectual property will belong to the employer, but unless the employer has specifically claimed the moral rights to the property, the musician will have the right to be identified as the composer and will have the power to block changes to the music. The economic rights over the piece of music would belong to the employer.

PROGRESS CHECK

1. Why might an employer require an employee to agree to an ICT code of conduct?
2. How can the monitoring of emails or web access be justified by law?
3. A technician uses a software monitoring system that enables him to track how software (and people) are working from his own screen. This can be done without employees knowing about it. Is this ethical?

1 The agreement made by an employee to follow specific rules and guidelines would protect the employer and employee from a range of potential ICT-related problems and issues. They would ensure that the employee knew about conduct in the workplace, and would also ensure that both employer and employee complied with legislative requirements.
2 The monitoring of emails or web access can be justified under the Protection of Children Act (1978) and the Criminal Justice Act (1988) since under these acts it is a crime to possess or distribute indecent photographs of children under the age of 16. Since comments sent by text, email or IM can lead to complaints of harassment or discrimination the monitoring could be justified under the Protection from Harassment Act (1997), the Sex Discrimination Act (1975) and the Race Relations Act (1976). There are defamation laws too that can be applied, as can copyright laws in relation to the use of material from the internet.
3 Any suitable answer, e.g. As long as there is an agreed code of conduct, it probably is. Employers need to be secure under the Companies Act of 2006 or the Bribery Act of 2010 that the activities their employees undertake on work premises comply with the law. The organisation can be considered at fault if data stored on their systems is found to be out of copyright, defamatory or discriminatory; ignorance is not considered a reasonable defence.

13.3 Careers in ICT

LEARNING SUMMARY

After studying this section you should be able to:
- describe the general skills needed if ICT plays a role in a job
- describe the skills needed if the work is ICT specific
- describe the skills needed to work successfully in an ICT team

General ICT skills

AQA **INFO 2, INFO 3**
OCR **G061**
CCEA **AS 1, A2 1**

For many workers the use of ICT is an essential rather than a desirable requirement.

Bank clerks need to be able to interrogate internal databases in order to check customer account balances, verify contact details or establish the need to send out a personalised letter. They may also be involved in supporting enquiries about a range of financial products, and would certainly need the support of ICT tools to help with calculations and cashing-up.

Teachers use ICT in a number of ways. They may use Internet facilities to support their research for planning lessons, word processing to prepare lessons and lesson materials, presentation software during lessons, and spreadsheets and database software for recording results, checking attendance and for administrative purposes.

Estate agencies are often cited as important users of ICT. They use databases to enable them to search for properties that meet their clients' requirements and they publish brochures and advertisements for their shop window or newspapers. They develop a website, offer financial advice to clients, and use diary management for their agents who show clients around new listings.

ICT skills are also required by other sectors, e.g. the health service, supermarkets and other retailing operations, kitchen planners and designers.

There are many generic software packages, tools and facilities available. You should be able to decide what are 'specialist' ICT knowledge areas and what people need to know as part of their general skills set.

The diagram below begins to analyse the range of general skills that you might have if you use spreadsheets on a regular basis. As you become more specialised in your knowledge areas you would use more complex procedures that a general user might not use.

Note that the knowledge areas shown in red are likely to be more specialised.

> It's useful to be able to describe the general skills that you have in word processing, flat file and relational databases, presentation software and Internet searching, and to know the difference between those skills and your more specialised ICT skills.

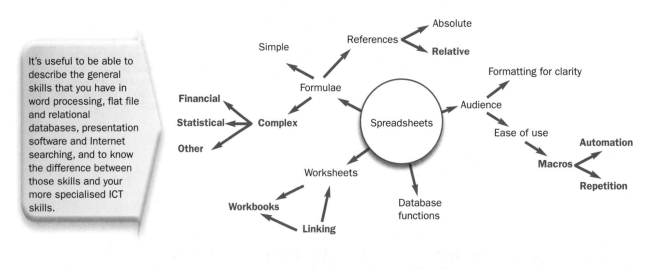

Using specialist ICT skills in the workplace

AQA **INFO 2, INFO 3**
OCR **G061, G063**
CCEA **AS 1, A2 1**

Within companies or other organisations that are focused on the use of ICT there is a large number of roles to consider.

Systems engineers

Systems engineering has developed as a specialist field of employment because many engineering companies, or clients that need an engineered solution to a problem, are unable to find a ready-made product that meets their needs and so have to commission a specially-made product. Most systems engineers have degrees and experience in mathematics, physics or engineering.

Systems engineers need to be able to understand and model the customer's requirements. They need to use their technological knowledge and skills to combine a set of integrated components into a purpose-built solution to their client's problem. The customer is likely to have high expectations that the engineered solution will not only work, but will be much better, more efficient and more cost effective than previously available solutions. Systems engineers work with designers at the start of the design process and need to produce specifications that are accurate, achievable and deliverable throughout the process from design, through to build, error checking and final delivery.

Usually, systems engineers develop additional specialist knowledge to apply their skills and solutions in such areas as battlefields (developing ICT-based solutions for the detection of roadside bombs), sub-sea oil fields (supporting the drilling process or detecting and capping leaks in situations where people could not work) and outer space (helping to repair space stations, deliver supplies, plan for longer voyages).

Key skills:
- Good interpersonal skills
- Careful and focused attention to detail
- Strong written and oral communication skills
- An ability to delegate and manage the work of others
- An understanding of the relationship between the needs of the client and the available or emerging technology

Project managers

Project managers organise and monitor the development of new ICT projects and systems. They see a project through from its inception (the identification of a problem or new service requirement) right through to its conclusion (the evaluation of the implemented solution). This involves overseeing the development of the system, testing the solution and the implementation. In many instances they will also undertake a follow-up evaluation to review the successes and failures of the project.

Key skills:
- Good interpersonal skills
- Careful and focused attention to detail
- A logical approach to problem solving (perhaps supported by the use of specialist software)
- Strong written and oral communication skills
- An ability to delegate and manage the work of others
- An understanding of the relationship between the needs of the client and the available technology

Computer programmer

Computer programmers design and write a 'coded' solution to an identified problem or service need. This coding ensures that the computer is able to perform the functions specified in the system design at the right time, in the right place and in the right order. They need to understand general programming structures and have specialist knowledge of programming languages such as C++, Visual Basic or Java script.

Programming has six main elements:
- Planning – defining a structure for the solution by identifying the main steps the solution will follow, identifying repetitions and iterations that can be set up as sub-routines, identifying opportunities to use existing codes.
- Coding – writing step-by-step instructions in the programming language appropriate for the job.
- Annotating – ensuring that each section of code is described so that other programmers can follow the structure of the program.

- Compiling – putting the written code together as a whole program and converting it into binary code.
- Debugging – testing the program for errors and correcting those that are found.
- Maintenance – amending the original if errors occur once the solution is implemented.

The annotation is important since many programmers find themselves working on the maintenance of programs that other programmers have developed.

Key skills:
- A logical approach to problem solving
- The ability to concentrate for long periods of time on one task
- The ability to learn new skills effectively and quickly
- Clear and focused attention to detail
- Clear and effective communication

Example – Java developers

Computer programmers with Java experience can apply their skills in a wide range of companies, development environments and technologies. Java is a fully object-oriented language used for the development of web services, desktop applications and to support the development of bespoke software solutions to meet needs and solutions required by end-users.

Working as a Java developer for an online company requires extensive practical knowledge of the latest web technologies as well as experience in developing and installing online solutions. As well as programming skills, a Java developer would need knowledge of and skills in database design and relational databases, and experience of working on a full life cycle development project.

As you can see from the Java developer case study, experience in computer programming can lead to a wide range of other careers in ICT. You should also note that capability in using and deploying generic ICT knowledge, skills and techniques is also very important for computer programmers.

Systems designers, analysts and testers

System designers specify the range of files and records to be used. They design the user interface and outline the sequence of processing. The designer also specifies the sequence in which the system will be put together, and in the same way as a project manager, will determine the timescale for development. They also design the format for onscreen views and for hard-copy outputs where these are integral to the system.

Systems analysts organise and review all the components of a system and design appropriate solutions.

Testers make sure that the system works and that it meets the needs identified by the end-user. Usually this leads to the development of a test plan, which ensures that all the elements the system is designed to cover work as planned. A range of test data is run through the system, results are logged and reviewed, and changes to specifications and designs are proposed.

Administrators

Website administrators manage and maintain an organisation's website. They have responsibility for keeping the content of the website up-to-date and for creating content (or including content from external sources). They are also responsible for developing and amending the structure of the site and should review the navigation regularly – pulling in test users where appropriate. They need to be able to run the web server software and to respond effectively to downtime problems or maintenance issues as and when they occur. Increasingly, they will need to manage communication software effectively and may even need to maintain editorial control of blogs, tweets and message boards.

Key skills:
- Adaptable as they have to be able to respond quickly when circumstances change
- Good design skills
- Able to make decisions quickly and delegate responsibilities so that problems can be resolved quickly
- Technical knowledge of the Internet
- Strong written and oral communication skills

Network administrators are responsible for the security and administration of networks. They are likely to oversee the commissioning and installation of new hardware and ensure that it is compatible with the rest of the network. They will maintain network hardware and will ensure that problems are fixed. They will maintain user accounts and passwords, focusing on the security of the network by validating all users. They will also implement regular and effective backup systems to ensure that company data is secure.

Key skills:
- Highly developed technical knowledge
- The capacity to learn quickly as systems change
- Practical problem-solving skills
- Able to understand the technology needs of the organisation and how they contribute to those needs
- Good interpersonal skills – they need to be calm and organised when things go wrong

Example

An emerging extension of network and website administration is the role of security consultant. There is a need for technology and infrastructure to be protected from external threats. Organisations that operate online are exposed to 'cybercrime' and need specialist security consultants to develop and maintain secure systems.

Data protection is extremely important as more and more data is stored and disseminated online. Security experts need to protect networks, software, Internet/intranet and other infrastructures, and also to develop policies governing the use of data. Security consultants would need, as a minimum, to know about:
- protecting against viruses and worms
- preventing website attacks
- developing and maintaining secure networks
- sourcing and installing security hardware
- managing internal security issues including the choice of secure passwords.

ICT function

The ICT function is responsible for the development, management and support of the ICT infrastructure of an organisation. This infrastructure will include the internal and external electronic communication networks: WANs and LANs. These networks link the operational systems within the organisation with the hardware and software systems used by managerial, support and frontline staff.

Staff roles within the ICT function include:
- network management
- technology and help desk support
- application and systems development
- project management and implementation
- system security
- staff training

> **KEY POINT**
>
> Many jobs require employees to be team players. Team players are good listeners and have well developed communication skills. They are seen as co-operative, but competitive for the company. They are adaptable to change and upbeat and optimistic. They are good at negotiating towards a solution.

Information technology training administrator

Information technology training administrators have responsibility for the administration of ICT training within an organisation. Typical duties would include the publicity for, and scheduling of, training courses, advice on suitable courses and all aspects of booking correspondence. They may also be responsible for maintaining a training database and associated website.

Technology and help desk support

Technology and help desk support would need to have experience and knowledge of Operating Systems and the software used predominantly within the organisation. They would need to have problem-solving skills and be able to undertake PC installations and support fault diagnosis and fixing. They would certainly need to be a team player and be able to work under pressure in very busy environments.

Junior computer support analysts

Junior computer support analysts or network support technicians assist in the implementation and commissioning of new computing equipment within the organisation. Tasks might include undertaking acceptance tests, installation, program installation, and the commissioning of computer and data communications equipment. They would also keep accurate records of work undertaken including the entry of information into asset systems. For some there would be a need to demonstrate the use of computer equipment to staff and to assist in the maintenance of computer equipment.

ICT trainer

ICT trainers ensure that employees have the required skills in the range of software packages used by the different departments within the organisation. Their role may also involve invigilating locally-based examinations, checking work, and managing and maintaining records. Such a post might also include training on a variety of other ICT courses that cover the use and maintenance of Operating Systems and the use of software packages such as word processing, spreadsheets, databases, presentation software, email and the Internet.

Application analysts

Application analysts may work in a variety of areas such as on the development of an electronic customer record system linked to a loyalty card for a major retailer. In this example, the application analyst would support the technical development and ongoing administration of the system. This type of post would probably require a degree level of education as well as a period of work experience in a relevant area. Someone working in this field would need to be able to work in a demanding environment, meet tight deadlines and be able to prioritise tasks and activities. Strong written and oral communication skills would be required.

ICT project and liaison managers

ICT project and liaison managers work closely with staff in the organisation and their role would involve either directly project managing or being involved with ICT projects. Project managers should understand the business objectives of the organisation and should be able to relate them to local and national ICT solutions. Good project management and communication skills would be essential to this sort of role, and a project management qualification would be highly desirable.

Network managers

Network managers usually need to be educated to degree level or equivalent standard and to have considerable experience of network management and protocols including TCP/IP. Additional requirements might include experience in the management of industry standard network Operating Systems, together with skills in the use of database applications such as Oracle, email server applications and PC applications.

Telecommunication managers

When large organisations move, or when they are involved in major reorganisations, there is often a need to design a new telephony system using the latest technology and involving a centralised service with a capacity for up to 5000 extensions. A **telecommunications manager** would manage the busy telecommunications department and assist in the development of the new telephony environment. Such a post requires excellent communication skills and experience of managing a large team. Extensive experience in telecommunications, including the management of budgets, would probably be required and the post holder would need to know about telecommunications developments.

ICT training managers

ICT training managers are responsible for the design and delivery of training to staff in the organisation. They would be involved as a full team member in the implementation of the identified developments within the organisation. Effective staff training is a key aspect of any implementation and will contribute to its success. Effective liaison with human resources (HR) is important in order to ensure that the development of ICT skills across the organisation meet the needs defined by the HR team. Good ICT skills and training experience would be needed for this type of role. Team work is important both in support of the departmental team and the wider system implementation team.

PROGRESS CHECK

1. What are the six elements of programming?
2. Why is it important to have skills as a team player in ICT?
3. What is the ICT function in an organisation responsible for?

1. Planning, Coding, Annotating, Compiling, Debugging and Maintenance.
2. Team players contribute to the success of ICT projects because they are good listeners, communicate effectively and work well as negotiators.
3. The development, management and support of the ICT infrastructure of an organisation.

Sample questions and model answers

This is an important point – the post is for a trainee, but the organisation will be looking for someone who can contribute early on.

It is important to acknowledge the nature of the company – many people they will deal with will be highly numerate.

Providing a reason for your choice of quality is important – and it is important that these reasons relate to the job under consideration.

1. Wize-up, an accounting software company, is looking to recruit a trainee for their help desk. The help desk and support manager for the organisation discusses the requirements with the human resources manager. What personal qualities will the right person for the job need to have in order to be effective in the role? **(8)**

A trainee new to the organisation will need to be able to demonstrate that they have the ability to learn software skills quickly. It is not necessary that they know everything about the company's software - but as trainees in an accounting software organisation they should be able to show that they are comfortable with numbers, familiar with spreadsheets and that they are able to communicate what they know clearly and carefully. They are likely to need to be calm under pressure: many people facing difficulties with computers need to be talked through solutions clearly and precisely. They will need to have good written communication skills so that they can keep accurate records of the faults and issues they are dealing with. As a help desk trainee they will also need to be able to work as a member of a team; playing a part in making sure that they can draw on the skills of others in order to reach a solution to an identified problem.

2. ICT professionals within a large organisation are given specific jobs within a team. Describe the roles of the following network management department team members.
   (a) network manager **(2)**
   (b) network support technicians **(2)**
   (c) network administrators **(2)**

Giving examples or expanding on an answer helps to ensure that you get the full marks available.

(a) A network manager would have to be familiar with the network Operating System used within the organisation and would have to be able to ensure that the Operating System was secure and stable. In many organisations this may include the use of database applications such as Oracle. They would also need to ensure that the email server applications were stable and secure and that users had support in place for the majority of standard PC / system applications.

(b) Network support technicians assist in the implementation and commissioning of new computing equipment within an organisation. Tasks might include undertaking acceptance tests, installation, program installation, and the commissioning of computer and data communications equipment. For some there would be a need to demonstrate the use of computer equipment to staff and to assist in the maintenance of computer equipment.

(c) Network administrators in large organisations would keep accurate records of work undertaken including the entry of information into asset systems. They would log purchases and repairs undertaken, and support the network manager in the scheduling of tasks.

Practice examination questions

1 Employees must be aware of the differences between legal and moral issues when considering the ICT code of conduct within the organisation. Describe three different issues that could be considered. **(6)**

_____

_____

_____

_____

_____

2 The use of video-conferencing has become an important business tool. Discuss three advantages of video-conferencing for business communications. **(7)**

_____

_____

_____

_____

_____

_____

3 ICT professionals are required to demonstrate certain personal characteristics in order to work effectively. For a systems analyst identify two personal characteristics, and explain why these characteristics are important for their role. **(4)**

_____

_____

_____

4 An increasing number of people are working from home rather than working from a central office. Describe three advantages and three disadvantages for an employee working as a teleworker. **(6)**

_____

_____

_____

_____

_____

Practice examination answers

Chapter 1

1. **(Any two of the following answers would be acceptable)**
   - It is important that the data is as up-to-date as possible (1 mark). If it is not, then the information generated may well be out of date (e.g. in a contacts list some people may have changed their address since the data was gathered) (1 mark).
   - It is important that the data is complete (1 mark). For example, if the gender data is missing from a list of customers, it will not be possible to target specific offers to just men or just women (1 mark).
   - It is important that the data is presented in a way that meets the needs of the audience (1 mark). For example, data presented in a graphical format is likely to be understood by a much wider audience than had it been presented in a written report (1 mark).
   - It is important that the data is accurate (1 mark). If the data includes errors and omissions, it will result in the generation of inaccurate (and therefore useless) information (1 mark).

2. **Any suitable answer, e.g.** Knowledge is the outcome of interpreting information (1 mark) (i.e. applying rules and logic to the information in order to derive knowledge) (1 mark). If someone states that "Tomorrow will be a good day for a picnic", this might be the knowledge gained by interpreting information supplied in weather forecasts (1 mark).

3. **Any suitable answer, e.g.** Encoding helps to simplify and speed up the process of entering data (1 mark). For example, in clothing the codes S, M & L can be used to represent small, medium and large. The codes can be entered much quicker than typing the full words, and it is less likely that the operator will make a mistake when entering the data (1 mark). Using codes requires less memory space, which makes data processing quicker (1 mark).

Chapter 2

1. **Any suitable answer, e.g.** Touch sensitive screens can be used without additional peripherals (e.g. keyboards and mice) (1 mark). They allow people to tap and/or drag items shown on the screen using only their fingers (1 mark). The main disadvantage of touch sensitive screens is that it is difficult to be accurate or control fine movements (1 mark).

2. **i)–iii) In any order:** They can be used for storing data (e.g. as a mini archive system) (1 mark); They can be used to keep personal copies of work in progress (e.g. backups) (1 mark); They can be used to transfer files from one computer system to another (e.g. when working on multiple sites or between home and work) (1 mark).

3. **Any suitable answer, e.g.** The four main features of a WIMP interface are windows, icons, menus, and pointers (1 mark). Multiple windows can be open at the same time, each of which can display a different program (1 mark). Small images in each of the windows (icons) are used to represent objects, options and controls (1 mark). The menus are lists of commands and options in text format (1 mark). The icons and menu options can be selected by using a pointer mechanism that can be moved around the screen using a mouse (1 mark). Items are selected using either single or multiple clicks (1 mark).

Chapter 3

1. **Any suitable answer, e.g.** A style sheet can be used to ensure that the font that is used is consistent across all publications that the school presents (1 mark). The standardisation could include having all headings in a larger-sized font (1 mark) so that they stand out and capture the attention of the audience (1 mark). I would ensure that the use of the school logo was standardised and was always on the front page of each document, and in the header of every 'chapter break' page (1 mark). I would ensure that the pages had consistent margins (1 mark) and that page breaks occurred at sensible points – setting rules for widows and orphans and the minimum number of lines to be carried forward (1 mark). It would be important to ensure that colours of covers were standardised (1 mark) to ensure that the school colours were consistently applied in the school handbooks (1 mark) and that each department was allocated its own colour (1 mark) to make it easier for users to identify the correct handbook (1 mark).

2. **(Any nine relevant points 1 mark each)** The screens and forms should be consistent (1 mark) with screen objects being in the same place, the same font and the same size (1 mark). If paper forms are used to support data entry then these should be consistent with the screen, with the fields matching and in the same place (1 mark). If the organisation uses other tailored screens and forms there should also be organisational consistency so that all users know what to expect (1 mark).
   They should be relevant (1 mark) and should require the minimum of input and actions from the user (1 mark) with no repetition (1 mark). Information on the screen should be useful if it is there at all (1 mark) and kept to the very minimum (1 mark). Support for the user is important (1 mark) but there is a fine line between too little and too much support (1 mark). The use of visual cues such as labels (1 mark), or auditory clues such as beeps (1 mark) should indicate progress made and/or errors – with appropriate error messages (1 mark).

Chapter 4

1. (a) **Any suitable answer, e.g.** Implementation contains three distinct phases: the construction of the system; the testing and installation (1 mark). Construction may include the purchase of additional hardware as well as bespoke programming (1 mark). This stage also includes training of all system users, and production of guides and manuals to help anyone who needs to interact with the system in the future (1 mark).

   (b) **(Any three relevant points 1 mark each)** Within the maintenance phase there may be a requirement to upgrade hardware where conflicts with upgraded software emerge; or to re-configure software where the system incorporated new hardware (the reconfiguring of printer drivers for example) (1 mark). Ongoing review meetings may require additional functionality to be added to the system (1 mark). Maintenance is likely to be necessary to deal with any operational errors that occur (1 mark), investigating to see if they have been caused by bugs in the system or by incorrect data that were not picked up during alpha, beta and user acceptance testing (1 mark).

2.

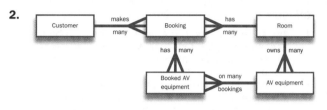

(1 mark is available for each correct relationship and 1 mark for each correct label.)

Chapter 5

1. Any suitable answer, e.g.
I used a nested IF to check the number of sick days that employees have taken to check that they are within an acceptable range (1 mark). If the number is between 3 and 5 then cell AI32 is coloured amber, if it is between 1 and 2 then it is coloured green, anything above 5 is coloured red and a warning message appears in the adjacent cell (Arrange back to work interview) (1 mark). I also used a VLOOKUP formula in cell B15 (1 mark) which reviewed the list of employees and provided a report on how many holiday days had been booked by an employee on entry of their employee number (1 mark).

2. Any suitable answer, e.g.
I used a combo box (1 mark) to select text from a pre-determined list (1 mark) and so reducing data entry errors (1 mark). This enabled me to increase the efficiency of data entry (1 mark).

3. Any suitable answer, e.g.
Data validation and error trapping can be supported by the use of option or check boxes (1 mark) which allow users to click in the cell to make a positive choice. This places a tick in the cell and helps to increase efficiency by saving time when making entries (1 mark). Spinners are useful in that they allow users to press up or down arrows to select a value from a pre-defined (1 mark) range. What would happen if interest rates went up by 0.25%, or by 0.5%? This lets users see how input changes alter the outputs in a model, and also see different outcomes quickly and easily (1 mark).

4. Any suitable answer, e.g. (to a maximum of 4 marks)
I put a range check of between 1000 and 2000 on my customer references number to ensure numbers were within the correct range (1 mark). I also checked that the numbers were unique. I used conditional formatting by putting a preset formula to work out the date for data in another cell (1 mark). I set the text length to 8 characters, and used an input mask to put a limit on customer postcode to prevent incorrect data being entered (1 mark).
I developed a macro to define the special print settings in the Page Setup dialog box and printed the invoice (1 mark) for requested customers (=VLOOKUP using the unique customer reference number) (1 mark). I also used 3D referencing formulas to summarise monthly delivery, payment and monies owing data onto the monthly and annual summary sheet (1 mark).

Chapter 6

1. Any suitable answer, e.g. A simple query contains just one parameter (1 mark) (e.g. LastName = "Patel") (1 mark). A complex query contains two or more parameters (1 mark), either in the same field (e.g. >= 20 AND < 45), or in different fields (e.g. First Name field = "Sanjeev" and Last Name field = "Patel") (1 mark).

2. i)–ii) In any order: The whole database could be stored on a number of different computers (1 mark) located at different sites (1 mark); Providing the computers are networked, parts of the data could be stored on different computers (1 mark) and the data could be synchronised on a regular basis (1 mark).

3. i)–ii) In any order: As a result of the process of normalisation the quantity of data stored is reduced (1 mark), therefore less money needs to be spent on data storage (1 mark); The process of interrogating the database (querying) is more straightforward (1 mark) because the data has been atomised (1 mark).

Chapter 7

1. (1 mark for describing the task and up to 3 marks for the features used)
Any suitable answer, e.g. I used word processing to produce form letters as part of my coursework (1 mark). I created a standard letter and put the company logo and address in the header (1 mark): this made sure that recipients could see that the letter was official.
In order to personalise the letter further I added word fields (1 mark) so that I could include additional comments for certain customers. I included a graphic of my signature so that I would not have to sign each letter individually (1 mark). I chose a sans-serif font (Verdana) (1 mark), font size 12 (1 mark) to improve the readability of the text.

2. (1 mark for each definition and 1 mark for each example)
(a) Hyperlinks take users to other pages within the website; or to pages in external websites (1 mark). They can be inserted as URLs (http://www.allaboutbigcats.com), attached to words (Big Cats) or to images (1 mark).
(b) Frames: in websites HTML frames break pages up into areas. Each area or frame consists of an individual web page. Frames allow the multiple web pages to appear on the same page/screen (1 mark). An example might be a web page for a search engine which has frames set aside for sponsored links, advertisements and video downloads (1 mark).

3. Any suitable answer, e.g. Master slides allow different people to work on the same presentation (1 mark). Because the master slide works in the same way as a template or a style sheet every presentation developed will have the same style when the slides are put into the same presentation (1 mark). Master slides also allow global changes to be made to existing presentations (1 mark); if you change styles on the master you change styles on all pages (1 mark). You can have a different master slide for the title slide and for handouts also (1 mark). This keeps the consistency in every aspect of the presentation (1 mark) not just the actual presentation itself.

Chapter 8

1. (a) Icons are meaningful images/symbols/pictures/shapes used to represent a program or option. The user selects an icon by using point and click to activate it. **(Any two relevant points 1 mark each)**
(b) Menus show options in a list from which sub menus can be obtained. A menu can be a drop down list or a pop-up menu. **(Any two relevant points 1 mark each)**

(c) Windows contain different tasks/applications. Many windows may be opened at the same time but only one is active at any one time. You can change the size of windows, open more than one at the same time, swap between windows, and transfer information from one window to another. **(Any two relevant points 1 mark each)**

(d) Pointers (also known as point and click devices) e.g. a mouse, use arrow head or cursor on screen to select choice. **(Any two relevant points 1 mark each)**

2. (a) **(Any two points)** Easy to use; Looks attractive; Easy to configure.

(b) **(Any two points)** Uses a lot of RAM; Uses a lot of disk space; Can slow the computer down.

Chapter 9

1. (a) **Any suitable answer, e.g.** If one machine fails, it may affect the whole system (1 mark). If adequate security procedures are not in place, security of data may be an issue (1 mark).

(b) **Any suitable answer, e.g.** All programs and files can be shared easily leading to easy communication and collaboration (1 mark). Fewer external peripherals are needed, for example one printer and one scanner between four users is acceptable (1 mark).

2. (a) **Any suitable answer, e.g.** All nodes in a ring network are connected to each other and not dependent on a central server (1 mark). The network makes use of a repeater to keep the signal strong as it is passed from one node to another until it reaches its destination (1 mark). Transmission in one direction means there is less chance of collision (1 mark).

(b) **Any suitable answer, e.g.** A star network has a dedicated file server (or hub) at its centre (1 mark). All data must pass through this central server, meaning that greater security measures can be put in place (1 mark). But if there is a problem with the server, the whole network is affected. Each node can be treated independently and have different transmission speeds and priorities (1 mark).

(c) **Any suitable answer, e.g.** A bus network is a relatively inexpensive solution (1 mark). No central server is required, yet a node will double as a PC and a file or print server (1 mark). They operate best when the length of cabling does not exceed 0.5km, though if there is a fault in the cable, it will affect the whole network. This solution is suitable for a small number of nodes as heavy usage will lead to degraded signals (1 mark).

Chapter 10

1. **Any suitable answer, e.g.** The Data Protection Act sets out a number of principles that apply to the collection of this type of data. It states that the data collected must be relevant, adequate and not excessive (1 mark). It states that the data should only be kept as long as it is needed (1 mark), and that it must be held in accordance with the rights of the person to whom the data refers (1 mark). In addition, the supermarkets are required to register with the Information Commissioner's Office, which monitors the appropriate collection, use and distribution of data (1 mark).

2. (a) Corrective maintenance is necessary for minor oversights such as column totals missing, or other mainly aesthetic problems which users have a preference to change (1 mark). These are referred to as reactive modifications of the software product, which are carried out to correct discovered problems, usually within the first few days (1 mark).

(b) Perfective maintenance is usually changes identified by the user. The system will perform as it was designed but the end-user will be able to identify where and how it may be better utilised (1 mark). Perfective maintenance is about making the system work more efficiently and effectively. There is normally no urgency on this and it may happen over a period of time. Perfective maintenance is modification of the software product to improve its performance or sustainability (1 mark).

(c) Adaptive maintenance is carried out over a longer period of time (1 mark). This is where modification of the software product is performed to keep it usable in a changing environment (1 mark).

(d) Preventative maintenance is where modification of the software product is carried out to detect and correct latent faults in the software product before they become effective faults (1 mark). This will take place by carrying out several tests of robustness, which will test the system in extreme situations (1 mark).

Chapter 11

1. **Any suitable answer, e.g.** Computers should be positioned so that lighting is advantageous when looking at the screen and the employer should make sure that all screens can be adjusted against glare (or have anti-glare filters) to avoid eye strain (1 mark). The employer should also make free eye tests available for users (1 mark).
The seats should be adjustable to suit the user's height and stature and back and foot supports should be made available (1 mark). Appropriate measures should be put in place to guard against RSI, e.g. using an ergonomically designed keyboard with wrist support (1 mark).
Electrical safety of peripheral devices should be considered, such as making sure that trailing cables are securely fastened down (1 mark) and taking care with food and liquids around electrical devices (1 mark).

2. **Any suitable answer, e.g.** Training may be carried out in-house – where a number of staff would benefit from a trainer being brought in to train them at the same time (1 mark). There may be Computer Based Training (CBT), which is either web-based or via a CD/DVD (1 mark), whereby individuals can learn at their own pace in their own time (1 mark). This can also take the form of online tutorials (1 mark). CBT will have been agreed at the implementation stage to make sure that the materials already exist (1 mark). Interactive training may take place (web-based, video or DVD) where learners' responses are used to feed into an overall score (1 mark). Some staff may be required to attend college/training centre courses on an evening, providing the course on offer covers what they are required to learn (1 mark). The factors determining the type of training used will be cost, location, size of operation and number of staff (1 mark).

Practice examination answers

Chapter 12

In order to gain full marks your answer will need to:
- **refer to all four of the factors in the question**
- **make a point and then provide examples to back up what you are saying**
- **contain few, if any, errors in spelling, grammar and punctuation**
- **use specialist vocabulary where appropriate**
- **be structured well so that sentences and paragraphs follow on from each other clearly and coherently.**

Model answer:

Social networking can be seen as dangerous because it raises a number of issues around the protection of personal data. Data can be given in order to set up the personal homepage on the social networking site. Many people are tempted to treat the site, and those who read it, as a 'real best friend' and can share more information than they might otherwise. This might mean that information such as birth date, mother's maiden name, address, phone number and other personal email are given. This type of information can be used by others to gain access to goods and services in your name and could very well relate to the type of 'secret questions' for banking. This could mean that your banking details and other things can be 'hacked' or our computers can be infected with a virus by so-called phishing.

There are moral and ethical concerns that arise here. The access to personal data is, in itself, morally questionable. But there are also concerns about the level of safeguarding within social networking sites, as there is no real way of validating that you are who you say you are. The use of alter-egos can be dangerous in that friendships that develop on a social networking site could, in the very worst cases, lead to paedophilia and child pornography. Students in schools are given plenty of examples of how this could occur by giving away too much information.

There are also elements of business and organisational ethics that have been highlighted by social networking. There are examples regularly in the press of people being refused employment, or refused an interview, because their social networking pages show them engaging in 'questionable behaviour'. Some may say that this is a valid use of publicly available information; others may say that it is an invasion of privacy and that what is done in personal time is of no interest to the employer.

Those who are enthusiastic about the use of the Internet for social networking firmly believe that social networking sites have become one of the easiest and quickest ways possible to form friendships and to widen their friendship groups among people from all over the world. While this may have many positive cultural benefits, it could be said that social networking sites have taken over face-to-face conversations. Like email they offer people the opportunity to avoid personal embarrassment that may arise when engaged in face-to-face contact – however, it does mean that we have to write carefully and precisely.

Social networking sites enable people who have similar interests to get together. This can be extremely helpful for people who have similar personalities to form friendships, maintain partnerships and even form long-term relationships. They are useful in maintaining contact between people who are separated by long distances. Of course there are other Internet-based resources that can be used to maintain this contact, but social networking sites provide a useful framework for short written communication, the sharing of pictures, for getting others involved, and for getting in touch with others who are members of the networking site. The key word perhaps is 'networking'. Email can be seen as following a linear and pre-defined communication pathway using defined friendship groups; social networking sites allow you to branch out and extend friendship groups.

Chapter 13

1. **Any suitable answer, e.g.** An employee may have the opportunity to use the Internet, email and telephones for personal purposes whilst at work. The employee has a moral obligation not to spend too long on personal activities since they are employed to fulfil a specific role (1 mark). There are legal implications if, for example, the employee uses email to distribute material that may be deemed to be offensive to others (Protection from Harassment Act – 1997, Sex Discrimination Act – 1975, Race Relations Act – 1976). (1 mark)
   Employees who attempt to gain access to an inappropriate website may find that their activities are monitored closely and that even if they were not permitted access they could be held to account. Their actions may be morally questionable (1 mark), but would be legally actionable if they were found to be attempting to access indecent images of children under the age of 16 (Protection of Children Act 1978, Criminal Justice Act 1988) (1 mark).
   Downloading and making copies of software for personal use may seem morally acceptable to some (1 mark), but the majority of software has licensing agreements that must be followed and employers are legally bound to ensure that the terms of their software licensing agreement are followed and applied (1 mark).

2. **Any suitable answer, e.g.** Video-conferencing allows for regular meetings between differently-located individuals (1 mark). This is important, for example, in multi-national organisations where face-to-face meetings might be considered as useful, but very expensive in terms of the cost of travel and the time in getting to and from meetings (1 mark). If an organisation has many centres, or if employees are distributed widely because the organisation supports teleworking, video-conferencing can help to maintain and enhance the company ethos (1 mark). It can be extremely difficult to maintain the kind of 'company feel' that people can develop in face-to-face interactions in the workplace; you can't for example meet over a cup of coffee or around the photocopier (1 mark). Video-conferencing can also be useful in that it can be used along with the Internet to facilitate the sharing of presentations (1 mark). Some information could obviously have been given by email, or over the telephone (1 mark) but the opportunity to see body language is often helpful in effective communication (1 mark).

3. **(Any two characteristics and two explanations from the following)** Good oral communication skills (1 mark) as the analyst would need to discuss and agree aspects of the project with the client using both technical and non-technical language where necessary (1 mark). They would need to be able to focus on the detail of the problem (1 mark) to ensure that all aspects of the problem were reviewed and resolved (1 mark). As they are likely to be leading a team (1 mark)

they need to be able to delegate and manage the work of others (1 mark). They will need good written communication skills (1 mark) to document the processes fully and to pass these on to the client as part of the systems training and support programme (1 mark). They will also need to be able to apply problem-solving skills in order to offer a range of alternative solutions to the client (1 mark).

4. Advantages of teleworking **(1 mark for each to a maximum of 3)**
   - Saves time and money on commuting to work.
   - Can choose where to live – not restricted by the time it takes to travel to work.
   - It is easier to work flexible hours – you might be able to start work early and work later in the evening to fit around family commitments.
   - It can be less stressful since you are not dealing with transport problems.
   - Many employees can set up their working space to suit themselves.

Disadvantages of teleworking **(1 mark for each to a maximum of 3)**
   - It costs more to work at home because you spend more on lighting and heating.
   - Some teleworkers feel isolated.
   - Some employers may decide that the pay rate for teleworkers can be lower.
   - There are fewer opportunities to meet other colleagues, to 'get the gossip', or to go out after work.
   - Some employees lose the distinction between work-time and home-time, or become distracted easily during the working day.

Index

Index